MAU MAU AUTHOR
IN DETENTION

GAKAARA WA WANJAŨ

Translated from the Gĩkũyũ by

Paul Ngigi Njoroge

HEINEMANN KENYA

Published by
Heinemann Kenya Limited
Kijabe Street, P.O. Box 45314
Nairobi

© Gakaara wa Wanjau 1988
First published, in the Gikuyu language, in 1983
This English translation published in 1988

ISBN 9966—46—354—2

Printed by
English Press Limited
Enterprise Road, P.O. Box 30127
Nairobi

CONTENTS

Acknowledgements   vii

Preface   x

Introduction   xv

1. The Beginnings of Tribulations, Kajiado, 21 October 1952 to 31 June 1953   1

We are given the rules and regulations governing our detention—Holding charges are prepared—We petition the Governor—Camp guards smuggle out letters for detainees—The big inspection which included body searches—Mau Mau fighters think of carrying a rescue raid on the camp

2. Across the Sea to Manda Island, 2 July 1953 to 1 September 1953   27

The journey to Lamu—The oppressive conditions of Lamu prison—We try to convince Lamu residents that we are not cannibals—We starve during the 'Kang'aari Famine'—We start a camp school

3. Serious Conflicts Over the Question of Work in the Camp, 24 September 1953 to 20 February 1954   51

The beginnings of divisions among the detainees—The white man who used a walking stick to conduct his prayers—Detainees are confined in punishment cells and beaten—Detainees arrive in Manda from Marsabit—We are divided into three categories—We dig a secret well in the camp building to save ourselves from death by thirst

4. Interrogations in Manda, 21 February 1954 to 24 June 1954   75

High-level discussions are held about the interrogation committee's plans to subject detainees to torture and beatings—Warũhiũ disagrees with the camp commandant—A camp farm is started and a camp fishing gang formed—A trained psychologist starts "rehabilitation" work at Manda—The camp gains 5 Abaluyia detainees

iii

5. New Regulations on Detainee Status, 1 July 1954 to 19 July 1955   107

Reorganisation of living arrangements for detainees—People are paid for work done but receive reduced food rations—Ohanga, Minister for Community Development and Rehabilitation, arrives —The Governor visits the Camp—The Advisory Committee on Detainees interviews some detainees—A warder is drowned in the sea—The commandant explains how detainees may "surrender" to the Government—The death of Gĩcaana

6. The Merger of Manda and Takwa Camps, 24 July 1955 to 5 April 1956   154

Detainees are divided over whether or not to accept "token" wages —We open a Camp school at Takwa—Fratèrnisation between detainees and Camp guards—Gĩkũyũ, Embu and Merũ elders become involved in rehabilitation—Rumours that our release is imminent fill the camp—Detainees from the "Jock Scott" operation are isolated from the main body of detainees

7. Brainwashing in Athi River, 5 April 1956 to 15 February 1957   175

Conflicts between the Rehabilitation Department and the Moral Rearmament movement—Towards the end of the rehabilitation "pipe line"—Confessions in mass meetings—Some of us receive "parole"—The Camp Newspaper, Atĩrĩtĩ—We perform anti-Mau Mau plays—J. M. Kariũki is beaten—A visit to Kamĩtĩ Women Detention Camp—I arrive at Karatina

8. My Exile in Hola, 2 May 1958 to 19 August 1959   198

My local community opposes my release—We settle into irrigation farming at Hola—Farming in the settlement village of "Kĩarũkũngũ" —The Hola massacre—Some detainees settle permanently at Hola —I am allowed to return home

9. My Life as a Restricted Person, 20 August 1959 to 19 May 1960   206

I am involved in communal work—I start working at Karatina— The operation of my restriction order—The special Commissioner for Detainees and Restricted Persons orders my trial—My restriction order is suspended—The Independent Government's policy of forgiveness

1. Nationalist Leaders—2. A List of Emergency Detention Camps—
3. An official memo recommending demotion down the pipeline—
4. Gakaara Wanjaũ's book *Roho ya Kiume na Bidii kwa Mwafrika*
5. Notes on the Mau Mau in Kenya: an official memorandum—
—6. Suspension of a Detention Order—7. Copy of a detainees'letter
—8. The Creed of Gĩkũyũ and Mũmbi—9. A facsimile from Gakaara
Wanjaũ's Holding Charge

DEDICATION

To the respectful rememberance of

My Father, Rev. Johana Wanjau, who was killed in the course of his Christian ministry during the War for Freedom.

With affectionate respect for

My loving mother, Rahel Warigia wa Wanjau, and my loving wife Shifira Wairire wa Gakaara, who were forced to drink out of the cup of suffering in Kamiti Women's Detention Camp. And for my children who were left to a life of deprivations when the Mau Mau War for Freedom took their parents away from home.

And also for

All Kenyans who were involved in many different ways with the struggle for freedom.

Acknowledgements

Although this book took basic shape several decades ago, when I put down in diary form my personal experiences during the Emergency, I owe a debt of gratitude to all those people who helped in refreshing my memory on certain matters and who cared enough to take the trouble to obtain old documents belonging to the period of our arrest and detention.

The following people helped me in verifying the happenings at these detention camps: Kajiado, Lamu, Manda and Takwa: Ex-Chief Gitahi wa Waciira, Kīhaato wa Kībuukū, Stanley Kagika Kuhutha, and Kinuthia wa Mugiia. I held enlightening discussions on happenings at Athi River detention camp with the following people: Nahashon Ngari Rūkenya, Linus Maina Githinji, Mohamed Mathu, Paul Mahehu Kibutu, Kame wa Muhoro and Kibuuthu wa Muturi. And I talked to the following "veterans" from Karatina and Hola: Moses King'aru, Wanjohi Solomon, Romano Njamuumo and ex-D.O. Kihoori Karuria. Many thanks to the following people who showed me old documents pertaining to Mau Mau detention: Mucooki wa Mbuitu, Rev. S. Chabangui Ngatunyi, Iregi wa Wanguku, and Tandeo Mwaura.

This book would not have seen the light of day without the loving care of my wife Shifira Wairire, who took good custody of the hand-written diaries which reached her hands in 1957, while I was still in detention. She also kept all my letters sent to her during my detention. The letters were an invaluable help when I came to filling in some dates in respect of recorded happenings. She and my loving mother gave me the facts about the detention of Mau Mau women at Kamiti Women's Detention Camp, as described in this book; they had been inmates in this camp.

I cannot find the words to express my deep appreciation for the altruism shown by that great and reknowned writer of books in English and in Gikuyu (*Ngahika Ndeenda and Caitaani Mutharabaini*), Ngugi wa Thiong'o. When word reached Ngugi that I had in my possession diaries kept during the Emergency, he travelled all the way to my home in Karatina to encourage me to have the diaries published. He strongly felt these diaries had great historical value. In his view most of the books already written on the Mau Mau War, by people like Waruhiu wa Itote, Karaari wa Njama, Kahinga wa Wacanga, Joram Wamweya, Gucu Gikoyo, Mohamed Matu and others, focussed most of their attention on the actual physical struggle. More materials should be brought to light on the experience of detention, in the manner of books written by J.M. Kariuki and B.M. Kaggia.

I wish to express my immeasurable gratitude to Maina wa Kinyatti, that great Kenyan patriot, who offered to read my materials and to edit them. At that time Maina was teaching as a senior lecturer in the history department of Kenyatta University College. He is the author of *Thunder from the Mountains*, which features in English translation the songs and hymns of the Mau Mau liberation struggle.

My thanks go to Waithiegeni wa Kirongothi who offered to type the manuscript in spite of her heavy duties. Her painstaking devotion emanated from her genuine patriotism.

I wish to record my appreciation for the work done by the following people in improving Gikuyu orthography: Karega wa Mutahi, a Kenyan linguist and a senior lecturer in the Department of Linguistics and African Languages at the University of Nairobi, Rev. John G. Gatu, Moderator of the P.C.E.A. Church, Peter Kiarii Njoroge of the C.C.M., Ngugi wa Thiong'o, Gerald G. Wanjohi, Kinuthia wa Mugiia, Ngugi wa Mirii, Magayu K. Magayu and Rev. John Mburu. I enjoyed working with these people on the written presentation of the Gikuyu language. I have benefited from these improvements and the new orthography is used in this book.

I must say that I felt deeply touched to see well educated people of the younger generation devoting themselves to the development of culture. These are the new people's warriors, carrying on the legacy of that older generation whose devoted work has shaped the Kenyan nation to what it is today.

The Gikuyu people have a saying: "Seeking and finding wealth is less demanding than conserving that wealth." We fought for independence with the intention of bequeathing it to our children. These children, this younger generation, are the guardians of our national development and our national wealth. They owe it to the nation to protect this wealth so that it benefits the Kenyan people who own this land; for the blood that was shed to redeem this land is an everlasting curse to those who would slacken their allegiance to it. If an impoverished home owner has to beg for charity from wealthy strangers in order to run his home, he should consider himself a home owner only by name. May God, the Owner of Brightness, lend vision to a deep understanding of the long term interests of the nation.

My prayer is that young people, including people in universities, should take more and greater interest in recording Kenya history and exposing the cultures and values of Kenyan peoples; for it was in the endeavour for national self-realisation that so much blood was shed in our country.

A nation which does not know its own history is a dead nation

Preface

"Son of Wanjau, you should never allow these happenings to go unrecorded." This is what the elders detained with me, former members of the Kikuyu Central Association, men like Wambugu wa Maina, Kirongothi wa Ndegwa, James Beauttah and others, would tell me.

These were some of the people who knew, and greatly valued this knowledge, that I was secretly keeping a diary. I kept this diary within the period 1952 to 1959. When some of my fellow detainees felt they had undergone an experience worth recording, they let me know. I would then enter it into my diary. They trusted me with their information for they were aware of my pre-detention efforts in spreading nationalist awareness through my publications. God willing, they hoped, we would leave detention alive and I would publish a book on the happenings in detention.

I was born at Tumutumu in Nyeri, in 1921. I went to primary school there, after which I joined Alliance High School in 1939. At the end of 1940, however, I and a few other students were expelled from the school by the colonial headmaster Carey Francis, who had just joined Alliance High School from Maseno. This is what happened. There was a kind of strike involving all students when the new headmaster ordered that we would no longer have sugar in our porridge. After this some of us were victimised for minor infringements of rules. I myself was expelled for making a mistake during a physical training lesson.

In December 1940 I joined the army. The Second World War (1939-1945) was in progress. My thinking at that time was that I had taken on a job, like any other. I knew that this war was not our war. I could not, however, stand aloof from the maltreatment of and discrimination against black servicemen practised by the British imperialists. It is not possible to give an indication here of the magnitude of that maltreatment and discrimination.

I was employed as a clerical officer. In the course of my work I met many Africans from the then British colonies, such as Nigeria, the Gold Coast, Tanganyika, Uganda, Nyasaland and Southern and Northern Rhodesia. I learned much from these people about the hunger and yearning for fredom of colonised peoples. And my distrust and eventual contempt for imperialists grew from my realisation that the British colonialists persisted in treating black people as slaves although they were shedding blood for the British cause.

x

One day in Addis Ababa, Ethiopia, I fought with a white sergeant-major who had insisted on interfering with my work in the office. When the case went to the commanding officer, a colonel, it was ruled that the sergeant-major was in the wrong.

I started writing little books, some on the customs of the Agikuyu and some on current affairs, in 1946 after we had come home from the war. In 1948 I took a job with a British company in Nakuru. My experiences in the Rift Valley—my witnessing of the virtual slavery to which African workers were subjected, including constant physical assaults and verbal abuse by white land owners, who seemed to constitute a government in Rift Valley Province—were the basis of a book in Kiswahili, which at the same time expressed my deep anger and exhorted Africans to show courage and defiance to their tormentors. The title of my book was *Roho ya Kiume na Bidii kwa Mwafrika* ("The Spirit of Manly Courage for the African" or "The Spirit of Manhood and Perseverence for Africans"). It enjoyed good sales locally and in Tanganyika. I returned to Nairobi in the opening years of the 1950's when the people's demand for land and freedom had reached white heat. I wanted my words of exhortation to reach the Agikuyu, and so I translated the book into Gikuyu under the title *Mageria No Mo Mahota* ("Make the Attempt in Order to Succeed").

Upto the time we were arrested I championed the cause of the Mau Mau revolt and published Mau Mau songs and its creed. I used the Gikuyu language in its idiomatic forms and exploited its proverbial turns of speech in order not to give myself away to those hostile to our cause.

The core of this book is the story of experiences of a representative sample of Mau Mau leaders, who were arrested on 20 October 1952, when the Emergency was declared, and taken to the Indian Ocean island of Manda, Lamu, and later to other detention camps in different parts of Kenya.

I was not able to put down each and every happening for each day. But I believe I managed to capture the major significant happenings of the detention camps, beginning with the Kajiado detention camp and the other camps of which I was later to go the rounds.

It is a well known fact that when the liberation war was over the colonialists put to the flame many documents and files that bore witness to the war crimes they had committed against the Mau Mau fighters. The colonialists destroyed these records of acts which would have earned them, had they become part of recorded history, international infamy and shame   acts of naked murder, plunder and robbery as well as acts of shameless and brutal inhumanity. But books such as mine will bear witness to some of these acts which the British imperialists and their lackeys committed against our people.

I am aware of the great interest many people, especially students from schools and the universities, local and foreign, have in the history of the Mau Mau movement. Such people have visited me for discussions. I hope this book will meet some of their study needs.

I have gone beyond the recounting of happenings in which I was personally involved, to recounting experiences in detention camps to which I may not have been as these experiences were related to me by people who were there. Witness is borne to the veracity of happenings and experiences by the mention of the names of the detainees who were involved as well as those of colonial and African personnel in the detention camps. Some experiences described here are complemented by those described in the late J.M. Kariuki's book *Mau Mau Detainee*.

No doubt, readers of this book, and especially former detainees who are familiar with the thorough checks and inspections to which detainees were subjected, will wonder how I managed to keep my writings concealed and how they reached my home. Let me tell you.

I was keeping my diary in sixteen page exercise books. I would then put these in a personal box, where they would remain concealed under a false bottom. It was a wooden box and the false bottom was a wooden board, cut to size, and held in place with small nails.

This box left my hands in 1956 when a camp worker at Athi river Detention Camp agreed to take it to his shop at Karatina. When my wife left detention in 1957, I wrote to her asking her to take delivery of the box. My wife took good care of it until I was released. What you are about to read, therefore, is thirty odd years old.

This book will reveal to you how loyal to each other the liberation fighters were and what great unity had been forged between them by the oaths of allegiance they had taken. You will see that while the Mau Mau forces continued to carry on their armed struggles against the British imperialists, the movement's political leaders continued to wage a political struggle in spite of their incarceration in detention camps. The detainees would even write letters and memoranda to the British Government, as you will see in this book, and have these sent secretly. Such letters would express our determination to face all kinds of persecution in pursuit of our ultimate goals: regaining both our land and our freedom.

As is well known the overall aim of Mau Mau was to wage struggle against the colonialists. For those of us who had already been put in detention the only avenue left to us to advance the struggle was to protest strongly, and at every turn, and in solidarity with each other, against colonial programmes, ideas and actions. Eventually, however, (and the truth must be told) as numbers of the detained increased, and as psychological weariness began to take its toll, a few people among us started to express views divergent from our general ideology, and sometimes to aquiesce to the acts of the detention authorities contrary to the stand of the majority. By mid-1954 such divergent views were the basis of many internal squabbles amongst us as well as deliberations.

And eventually many of us came to appreciate the nature of opportunistic leadership: there were those leaders who, before the mass detentions, spoke to public meetings with a tongue coated with patriotic courage; but when the struggle intensified into bitter confrontation and they were put in they showed their cowardly face and started to collaborate with the colonial authorities, to the detriment of the other inmates. But the opposite was also true. There were people who had never attained public stature outside detention who now drew from great reserves of courage in resisting the colonialists, who then responded by subjecting these patriots to torment and torture, including beatings and confinement in cells; when there were protests these people were invariably accused of being the ring leaders.

The general methods of resistance to the authorities in Manda Detention Camp, as described in this book, were similar to those employed in other camps — Mageta, Manyani, Athi River, Lodwar, Malingat, Mwea, Kamiti, and others all over Kenya. Acts like boycott of manual work, hunger strikes, writing secret memoranda, holding secret inmate councils, and holding mutual self-education sessions were met with confinement in cells by the colonial authorities. And when the authorities started to enforce manual labour and to force people to make confessions about the oaths they had taken, there was a major and bitter split between those who insisted on resisting and those who joined the ranks of the collaborators. It is to the credit of the detainees that they didn't carry that bitterness to their life in freedom.

In those far off days when I started keeping my diary, my aim was that I would be able one day to publish a book which would give an objective picture of life in Mau Mau detention camps. Today I consider my account objective and as such of considerable historical and national value. It is definitely not part of the intention of this book to make

unwarranted praise of individuals or groups of people, or to cast any
aspersion on any group of people or any individual. I am confident the
reader will study this book in that spirit.

Gakaara wa Wanjau
Karatina, Nyeri
October 1981.

Introduction

The struggle for Kenya's national liberation from British colonialism was waged by two successive generations. The first generation consisted of people who witnessed, as young children or as young adults, the advent of the colonialists. These people witnessed the white man's forcible alienation of their land, without so much as paying for the right of use, and, as if this was not enough they found themselves conscripted as slave labour to work on this land. Then British colonialists went ahead to seize the government of the land from the people.

From this generation some people resorted to political organisation in order to agitate for the return of their stolen lands. The East African Association under the chairmanship of Harry Thuku, and the Kikuyu Central Association under the chairmanship of Joseph Kang'ethe and with Jomo Kenyatta as its secretary were such political organisations.

These early organisations used peaceful and legal means of struggle and they would send petitions and memoranda to the colonial authorities; many such petitions and memoranda were treated with colonialist contempt. Within the KCA movement were people who placed the emphasis of their struggle on the preservation of the cultural values of the Gikuyu, Embu and Meru peoples; female circumcision became a central issue as a symbol in this struggle. The cultural concern was expressed in the *muthirigu* song and dance, which became very popular in 1928, as well as in the setting up of schools, under the Kikuyu Karing'a Schools Association or Kikuyu Independent Schools Association, which were independent from the colonial educational system. Independent churches with ministers from the cultural movement were also set up.

It is the KCA which sent Jomo Kenyatta to England in 1931 to air their grievances. When the Second World War broke out in 1939 some of the prominent leaders of the KCA were incarcerated in a detention camp at Kapenguria. They were not released until the end of the war in 1945. The KCA was proscribed, but these leaders did not give up the struggle after regaining their freedom. I have told the story of the KCA and its patriotic leaders in my book, *Agikuyu, Mau Mau na Wiyathi* ("The Agikuyu, the Mau Mau, and Kenya's Freedom"). When the Emergency was declared on 20 October 1952 some of the KCA leaders, now elderly men, became the first people to be picked for detention under the suspicion of being the managers of the secret organisation of Mau Mau.

But following on the proscribing of KCA another organisation had been created in 1945 — The Kenya African Union. Kenyatta had returned from England in 1946. The ranks of KAU were filled by the second generation of Kenya's freedom fighters — the sons of the KCA people, who wanted to advance the struggle started by their fathers. A good number of these people, I being one of them, had been in the Second World War and had acquired good experience in jungle warfare, having been involved in campaigns conducted in the forests of Burma and in the Ethiopian highlands of Gonda. They had also acquired skills in the manufacture of fire-arms, grenades and ammunition.

When the Mau Mau movement flowered within the general KAU organisation these young men served the movement in their capacity as the movement's youth wing. They became ardent oath administrators in their bid to create awareness and courage and loyalty to the overall KAU programme of seeking to reacquire our stolen land and our national freedom. These young men constituted the second generation of Kenya's nationalist freedom fighters, and they were also, like leaders of the first generation, swept in the first wave of Emergency arrests under "Operation Jock Scott". They, too, were regarded as part of the top leadership of Mau Mau.

Appendix I of this book carries a list of the names of most of the leaders who were swept into detention camps; indication of their public work is also given. As you can see from Appendix I, many of them were the leaders of organisations which had been lawfully registered by the Registrar of Societies. But many of them were involved in secret Mau Mau associations. I have explained the nature of the secret associations of Mau Mau in the second chapter of my book in the Gikuyu language, *Agikuyu, Mau Mau and Kenya's Freedom.*

Mau had a very broad leadership elected from the grassroots of every localised community in the breadth of Gikuyuland, Embu and Meru. A central and national committee had been elected from the broad strata of lower cadres. This committee may be said to have been led by the following people: Eliud Mutonyi, Isaac Gathanju, J.P. Kali, Fred Kubai, B.M. Kaggia, Hiram Kinyeru, Charles M. Wambaa, John Mbiyu Koinange, Mathenge Mirugi and Njue Kamumbu. Although many people in the leadership structure of Mau Mau were arrested, the movement was never left leaderless, for other people were found to step into the shoes of those taken away; these new leaders, as yet unidentified by the colonial authorities, were charged with the duty of carrying on with the Mau Mau programme. There were leaders in political work, in matters of the armed struggle as well as administrators of every day communal life.

There was, therefore, a good number of leaders who were not netted in the night of 20 October 1952, simply because they were not then known to the colonial authorities. Others, however, were not taken in on that particular night for different reasons, although they were known to the authorities, some of them having been betrayed by collaborators. People like Ex-Senior Chief Koinange and Jesse Kariuki Curang'a had been exiled earlier on in remote parts of Kenya. Others, like James Beauttah, Rev. Petro Kigondu, Dedan Mugo and Issac Gathanju, were already in prison, while people like Peter Mbiyu Koinange and Henry Mworia had left the country. And yet others who were in the arrest plan and were even blacklisted, like Dedan Kimathi, Mathenge Mirugi and others, had disappeared into the forests, there to start a "dialogue of bullets" with the colonialist oppressor.

But many who escaped the first operation soon joined us in detention. And it is obvious that the first operation was designed to net far more than 87 Mau Mau leaders, contrary to claims in colonialist records.*

Most of those first generation KCA leaders whose names appear in Appendix I are already dead. However, they deserve a revered niche in our national memory and history, for they were the architects of the movement for the struggle for independence.

Life in detention became a continuation of our nationalist struggle and colonialist resistance to this struggle. As you will see from the diaries, colonial functionaries would subject us to much verbal abuse and impute all kinds of evil motives; we were leaders unto darkness, managers of a secret society of murderers, even members of a Satanic cult. It would have been better if none of us had been born, they said.

On our part we knew why they insisted on such distortions. They were afraid. We had torn off the mask of colonialist benevolence and exposed the colonialists for the naked robbers and plunderers they were. They were hurt in the raw because we dared to call them robbers to their face.

But there were also attempts at dialogue. Servants of the colonial government would visit us and listen to us; and representatives, sent from Britain to investigate the root causes of Mau Mau, would find it necessary to talk to us. We would willingly talk to those who had come

*The colonial press (*The East African Standard, The Colonial Times*) reported that the authorities had been out to arrest 87 key Mau Mau leaders. Obuor in *White Highlands No More* seems to accept this version of events.

from overseas and sometimes we would make them the bearers of our petitions, or we would send petitions and memoranda through them after they had gone back home.

The image that emerges of the average Mau Mau leader is one of genuine self-sacrifice. They showed neither a greed for quickly acquired wealth nor hunger for power and authority. They would readily use their money and material amenities in the promotion of national awareness and patriotism. The followers of the movement in their turn joined hands with this selfless leadership to work for the common cause of fighting colonial slavery. Since monetary self-gain was never an acceptable motivation, elections to positions of leadership were based on patriotic merit; leaders were elected to patriotic service.

The oaths of unity administered by Mau Mau played their part in instilling patriotic courage and in driving people to the greatest heights of dedicated service such that people gladly shed their blood for their land and people. And the truth is that bitter divisions among one people were inevitable in the height of struggle, between the patriots on the one hand and those who had chosen to collaborate with the colonialists. We saw these latter in their own reactionary camp and we regarded them as traitors to their own people, for they had sold out.

And selling out was a vital issue. Mau Mau found it necessary to wage an unrelenting struggle against this trend and deal ruthlessly with individuals whose selling out amounted to holding positions of authority in the colonial government.

But the concept of selling out against one's own people is a large one and may not be confined to a historical period. For what is selling out? Selling out is when an individual turns against his people, the Africans of Kenya, takes unfair advantage of them and uses his abilities to enrich himself and his immediate family, knowing full well that his actions result in the general impoverishment of his own people as well as in general discontent. To make private use of money acquired in public trust is to sell out. For people in positions of national leadership to allow aliens to grab opportunities in commerce, in acquisition of land and other kinds of property, to the disadvantage of the indigenous African people, who cry out for opportunities, as burdened as they are with poverty: this is to sell out. And the ultimate sell out could happen if little by little the majority of Kenyan Africans were allowed to descend to the level of beggars asking for charity from wealthy aliens. This would happen if we allowed ourselves to be mentally bought to such an extent that our desire would be to give succour to the aliens and to slavishly minister to their interests. God forbid that this should happen in this our land of Kenya which was redeemed with so much blood and sacrifice.

1

The Beginnings of the Tribulations

Kajiado, 21 October 1952 to 31 June 1953

October, 1952

21 October 1952

At about 5.00 a.m. we were put into two prison trucks whose sides were built with wire mesh. We had been handcuffed in twos and then chained in groups of six. There were four armed soldiers in each lorry. All of us had been rounded up in Nairobi and Kĩambuu. There were thirty men and two women. We had no idea where they were taking us. We were driven in the direction of Athi River. At around 10.00 a.m. we arrived at Senya Prison Camp. This was then being referred to as Kajiado Detention Camp. It lies about 30 miles from Nairobi.

All the way from Nairobi our convoy had been tailed, from a distance, by a taxi on whose body stripes had been painted. Some of us were aware these were our people coming to verify our destination. When we entered the prison gates, the taxi turned away.

A British prison officer and a group of African prison guards were waiting for us. After they had removed our handcuffs, the imperialist officer ordered us to sit on the ground before he addressed us. We had been held and would continue to be held, he told us, under Emergency regulations promulgated by the Governor of Kenya. We should obey the following regulations: No detainee should attempt to escape; no detainee should as much as touch the barbed wire surrounding the camp. Detainees should keep well within a one-wire boundary which lay 3 yards away from the main barbed wire fence. If any detainee put a foot over that wire or touched the barbed wire he would be shot. Detainees should not cause any breach of order or any riot. An officer who would be solely concerned with our affairs would be arriving shortly.

Each of us was issued with the following things: an iron-bar bed; an old and used sleeping mat; and two old and used blankets. We would obtain a daily ration of food stuffs, from which we would cook our meals.

All the men were locked in house no. 1, a hall built on all sides with corrugated iron sheets. The women were put in a similar shed, house no. 5. We would

1

not be able to go out except when guards escorted us to the lavatory or to the washroom or to eat.

That night prison inmates prepared our meal. We had rice, black *ndengū*,* meat and tea.

At around 4.00 p.m. thirty-one more detainees arrived. They had been rounded up from Nyeri, Embu, Nanyuki and Meru. They were given food and locked up in house no. 2 so that we wouldn't get an opportunity to talk to them. But we were able to communicate with them once the guards had locked us up and gone, for number 2 adjoined number 1—we were merely separated by a corrugated iron wall. They gave us their names and we gave them ours. Many people from both halls knew each other, having got acquainted while carrying out work in various political organisations. The house-2 inmates told us they had first been herded into Nyeri Prison before being brought here. They were brought all the way from Nyeri in handcuffs and chains, lying on their stomachs on the floor of a lorry, with three armed soldiers guarding them. Two armoured cars had driven in front of their lorry and two police vans full of soldiers had followed the lorry that carried them. And they had even been guarded from the air by a military helicopter.

On that first day people, even if they hailed from the same ridge back home, appeared suspicious of each other. Many of us suspected there could be government informers among us. So people in general talked about what wasn't compromising; each detainee would describe how he had been arraigned by a pack of colonial troops, British and African, who were armed to the teeth. Stories were told how on the night of 20 October 1952 all manner of motorised traffic had been stopped at midnight; with the exception of police patrol cars which were hunting for specified Mau Mau suspects. Those people who were well known to each other would engage in mutual speculations about the nature of their offence and wonder whether they would be charged in court or whether they would face the fate of KCA leaders who had been detained without trial in 1939. Some people said we would all end at Mahiga Mairū,* like all those people rounded up in Olenguruoni.

For my part, I suspected I would be tried for publishing the "Creed of Gīkūyū and Mūmbi" (see Appendix 8). I had seen a card, on which this creed was printed, pinned to the warrant of my detention order which had been signed by the imperialist Governor of Kenya, Sir Evelyn Baring.

---

*a Pea-like vegetable.

* Between 1945 and 1948, many people from Tigoni, Limuru, Kiambuu, had their land seized. These people were forcibly relocated in Olenguruoni in the Rift Valley Province. When they revolted against harsh regulations imposed on the way they should practice farming, some of them were further exiled to Yatta area in eastern Kenya—a land of black rocks and stones, hence the name *Mahiga Mairu*.

22 October 1952

At 8.00 o'clock in the morning 16 people from Mŭrang'a and the Rift Valley were brought to the camp. As they narrated later, those from Mŭrang'a had arrived in Nairobi the previous day and had joined the Rift Valley group who had spent the night at the Nairobi police headquarters. The Rift Valley detainees had been brought in a pick-up in which they had been forced to lie on their backs. They were guarded by four armed soldiers, and they had a police motor-cyclist leading the way as well as a helicopter escort. Those from Mŭrang'a had similarly been chained together and had been made to lie on their backs. They were brought to Nairobi in a lorry. They were escorted by two police vehicles, one leading and the other following behind.

When they arrived at the camp we climbed to the rafters to get a vantage point to watch them. After their chains had been removed they were taken to the eating hall. They were then thrown into house no. 3.

In the afternoon the prison camp officer told us we might elect a camp leader. We elected Anderson Wamŭthenya. Then we chose our kitchen staff: Daudi Wanyee, Ndibŭi Wawerŭ, Mwangi Baarŭ, and Paulo Ndŭrŭ.

When we left our enclosures for lunch at around 1.00 p.m. people from the different "houses" had an opportunity to greet each other and get to know one another a little more.

Back in our lock-up Kŭngŭ wa Karŭmba and Charles Mŭnyua Wambaa suggested that it would be a good idea for us to introduce ourselves to each other to allay mutual suspicions. Keeping quite alert for any intrusion from outside, each one of us would stand, mention his name, say where he came from, mention the names of people known to him in our place of detention, and disclose his trade or profession before detention, including involvement in public or political work.

People would have been keen to discern from each individual's story whether he had been initiated into nationalist leadership through the oaths of unity. For people who had taken the oath knew how to give an unmistakable hint to others like them by the use of proverbial language. One could say things like that he was not an outsider or that he was an unblemished Mŭgĩkŭyŭ, or that he was privy to the secrets of the people, or that he belonged to Gĩkŭyŭ and Mŭmbi. Such statements gave a clear indication to the initiated that you were committed to the struggle against the imperialists and their local slaves.

But when some people in a round-about way suggested the need for these disclosures, other detainees refused to support this procedure. People who had earlier been either in detention or prison indicated it was foolhardy for people to reveal themselves, even in figurative language, for there were normally spies keen to exploit such situations. So we all declared that we had been arrested for involvement in legal agitation for land and political freedom. Any other insinuations against us were false.

When we went for four o'clock tea we requested a Luo prison sergeant to consider allowing us to go out of our enclosures for a dose of fresh air and sun. The sergeant let us know he had no powers. However, he disclosed, a British officer in charge of all our affairs would be coming tomorrow.

I had been composing a song. Wamũtĩ wa Mũhũngi, Gacangi wa Gĩkaru and Mwangi wa Wawerũ and I practised singing the song. Then we sang it to the whole assembly in house no. 1, and everybody loved it. They started learning it. The title of the song was "Ũtukũ Mweri Mĩrongo Ĩĩrĩ" ("In the night of 20 October") and these are its words:

1. It happened on the twentieth of October
   When the patriots of the nation were in their beds
   They swooped on them and arrested them all
   And chained them for delivery to the captors' camps.

   There was great sorrow among those left behind
   Parents, children and friends wailed and wept:
   "Ũũi, ĩĩya, Our God help them!
   Take care of them until they return to us!"

2. They took each patriot in a different way
   Those captors loaded with weapons
   They bore rifles and revolvers and clubs
   And rounded patriots into one place in the night.
3. That same night they arrested the Great Leader
   The white soldiers came in convoys of cars, loaded with arms
   They told him, Pack up your cases and your clothes!
   They wouldn't even allow him to bid his family farewell.
   When the patriots arrived at the captors' camps
   They were made to sign pieces of paper
   Their photographs were taken, each patriot was given a number
   They had prepared numbers before their swoop.
   Thaai.*

24 October 1952

An interrogation committee arrived. Chaired by an officer named Mitchell, it had four other members: two British officers, a Gĩkũyũ police inspector named Gĩthieya and a Mkamba police officer. Some of the detainees knew the

*Thaai is the Gĩkũyũ equivalent of "Amen"—may it be so: it is generally used to close solemn words of prayerful invocation.

British officers: they were senior people from C.I.D. Headquarters, Nairobi.

They would summon the detainees individually to an office. The detainee would be given a seat and the interrogation routine would start: Name? Where do you come from? Your profession or trade? Have you taken the Mau Mau oath? How come you haven't taken it? Are you one of these political agitators demanding land? Are you a member of KAU? KCA?....

It is these officers who drew up holding charges against each of us. For it was clear that they had carried out arrests *en masse* of alleged Mau Mau leaders, without any specific allegations.

Two people from Mombasa, Kĩnyanjui wa Kĩmani and Saidi Mohamed, were brought to the camp. Then they brought in a very eldery man, one Cege, whom we eventually came to call "Cege, the Venerable Politician". It came to appear later that Cege had been picked up in error, in place of his son. These new detainees were put in house no. 4.

Officer Mitchell suggested that each house elect one representative who would be given an opportunity to listen to the radio at Mitchell's house. The following people were elected: John Cege Kabogoro, Mwanĩki wa Mũgwerũ, Romano Njamumo and J.D. Kali. It later did appear that Mitchell would make sure the news would be safe; at times he wouldn't allow the detainees to listen to the radio.

27 October 1952

Rev. Stefano Waciira from Nyeri and Solomon mtu Mwiricia from Meru were brought to the camp. They were put in house no. 4. On this day alone twelve people were interrogated. Each person would take a relatively short time at the interrogation office.

28 October 1952

Detainees who had taken ill were taken to Kajiado Native Civil Hospital. The men were put in handcuffs, but they spared these for the women patients. An opportunity offered itself for smuggling letters out with these people for posting at Kajiado Post Office.

We started to strike up an acquaintance with the African prison warders.

31 October 1952

Kamau wa Mwerũ, Gregory Mbiti and Babu Kamau were brought in in chains. They were put into house no. 4.

Each time new people came in, we would find a way of asking them about the situation outside. They would let us know that the armed conflict was escalating.

November, 1952

1 November, 1952

A prison warder of some rank got the surprise of his life to find Kamau wa Mwerŭ, a wealthy man in the transportation business from Mŭranga, in the detention camp. They had last met three years back. The prison corporal marvelled: "Have you also been brought here? Aren't you a man of means? Or you have been an underground agitator?" And since he still held him in high regard, he added: "Are you experiencing any problems? If you need anything outside, feel free to send me."

Kamau thanked the man. He would ask for help when the need arose. When the corporal had left, Kamau offered to ask him for assistance when any of the detainees needed to make contacts with Nairobi. We agreed that we would treat this corporal as a friend.

Mwanĩki wa Mŭgwerŭ composed a song, *Ithaka Ciitŭ Andŭ Airŭ* ("These Lands of Ours, Black People"). He taught it to the inmates in house no. 2. They sang it for us and all of us liked it and we were all soon familiar with it. This is the way we used to sing it:

1.   These lands of ours, black people, were all taken
     And we and our children were given to wailing.

     We will never stop wailing, with no land to till
     And denied our freedom in this our land Kenya.

2.   This is why we were sent into exile, when we expressed deep care for
        our children
     They took us into the wilderness, a land of masses of sand.

3.   Tears flowed from our eyes, when we were forced into exile
     But God has given us comfort and promised us victory.

4.   Oh, the wailing of our children, in the grip of the throes of hunger
     Without land to till, how can we help our children!

5.   And you traitors, haters of your own children
     Caring only for the satisfaction of your stomachs, you are your
        people's biggest enemy.

6.   Whether you keep silence or speak, we ourselves will always cry out

We will be like our patriots, the true leaders of our people.
Thaai

2 November 1952

We were having our lunch in the open at one o'clock when the corporal who had befriended Kamau wa Mwerŭ said to the sergeant-in-charge: "Here is the man of means I talked to you about." The sergeant replied: "You shouldn't underestimate most of these people." He pointed at Solomon Meemia and asked, "You come from Kĩambuu, don't you?" Meemia replied, "I also do know you." The sergeant pointed out Kahũgĩ wa Gĩturo and Ngũgĩ wa Mũibũ and all of them admitted they were known to him. He had served in the colonial government in Kĩambuu for a long time.

Striking a friendly dialogue, the sergeant said that most of the personnel at this camp were retired officers of the government; they had been recalled into service after the declaration of the Emergency. Many of them had worked in Gĩkũyũ, Embu and Meru areas and they knew that our involvement in nationalist politics was genuine and deep.

The sergeant's words pleased us.

When they had gone we came together for deliberations. We agreed that we should avoid as much as possible doing things which would antagonise the African prison personnel. Those elders who had been detained during the 1939-1945 World War, among them George Kĩrongothi Ndegwa and John Mbũgua Kĩmotho, told us that their good relations with prison personnel had enabled them to enjoy many privileges. Our resolution was worded as follows: "We bear no deep-seated hatred for these people who consider they are carrying out work in the line of duty; but we should when possible impress on them that we are involved in a struggle for land and freedom, a struggle which should also be their own." So we resolved to maintain friendly relations with these people so that they might willingly carry out errands for us. And when we sent them on errands we would put a small token, "roast intestines for the messenger", into their pockets.

3 November 1952

Those detainees who manned the kitchen informed the others that they had on several occasions seen Kũng'ũ wa Karũmba's country buses, which used to run from Nairobi to Namanga, stopping on the road, about 300 yards from the Camp. Detainees started to make use of these buses. These buses would deliver parcels from Nairobi for detainees. Warders would collect these from the road, keep them in the houses, and deliver these secretly to the detainees at night or even during the day.

4 November 1952

Some detainees received parcels sent collectively from their extended families or from their immediate community. Sometimes a location-wide collection, or a division-wide collection was made for detainees from a particular administrative location or division. A parcel would bear the name of one individual detainee. Inside the parcel there would be a letter suggesting how the donation was to be shared. A parcel would contain items like cigarettes, home-made smoking tobacco, money, under-wear and newspapers.

6 November 1952

It was deliberated that every detainee should be involved in cooking; people should take turns in the kitchen, and a system should be worked out following the arrangement of beds in each hall. More and more detainees had been brought in and preparing food was difficult work. And to make matters worse the available firewood was not dry enough and the kitchen would become a hive of irritating smoke; kitchen workers would emerge from the kitchen with red and swollen eyes. It was torture for some people to be in the kitchen, what with the great heat and the smoke. Food would be prepared in drums whose top half had been cut off. Carrying these from the fire to the serving area was difficult work.

The elderly people and sick people were normally exempted from kitchen duties. But sometimes arguments would break out: how old was old enough for exemption from the kitchen? Sometimes able-bodied people would make out they were too old to cook. So it was finally resolved that only those people who were seventy and over would be exempted from cooking. They would, however, do the following types of light work: sweeping the floor, and washing plates. Quite a large number of detainees, forming part of the old leadership of the nationalist movement, were elderly. It must be mentioned that the younger men very willingly sacrificed themselves in carrying out the heavier work, for they considered themselves the children of these older people.

14 November 1952

At about 8.00 p.m. Kũng'ũ wa Karũmba was taken away. They told him to take all his things with him. We couldn't hide our worry, for we didn't know where they were taking him. While bidding us farewell, he said: "Have courage, brothers!" We told him to go in peace, God would be his guide.

(We did learn the following day that Kũng'ũ was being taken to Kapenguria, there to be tried with Mzee Jomo Kenyatta. We did not know at this time who else was to be put on trial. But we felt convinced that we ourselves would be taken for trial. I myself thought I would follow Karŭmba, for while Karŭmba had been given Number G.D.O. 14, I was Number G.D.O. 15.)

About 50 people were brought in at around 10.00 p.m.; they had been expelled from Arusha, Tanganyika, for allegedly being members of Mau Mau. They had taken whatever pieces of property they could carry with them; most of their property was left behind.

Some of these people were not only not members of the Mau Mau movement but they were not even aware that there were oaths of initiation into the movement. The fifty people included men, women and children, some of them mere infants. They were perplexed to find us at the detention camp, for they had not been aware of the mass arrests. They had suspected that their expulsion had been engineered by the government of Tanganyika. They had harboured hopes of seeking redress from the government of Kenya. Some of these people had been evicted from their lands in Limuru and Tigoni when these were alienated from them. They had first been settled at Olenguruoni, from where they had later been expelled. They had wandered and lived an unsettled life, like water on an arrow root leaf, until they had sought solace in Tanganyika.

They were put into houses Nos. 5 to 7.

15 November 1952

Officer Mitchell granted permission to detainees to prepare 10.00 o'clock tea for themselves; the women were allowed to individually prepare home-like meals for themselves and their children. Water would be boiled in the communal kitchen by the detainees on cooking duty. Those who wanted to brew their own tea or coffee or cocoa would get their share of the hot water.

Officer Mitchell brought in a black-board for use in giving instruction, as well as a volley ball, a foot ball, and a tenniquoit. From this day the detainees were allowed to remain outdoors for purposes of holding mutual-instruction classes as well as doing sports and games. The detainees started to use this freedom to get acquainted with each other as well as to renew links with old friends and acquaintances.

By this time about half of the G.D.O. detainees had already been subjected to interrogation. Most of us had become well aware of the general thrust of interrogation.

16 November 1952

The friendly prison sergeant asked Anderson Wamŭthenya, the detainees' elected representative, to talk to the detainees and ask them to limit the use of warders as errand runners; for the superior authorities had become aware that warders were being sent by ourselves to Kajiado and Nairobi.

We agreed with the sergeant's sentiments that we should use the privilege he had allowed us with restraint and discretion. And it was true restraint and caution had not always been the watchword, for the warders had become over-enthusiastic and gratuitous. They were keen to offer themselves for errands, especially to Nairobi, since they would be given money to take care of their journey to and fro as well as their other needs. On many occasions they would be sent to Kiburi House which used to house the office of a wattle-buying co-operative as well as the offices of many different trade unions. Kiburi House used to act as the meeting place of Gĩkũyũ people from all corners of the land.

A prison warder would arrive at Kiburi House carrying, say, ten letters from ten different detainees. He would be warmly and hospitably received. He might be treated to drinks as well as receive gifts in cash. Sometimes, prison warders would be put in cars and taken to homes near Nairobi, say in Kĩambuu or Thika. They would carry parcels as requested in detainees' letters. Sometimes they would come loaded with such parcels, which they would deliver to Kajiado and initially keep in their houses for safe custody.

Considerable fraternising between the detainees and the African prison personnel had been the result. After being shown hospitality by members of the detainees' families, some of these people could no longer treat us as prisoners. And when they came to appreciate that some detainees came from wealthy homes, they could no longer feel we had been detained on trivial matters. Some of them were given doses of political education by the detainees and they developed nationalist resentment against colonialism.

Dealers in soft drinks were allowed to drive their lorry right up to the camp gate and we bought sodas from them. Some detainees bought bottles of soda in bulk and they would sell to others at a profit. The detainees, men and women, enjoyed buying one another a bottle of soft drink.

17 November 1952

I was summoned to the office for interrogation. I found all the books and period-icals I had published laid on the table. The first question they asked me was when had I taken the Mau Mau oath. I denied ever having taken the oath. I was asked how come I had not taken this oath. I replied I had had no idea where the oath was being administered, leave alone knowing the purpose of taking the oath. "And how come you publish Mau Mau propaganda if you haven't taken the oath?" they demanded. I replied that I had all along taken it that I published matters of national concern and not Mau Mau matters. I was told: "Yes, that is the point: those matters of national concern you express as subversion against the legally constituted government, and that is exactly the concern of Mau Mau!" I said: "My writings are admittedly of a political nature but they express concern with the fate and cultural values of my people, and they have absolutely nothing to do with the Mau Mau movement." "Why did you write 'The Creed of Gĩkũyũ and Mũmbi'?" I replied I was trying to express my deep convictions and aspirations. "Why do you express faith in the leadership of Jomo Kenyatta?" I said it was because I considered Kenyatta a great leader of our nationalist movement, the Kenya African Union (KAU). Since I had expressed strong convictions about alienated land in my book *Roho ya Kiume na Bidii kwa Mwaafrika*, had there been any family land which had been taken from us by the British? I replied that we had lost clan land at Tũmũtũmũ, and, I had also been told, at Naromoru. "Aren't you the man who has blasphemously substituted the name Jomo for Jesus in the Christian hymn, so that you now say 'Jomo is the shepherd of his flock' instead of 'Jesus is the shepherd of his flock'?" I said, "No!" They asked me when I had started writing books and how many people had worked with me in my publishing venture.

I was then dismissed. I would be summoned later, I was told.

22 November 1952

Fourteen people, 13 men and one woman, were brought in. They had been rounded up from Kilimanjaro, Tanganyika. They were taken to shed No. 7, where some of the Arusha detainees were. One venerable elderly man, Gakami wa Mũthoondu, was held in great esteem by these Kilimanjaro detainees; they would treat him as their leader although he did not appear to possess much modern formal education. He was apparelled in an expensive *shuka* (plain cloth) and would wrap himself in an expensive blanket. We were told he had left great wealth in Kilimanjaro.

27 November 1952

Twenty men and six women were brought from Nairobi. The men were chained in sevens and the women in twos. Cecilia Wanjikũ was one of the women. And also among the women was Josephine Mũthoni, who was very well known as the proud owner of several homes and buildings in Nairobi.

29 November 1952

Judith Nyamurwa, Henry Mworia's wife, was brought to the camp with her young son, Kĩnyanjui. Nyamurwa had assumed the editorship of *Mũmenyereri* from the time her husband left for England, just before the state of Emergency, until it was proscribed. Mworia was on the blacklist of those who would have been arrested on the night of 20 October 1952. Nyamurwa was arrested at the office of *Mũmenyereri*. She was found packing up with a view to closing the business, after the Emergency had been declared.

December, 1952

8 December 1952

We hatched the idea of forming a detainees' committee to solve problems which arose among ourselves. This idea emanated from the misunderstanding that arose when M'Angaine refused to cook when his turn came. Then those who should have cooked with him said they wouldn't cook either. Wahome wa Kĩĩhĩa solved the misunderstanding when he offered to cook in Angaine's place. Angaine gave Wahome a present in appreciation of this show of genuine friendship, for he said he was feeling unwell and was not in a position to help in the kitchen. Our detainees' committee, conceived without the knowledge of the officer in charge of the camp, would in future sort out such problems.

12 December 1952

Waigera Kĩmaathi and J.D. Kali were elected to teach other detainees proper cooking, and especially preparing fried dishes flavoured with onions. These two people had good experience in preparing the right cuisine since they had been in the hotel business before their detention: Waigera had worked in his own hotel and Kali had worked in his father's hotel.

16 December 1952

Fifty-four men and one woman, who had been arrested in Kĩambaa during the months of November and December, were brought to the camp. They told us that an armed struggle was being waged in earnest. All the young men had taken to the forests and the colonialist authorities were terribly worried for they hadn't foreseen this eventuality.

Some of these new detainees were leaders of KAU and KISA*, or of other Gĩkũyũ organisations.

25 December 1952

On Christmas day the detainees were allowed to entertain themselves. There was plenty of soft drinks, bread and tea as well as meat prepared for sharing in groups. Some of the younger people even enjoyed alcoholic liquor, smuggled into the camp by the warders. People participated in traditional dances like mũcũng'wa and kamanũ as well as modern dances. The women performed a play depicting a love suit which the detainees found very entertaining. In the morning the women had prepared a nice Gĩkũyũ dish with njahĩ and green leaves; the detainees shared this dish which aroused deep memories of sweet home.

*See Appendix 1

26 December 1952

I received a telegram message from my brother, Isaac Hunja, that my Father, Rev. Wanjaŭ, had not been seen since 23 December. Aware of the implications of such a disappearance in those troubled times, I shed tears of sorrow. When my fellow detainees came to know of the message, they crowded around my bed and mourned with me. My father was a church minister with the Church of Scotland Mission (C.S.M.), Tūmūtūmū. As it turned out my father had been killed by Mau Mau at Mīhūtī, in Mŭkŭrweinī, Nyeri, where he had been assigned by the church.

27 December 1952

I went to see Mitchell and his screening committee to seek information on how my father had met his death, and to seek permission to be escorted home. Mitchell sarcastically remarked that my father had met his death at the hands of people who belonged to my own movement. It was only the Governor of Kenya, he let me know, who was empowered to grant permission to leave the Kajiado detention camp; if I so chose, I could write to the Governor for such permission.

28 December 1952

During the month of December, they were constructing two more detention sheds, we did not know for whom. But we presumed more and more people would be brought from outside for detention. The sheds were being constructed by prisoners under the direction of an elderly British officer named Dennis. The building materials were brought in by lorries owned and driven by Africans; some drivers were even known to the detainees.

A dispensary and a store were also constructed in December.

January, 1953

1 January 1953

On New Year's Eve the detainees sang songs. In the morning of New Year's Day, a group of detainees from Shed No. 3 made the rounds of the other Sheds singing, "How happy we all are, it's the new year!" People would remark that indeed it should be a happy occasion, but to consider that we were actually happy, locked as we were in a detention camp, was sheer self-deception.

We participated in games and dances. Mahuti wa Gĩcũhĩ led the *mũcũng'wa* dance.

Then we had prayers in which all of us participated. We all held hands and faced Mount Kenya and elder Gĩitwa wa Ndimũ led us in prayers. We prayed for all the loved ones we had left at home as well as for our heroes who had gone to the forests; and we prayed for ourselves and for victory against colonial slavery.

—*Thai Thathaiya Ngai, Thaai.* God, let it be so, Amen!

2 January 1953

We were informed that the colonial Governor of Kenya, Evelyn Baring, would visit the camp on 3 January 1953. We decided to appoint five representatives who would draft a memorandum on our behalf: Cege wa Kabogoro, Mwanĩki wa Mũgwerũ, J.D. Kali, George Waiyaki and our overall camp representative, Wamũthenya Kang'eri. We told them to raise the following points in their memorandum: to demand to know why we had been detained; what assistance could we expect for our people back home?; the collective punishment that was being meted to our people; access to newspapers; the detention of infants with their mothers; could Gakaara be allowed to go home, under escort, since his father had died? Ngigĩ, the young boy, and Cege "Mũteti", the elderly detainee, should be released; the problems of the sick; access to our families.

I had already written a letter to the Governor and delivered it to Mitchell.

3 January 1953

We were collected at one place outdoors when the Governor arrived. He was shown inside all the dormitories and he made a tour of the lavatories and the kitchen in the company of a large group of British officers and reporters from the loyalist press. It was decided that the five representatives we had elected to draft a memorandum would also be the ones to have an audience with the Governor in the office, before presenting our memorandum.

The Governor did have an audience with our representatives and address the points raised in our memorandum: We had been arrested and detained because the Governor had determined that we were a dangerous threat to peace and security in the present unsettled circumstances. But he issued an assurance that the property of detainees would no longer be confiscated. He would go and make arrangements for us to get a camp doctor. On the question of receiving family visits, he said he would consider allowing our families to receive our letters through senior prison officers. He would go and think about all the other matters raised.

8 January 1953

We received a schedule of daily food rations per person. This was one of the issues raised in our memorandum to the Governor. The schedule was as follows:

Wheat flour	12 oz.	Meat	4 oz
Rice	6 oz	*Ndengũ**	3 oz
Potatoes	3 oz	Cabbages	8 oz
Cooking fat	2 oz	Carry powder	$\frac{1}{8}$ oz
Tea leaves	$\frac{1}{4}$ oz	Onions	$\frac{1}{2}$ oz
Salt	$\frac{1}{2}$ oz	Sugar	2 oz
Milk	10 oz (1 pt.)		
Fruits:			
Bananas	2		
Oranges	1		

The allocation of firewood fuel would be reckoned in terms of its weight.

9 January 1953

The first baby was born in Kajiado detention camp. Her name was Nyokabi.* People marvelled at this strange coincidence, for Nyokabi had been reborn in Maasailand. We made a collection for a tea party to celebrate Nyokabi's birth, and four men delivered our collection to the women's dormitory.

Kagĩĩka composed this little song for little Nyokabi:

Let us rejoice at little Nyokabi's birth
Here at Kajiado camp in these times of troubles
Nyokabi, you were born in the thick of our freedom struggle
You should grow in deep devotion to our land.

There were other babies and children in Kajiado camp. Baby Kariũki had been christened *Warũrũng'ana** by detainees. There were also Ngũgĩ and Kĩnyanjui.

17 January 1953

Thirty people arrested from Mũrang'a were brought in, among them Timothy Maina and Gĩcohi Gĩthua. They told us stories that gave us courage and put new life into us. They told us that many of our people had gone to the forests to form many battalions of freedom fighters. Young men and women were leaving school everyday to join their ranks.

The new detainees were put in shed No. 4. They were not locked in.

*In Gĩkũyũ tradition, a child is named after a kins man or woman. The name Nyokabi means 'of Masailand', for the original owner must have been a Maasai woman. Kajiado is in Maasailand.
*This was a nickname given to Mau Mau people by Boran colonial soldiers.

20 January 1953

I composed a hymn which sought to express the emotions aroused by the information that had been coming to us from Gĩkũyũland, since our detention. We would sing this hymn with a combination of pain and sorrow, as well as courage borne of a spirit of bitterness in resistance. The hymn took its title from the words of the first verse:

1. The rule of the emergency came to Kenya
   And everybody—black, white and red people—
   Set their ears in alert like hunted animals.

2. The land of Kenya was filled with sorrow
   Mass detentions and imprisonment took place
   There was bitter war and numberless deaths.

3. In the countryside people's livestock was raided
   Market places and shops closed their doors
   And the newspapers ceased circulation.

4. And they put women in detention camps
   Some of them with their infants
   All of them were put in the place of troubles.

5. From the Rift Valley farms, squatters were expelled
   Goats and cattle were confiscated
   And the squatters' property was sold off.

6. Many people were shot at Kĩrwara
   In accordance with a young man's prophecy
   And people consolidated their unity and defiance.

7. Almighty God, hear our prayer
   Do not allow us to lose our birthright
   May we see the day of freedom.

24 January 1953

Wamũthenya and Wahome Kĩhĩa were taken to Karatina, allegedly to confront many people from their home in Mathĩra, Nyeri, who claimed Wahome and Kĩhĩa had administered oaths to them. J.D. Kali became camp leader in Wamũthenya's stead.

27 January 1953

A British officer named Davine took overall charge of Kajiado prison camp. Since he had a habit of shifting things all over the place, we named him the Fastidious Arranger.

30 January 1953

The following people were removed for transport to Kapenguria to give testimony during Kenyatta's trial: George Waiyaki Wambaa, Willie George Kamũmbũ, J.D. Kali, Joram Wawerũ and Samuel Kĩhara. We couldn't guess what the authorities expected them to say at the trial. But we learned later that the idea was to demonstrate in court that they had been Kenyatta's collaborators in acts that were the subject of the trial. For these people had at one time or another been Kenyatta's associates: G.W. Wambaa had at one time served as the Principal of Kenya Teachers College, Gĩthũngũri. W.G. Kamũmbũ had been a member of the Kikuyu Central Association and had been the chairman of the Night Watchmen Union; J.D. Kali was an editor with the KAU newspaper, *Sauti ya Mwafrika;* Joram Wawerũ and S. Kĩhara were leaders of KISA.

31 January 1953

Four detained persons were released after satisfying Mitchell's interrogations committee that they had not taken the Mau Mau oath. These were: Isaac Kitabi, Jackson M'Angaine, Saidi Mohamed and Benjamin Kariũki.

February, 1953

5 February 1953

Three men and two woman were brought from Thomson's Falls, Laikipia. One of these women was the wife of Onesmus Gacoka. Gacoka had been the chairman of KAU, Laikipia, until his arrest on 20 October 1952, and subsequent detention at Marsabit.

The men were put into Shed No. 4, and the women with the others in Shed No. 5.

6 February 1953

The following people were brought from Nakuru: Joel Warũĩ, John Njenga and Gathogo. They were put into Shed No. 4

8 February 1953

Rev. Stefano Waciira performed Christian baptism on baby Nyokabi. People sang Christian hymns and said Christian prayers.

9 February 1953

British officer Dennis came to the camp and met Willie Jemmie Wambũgũ Maina, whom he regarded as belonging to his age group. He greeted him in the greetings of the Irũngũ generation: "*Wanyua kinĩ!*" They had got acquainted with each other at Tũmũtũmũ, where Dennis was running a course in house building, and where Wambũgũ was an adult student. Dennis proverbially quipped to Wambũgũ that housed together in this camp were leopards and goats. We construed this to mean what we had all along suspected: that there were government informers locked with us. We couldn't put our finger on who these informers actually were, although we suspected there wouldn't be more than three. But we were not unduly worried for we did not consider these informers were any cleverer or more cunning than the rest of us.

10 February 1953

After listening to stories, told by new detainees who had already witnessed the armed struggle in the countryside, about the courage of young men who were daily streaming into the forests, a group of young men hatched a plot to break out with a view to eventually finding their way to the forests to join the war effort; it was futile, they felt, to sit it out in idleness in a detention camp. This group was led by young people who had worked as drivers for Overland Transport Company. Their plot couldn't work. For it was felt that even if those people could in fact make good their escape, they would expose those older men, women and children left behind to dire jeopardy, for they might all be killed in ruthless reprisal. After secret deliberations among the young people, the idea was given up. Our elders were not aware of these plans, although we did reveal them to them later.

11 February 1953

The detainees' committee decided that it was important to establish an equitable method of dividing out food when meals came to be served so that some people did not take unfair advantage over others. Gĩtahi wa Waciira was charged with the responsibility of making sure that each person took one piece of meat when meat was being served.

The committee also directed that children should be given milk every morning; only the mothers of children would be allowed to go to the kitchen to prepare special food for children. Other women would not be allowed to use the communal kitchen to make special meals. The women were not pleased with this ruling, but they accepted it.

14 February 1953

The women were moved to one of the new sheds that had been under construction in December. The women had complained earlier about lack of their own bathing facilities and the fact that they had to share lavatories with men. (These facilities would now be available.)

Officer Davine, nicknamed *Kabangi* or Busy-body Arranger, poured down food women had prepared for themselves, to the great annoyance of the women.

Three people were removed for transport to the Kapenguria trial: Mbūrū Mūgwīra, secretary of KAU, Mūrang'a; Rev. Ephantus Waithaka, a church minister with KISA, and Kĩnyanjui Kĩmani, a member of KAU, Mombasa.

15 February 1953

Seventy-four detainees were picked out from shed No. 1 for transfer to a new shed that had been constructed about 100 yards from No. 1. Those detainees who were not for transfer were ordered to stay outside in the backyard of Shed. No. 1. Those of us on transfer gathered our belongings and we were escorted by guards, without this time being put into chains. We remarked that the authorities had determined we were not the type of people who would try to run away.

Our separation had taken place as a result of categories established by Mitchell's interrogation committee.

17 February 1953

In the evening, the camp Officer, "Busy-body Arranger" Davine, instructed detainees from Sheds No. 1 and 2 that they should start waking up early in the morning for drill. The detainees said they would have nothing to do with drill. They were not school boys but elderly men.

18 February 1953

"*Kabangi*" appeared very early in the morning, at about 6.00 a.m. clad in sports clothing, but all the detainees declined to participate in drill. He stormed away in a rage.

19 February 1953

"*Kabangi*" issued a directive that all of us should be deprived of our beds' since no beds had been issued to any detainees locked up after the "Jock Scott" operation.

We fiercely opposed this move. When "*Kabangi*" attempted to physically carry out the bed used by Mburati Njogu, there was a tussle between him and Mburati and "*Kabangi*" failed to move the bed. He stormed out looking upset.

We expected that he would come back with prison guards but he didn't return. When Officer Dennis came to see us, Wambūgū Maina complained to him about "*Kabangi*'s" attempts to deprive us of our beds: the same *Kabangi*, Maina said, had maliciously poured out women's food the other day. Wambũgũ asked Dennis, "Have you people left us to the mercies of young upstarts?"

Dennis left for Nairobi the same day. When he came back he let us know we would not lose our beds.

20 February 1953

We learned that Officer Dennis had been given the position of Welfare Officer over us; he was charged with our welfare because he was supposed to be familiar with Gĩkũyũ ways. The story had it that Dennis had come to Gĩkũyũland around 1900. As a young man he had fraternised with young Gĩkũyũ men. He had been picked to work among us so that he would make a good study of us. He, therefore, made out to be a good friend of the detainees. On our part, we learnt to use his own words to place him—"the leopard among the goats".

25 February 1953

Sixty-six more detainees were transferred from shed No. 1 to our new shed. Our number rose to 140.

26 February 1953

During the month of February 1953 a large number of detainees, who had been brought from Tanganyika, were released and allowed to go home. Some expellees from Tanganyika were, however, not released, for the authorities continued to hold them on suspicion that they were Mau Mau. They told us that those who had been released knew no home in Gĩkũyũ-land; they would, therefore, have to go back to Tanganyika and face the danger of being expelled again.

March, 1953

1 March 1953

Those of us who had moved to new shed No. 2 requested Officer Dennis to supply us with a black-board for use in giving reading and writing lessons; we had left the board, supplied earlier, in the old shed No. 1. Dennis made a trip to C.M.S. Bookshop, Nairobi, and came back with two boards, exercise books and pencils, as well as reading materials for a lending library; we were allowed to buy the exercise books and the pencils, and started using the library facilities.

4 March 1953

A committee made of Col. La Fontaine, David Warŭhiŭ, Dennis, and two other British officers started to carry out interrogations. They used the camp commandant's own house as the venue of their interrogations. We had heard on the grapevine that a court had been set up which was empowered by the Governor to try people, release those it found innocent, and imprison the guilty or even recommend continued detention. We assumed this committee was that court, come to get all of us imprisoned.

6 March 1953

We heard that a prison warder had been found in possession of letters for detainees and had as a consequence been dismissed. Some of the warders confided to us that the man in question was from the Athi River detention camp.

On this same day Dennis came to see us and mentioned to his "friend" Wambŭgŭ that the prison authorities had discovered we were using camp personnel to run errands between ourselves and Mau Mau people in Nairobi. Wambŭgŭ declined to comment on this accusation. When Dennis was leaving he issued a warning to Wambŭgŭ: "Take care what you do!"

7 March 1953

A teaching programme was drawn up by Ndeng'era Mŭrĩithi, Timothy Maina, Tandeo Mwaŭra, John Cege and Babu Kamau, all of whom had been teachers at one time ,before their detention. They were assisted by other detainees. Four classes, one to four, would be operative. Lessons would be provided on the following: arithmetic, English, reading and writing, health and hygiene, agriculture, and current affairs.

And Ndeng'era wa Mŭrĩithi started to give physical training lessons to detainees in the mornings.

8 March 1953

We learned that the Legal Adviser to the British Colonial Secretary had arrived in Kenya. We promptly held a meeting and decided to present a petition to him, in which we would indicate the nature of our political grievances which had led to our detention. This was the only way we could further the political struggle; although we were physically incarcerated our mind and our will were free.

A petition was drafted and smuggled out of the camp, through a prison warder, to Kiburi House, from where it was to be handed to the colonial officer before he left for England.

13 March 1953

I was indoors reading a book when I got information that Officer Dennis wanted to see me. Outside Dennis greeted me in the Gĩkũyũ language and engaged me in a chat. He had known my father, he said, since he had lived at Tũmũtũmũ in the past; during those days I must have been a mere child. He had seen my name on the list of detainees and he had been struck with the coincidence that my father had been murdered by Mau Mau. I replied that I had been told my father had died at the hands of Mau Mau, and I had petitioned the Governor for permission to travel to my home, but up to now my petition had not been responded to. With his gaze fixed on the ground he shook his head. Were they considering releasing us soon? I asked him. He told me our fate was in the hands of the Governor. His (Dennis's) committee was simply charged with playing an advisory role. If he (Dennis) was satisfied that an individual was repentant he could recommend his release.

Other detainees had joined us. Henry Wambũgũ asked Dennis, "Do you present each individual case to the Governor?" Dennis replied, "Indeed, yes, we do. Didn't the Governor release some people just the other day?" But he added quickly, "But the country just now is in a state of war."

We interpreted this to mean we could not be released in the thick of the conflict.

21 March 1953

There was a physical tussle in the kitchen. It happened like this. Waciira wa Inoga was making the fire on which he would cook some tea. A warder wanted to collect some live coals from the fire place for use in the iron box. Waciira wouldn't let him, and the warder pushed him. Waciira reacted violently and would have pushed the warder into the fireplace had Gĩtahi Waciira not caught him just in time.

The warder reported Waciira wa Inoga to the sergeant-in-charge. We jointly accepted Waciira had been in the wrong and pleaded with the sergeant not to punish him since this was the first time we detainees had wronged any camp personnel. Waciira was asked to apologise, which he did. And the matter was closed.

30 March 1953

I requested Dennis to deliver a manuscript I had written at Kajiado, with the collaboration of Benson Gatoonye and Gĩitwa wa Ndimũ, to Nairobi publishers.

It featured a traditional Gĩkũyũ medicineman. Its title was *Tahĩka Waariga* which literally means "Vomit it out", a phrase medicineman would use in ceremonies of cleansing.

Although Dennis offered to deliver the manuscript, he never did.

April, 1953

2 April 1953

A Maasai church minister, Rev. David Mukinyo, came to conduct a service in the camp. He prayed to God to help us to obtain our release so that we could go back home. It was God, he said in his prayer, who had decreed that Gĩkũyũ people would find their fulfilment cultivating their land, while the Maasai people would live by keeping livestock. We were now unnaturally being kept in Maasailand, away from our land, unable to take care of our land.

He exhorted us to put trust in God who would see to it that we were freed from all our troubles.

10 April 1953

We discovered that Col. La Fontaine's interrogation committee was not itself the advisory committee on detainees' matters. It was charged with the preliminary duty of arranging individual cases, for presentation to the Advisory Committee.

Col. La Fontaine's committee did not manage to question all the detainees at the camp.

21 April 1953

Information got to us that Kiburi House had been besieged by government security forces and that the house had been subjected to a thorough search, in an attempt, so we were told, to recover some of the secret letters we had sent to the leaders of the Mau Mau armed struggle. A number of people who were actually found in the house had been arrested.

There had been rumours that Mau Mau fighters had vowed to conduct a rescue operation for their political leaders at Kajiado and Athi River detention camps. Those warders who had run errands for us were now afraid to do so. They said the situation was bad.

29 April 1953

Thirteen people, allegedly belonging to the inner core of the Mau Mau committee, were brought to the camp and locked up in Shed No. 1. We were told these people had been responsible for a state of great insecurity and disruption in Nairobi. Some names among them were: Lawrence Karugo, Hiram Kĩnyeru, Mũgo Mũratha, and Nyamũ Mareea.

Mwinga Chokwe and Karũũga Koinange were brought into the camp. They had been brought to hospital in Nairobi, from their detention in Marsabit; instead of being returned to Marsabit they were brought to Kajiado.

They described Marsabit as far hotter and drier than Kajiado. There had been fewer than twenty people at Marsabit, they told us; this made cooking more convenient than here.

30 April 1953

Charges against us started to be laid, prepared in accordance with the manner of each detainee's arrest. When we were arrested the colonial authorities were obviously unclear about which particular charges to make against each of us. We had been arrested on the unspecified charge of involvement with the Mau Mau movement. Many people detained under the Governor's Detention Order were charged with acts done more than twenty years back. For example, a detainee could be held for having been, those so many years back, a member of the proscribed K.C.A.; or for having been associated with a leader of KISA which allegedly sought the disruption of Church mission-run schools.

My own case is a good illustration. I was detained on charges that in 1948 I had published a book in Kiswahili, *Roho ya Kiume na Bidii kwa Mwafrika*, which sought to instil hatred against white people. And again in 1952 I had published the "Creed of the Agĩkũyũ" which was calculated to instil a spirit of disobedience against the authority of the Government.

May, 1953

7 May 1953

A thorough search of our living quarters was sprung upon us unawares. It affected Sheds number 1, 2 as well as the women's quarters and it lasted between 5.00 a.m. to 11.00 a.m. A platoon of British officers from the Kenya Police Reserve, specially set up for the Emergency, had arrived at night in armoured cars. Powerful searchlights were mounted to light an area of the camp, within a radius of 100 yards. Some officers conducted a search of the compound, while others came into the living quarters.

All of us men detainees, prisoners and women detainees, were stripped to the skin; police women carried out the search on the women.

Babu Kamau and George Waiyaki were found in possession of many letters and documents and they were badly assaulted; Babu lost a tooth in the process. From other detainees they confiscated various items: cameras, books which had virtually formed our library, writing paper, even knives for peeling potatoes. They even drilled into the ground in shed number 2, using a machine we nicknamed the "scenting machine"; they were presumably searching for arms, may be ammunition and grenades.

An amount of more than Sh. 6000 was taken from the detainees.

We assumed that the whole exercise had been prompted by rumours that Mau Mau fighters had vowed to carry out a rescue operation on the detention camps. We also heard that a warder from our camp had been caught red-handed handling detainees' letters.

We started cooking our lunch at 12.00 noon and the meal did not get ready until 3.00 p.m. That day we ate only one meal.

12 May 1953

This was the first day detainees were given an opportunity to travel to Nairobi to appear before the Advisory Committee on Detainees. Those who were travelling to Nairobi on this day were awakened very early and travelled under very tight security, like criminals being taken to the high court on a capital charge. The following people appeared before the Advisory Committee on this day: Charles Mũnyua Wambaa, Mũũgĩ Cege, Joshua Njũgũna, Mĩnyarũ Kahĩa, John Ng'ang'a and Ng'ombe Gakũrũ.

It transpired that this appearance took the form of a trial without witnesses or defence counsel; the Committee had final jurisdiction over the fate of detainees: they could order release or continued detention.

Those who went to Nairobi were not given lunch.

14 May 1953

It was ruled that detainees at Kajiado would no longer be served with tea; instead porridge would be served. People refused to take porridge, and trouble appeared imminent. People with money bought their own sugar, cocoa, or coffee, or tea leaves. On that day some people drank black tea.

Our rations of food were also cut. No explanation was forthcoming.

20 May 1953

Those of us in new shed number 2 received some encouraging news. That news was passed to us by some of our group who had received it from women detainees when they met at the camp dispensary, where they had gone for treatment. This was a favourite place for exchanging news among detainees.

The news was that two "Tanganyika" detainees who had been freed from Kajiado had not only returned to Tanganyika, but had taken the trouble to gather together the property of people who had continued to be detained in Kajiado. They had arranged through a camp warder for clothes and money to be delivered to the other Tanganyika detainees. This news filled us with joy.

29 May 1953

Twenty people who had been detained after the Jock Scott operation were told to pack up their things as they were to be moved from sheds number 1 and 2 to the Athi River detention camp. We had grown close to one another after living together and sharing political ideas and this enforced separation filled us with sorrow.

We said farewell to each other amid exhortations that we should be for ever faithful to our cause whatever the venue of our detention.

Some of the people who were transferred are: Solomon Meemia, Wamũthenya Kang'eri, Romano Njamumo, Joel Warũĩ, Mwanĩki Mũgwerũ, Rev. Arthur Gatũngũ and Kamau Itũtĩre.

30 May 1953

I composed a song based on the questions asked and answers given during a typical interrogation session:

"You! Who told you to join nationalist politics?"
"It is the pain and bitterness of losing our land which turned me into a nationalist!"
"And political freedom: why do you demand it?"
"Because I cannot accept to be a slave in my own land!"
"Freedom and land: from where will you get them?"
"Our party KAU will win its case, for its case is just."
"You in KAU: what are your ideals, what is your programme?"
"In KAU we believe in justice and we put our trust in God."
"So your ultimate objective is genuine peace?"
"God, let it be so, Amen. God, let it be so!"

June, 1953

16 June 1953

A woman named Rebeka Njeeri developed an ailment of the intestines. Some people in the camp had blood-stained diarrhoea. Dr. Likimani came to the camp, gave all of us drugs and innoculated us. Some people had swellings where they had been injected; we said this was a sign that a serious infection was in its early stages.

We felt that Dr. Likimani had given us very good treatment and had shown great patriotic concern for us, we who were involved in the struggle for freedom.

2

Across the Sea to Manda Island
2 July 1953 to 1 September 1953

July, 1953

2 July 1953

Trucks belonging to the Public Works Department (PWD) were brought at around 5.00 p.m. to transport us. Their bodies were constructed with wire mesh. Twenty guards were ready to put handcuffs and chains on us before transportation.

When the British officer who was to oversee our transportation arrived, we respectfully made representations to him, assured him that we would on no account attempt to escape, and requested him not to put us in chains. Some elderly detainees asked Cege Kabogoro, who had become the camp leader, to put their case in English to the officer asking him to respect their age. The officer ordered that we should be transported without being handcuffed or chained.

At around 6.00 p.m., 13 of us were driven towards Athi River, without, however, being told where we were being taken. When we arrived at the Athi River railway station we were made to wait until 8.00 p.m. when we were ordered to board two train coaches. There were 69 detainees and 10 guards in each coach. The train steamed with us towards Mombasa.

3 July 1953

We arrived at Mariakani railway station at around 1.00 o'clock. We alighted from the train and were loaded into Public Works Department trucks. There were very many people here at Mariakani. We talked to some railway employees who were known to us. They told us that a crowd had collected here because information had gone out, courtesy of the colonialist propaganda machine, that cannibal Mau Mau people were being brought; they had come to see the cannibals with their own eyes.

Many of these Taita people appeared quite surprised to see us, who appeared quite normal people, willing to hold normal reasonable conversation with them. We let them know that we were being persecuted because we had refused to accept the loss of our land, and hinted to them that they would themselves face a similar problem in the future. Some of them were eager to learn about the

27

fate of their countryman, Mwinga Chokwe, but we were hardly given enough time to have a good chat.

We left these people shaking their heads: how could they have been so duped by the colonialists!

We were driven through farmland roads and along roads that went through uninhabited bushland until we reached Malindi, at around 6.00 p.m. We were put inside a badly ventilated shed constructed along the sea shore. We were brought supper of *chapati* and relish, but we couldn't enjoy our meal, what with the sweaty overcrowding and overwhelming heat. People were so oppressed by the heat at night that they felt they would faint, and we were tormented throughout the night by a swarm of mosquitoes.

4 July 1953

In the morning prisoners brought porridge to us which we declined to take. They put us into trucks again and drove us along a road which was being constructed by prisoners convicted on charges of belonging to the Mau Mau movement. The trucks found if difficult to move on the muddy and slippery roads for it had rained heavily. At first the guards would push the trucks on their own when they got stuck in the mud; but finally they asked us to come down and help. They had to forget that we were prisoners and they invited us to share the troubles of the journey. As we entered into conversation we would tentatively touch on the nature of our political grievances, seeking to show them that we had been made to suffer for asking that our lands be returned to us; and they would agree that there was justice in our cause.

We stopped at "Lango la Simba" prison, which was situated right in the depth of the forest. We became friendly with the prisoners, many of whom were known to us, and had interesting conversations with them. Showing a touching regard for us, they prepared the midday meal for us. They spoke bitterly about the way the British imperialists were disrupting the lives of the people in the whole country. Most of these people had been imprisoned after being convicted on false charges devised by traitors who for their own reasons wanted them removed from the life of their communities.

Their militant courage made a deep impression on us, who almost felt that we were wanting in similar courage. They sang songs which expressed a spirit of daring defiance. They told us that there were people who were fighting a ruthless war trusting in the guidance of our ideals; we should resolutely continue to give ideological guidance until final victory.

5 July 1953

At 6.00 a.m. we climbed into the trucks and we were driven in the direction of Lamu. We crossed the Tana river by ferry at Garisseni. We arrived at Mkowe, on the shores of the Indian Ocean, at around 3.00 p.m. People who had never seen the open sea before were horrified at the prospect of having to step into the water. One old man shed tears overwhelmed by the fearful thought that the imperialists had planned it all—to exterminate us by throwing us *en masse* into the ocean. Would he be forced to part for ever with all that wealth he had acquired with toil?

But another elderly man, who was full of courage, remarked that this grief was misplaced: "You weep because of your property," he remonstrated. "Shouldn't you weep for our lives and the lives of these young men? Why don't you reserve your tears for our people who are being massacred by the British imperialists?"

We could see the town of Lamu lying on an island that appeared to be about seven miles from our location on the mainland. A motor boat was anchored some distance from the shore. They put us in rowing boats and rowed us to the motorboat which rode the waves until it reached Lamu Island.

The road leading from the boat-landing to the prison was heavily guarded by soldiers who lined both sides of the road. We marched in the middle of the road, our luggage carried on our shoulders. Almost all Lamu residents had crowded along this road, to have a glimpse of us, alleged Mau Mau cannibals who, so the story had gone out, relished the flesh of infants and women's breasts.

We were put into an immense building. A long time back, slaves waiting for shipment had been locked in this same building. Today it served as the main prison in Lamu. It was a one storied building with numerous cells, and enclosed a large court.

They crammed many of us, with our belongings, into 10 by 10 foot cells; each cell would be loaded with ten or eleven detainees. One wing of this prison building housed people who had been convicted in courts for belonging to the Mau Mau movement: many had been sentenced to long prison terms of ten years and over, and yet others had been given life terms.

We were locked up for the night at around 8.00 p.m., after we had eaten. They had put a pail in each cell for our calls of nature. It was an uncomfortable sleep with people sleeping with their limbs literally interlocked, and we woke up with aches and exhaustion.

6 July 1953

They unlocked the cells at around 7.00 a.m. and carried out a head count. We complained bitterly about the degradation we had been subjected to—sleeping in cramped conditions, using a pail for our calls of nature and sleeping amid the stink of our own shit. The convicted prisoners took out the pails, to go and dispose of the waste in the sea, and to clean up the pails.

The officer in charge of this prison was an elderly white man. Some detainees recognised him as one "Commander" Stancey-Marks, a prominent landowner and member of the British settler community. When he came to see us in the morning, he asked us to choose three people who would cook our food. We chose Cege Kĩraka, Kĩhaato Kĩbuukũ and Gacangi Gĩkaru. There were now two kitchens—one for the convicted prisoners and one for the detainees. When we complained about our sleeping conditions, Stancey-Mark dismissively told us there were no other sleeping quarters.

The conditions of the journey, the bad food and terrible sleeping conditions, as well as the strange climate, all started to take their toll. A number of detainees were taken ill and they were escorted to Lamu Native Community Hospital. Most of them were treated and released, but three patients—Gacuĩrĩ Kĩariĩ, Kagĩĩka Kũhũtha, and Joram Wawerũ—had to be admitted, under guard, as in-patients. Those patients who returned brought the news that they had made the acquaintance of a Mũgĩkũyũ hospital worker, a resident of Lamu. We decided that we would cultivate this man's friendship and use his assistance in getting our letters sent out through the post office.

At 1.00 p.m. two detainee cooks, Cege and Kĩhaato, took food to the admitted patients. They would try to gather more information about the Mũgĩkũyũ hospital worker.

In the evening convicted prisoners who had been working outside returned. They told us they were preparing a place for our detention on Manda island. According to them Manda island was uninhabited and had been uninhabited for 300 years, since when people had mass-emigrated to escape from the diseases and natural hazards that were rampant on the island. The island was inhabited by poisonous creatures like scorpions, snakes and red-headed lizard-like reptiles.

We were filled with apprehension. The colonialists had designed the place of our end, we decided. We contemplated resisting our transfer from Lamu prison to Manda island, even if this meant our mass extermination in Lamu prison. But after long deliberations among ourselves, we decided we would accept our transfer and put our trust in God, the guardian of our lives.

7 July 1953

Many detainees, seeking an opportunity to get out and to see Lamu town, made out that they were sick. The guards were aware that a good number of these people were not actually ill, but they did not want to make a fuss. What they did was to divide the "sick" into groups of about ten, so that each group would be taken in its turn.

The hospital was built near the backyard of the prison. From the hospital one could see the back prison gate, from where slaves used to be loaded on to sea-bound ships.

Many Lamu residents came to the hospital to have a good look at "Mau Mau cannibals". The detainees talked patiently with these people and proved to them the colonialists had created adverse rumours about the Mau Mau in a bid to drive a wedge between the peoples of Kenya. The inpatient detainees did a good job in establishing mutual understanding between the detainees and the local people.

The doctor in charge of the hospital was one Dr. Shah, an Indian.

8 July 1953

I composed a song to the tune of an Italian song in a record I had bought at Addis Ababa during the War in 1942. It was based on our experience of transfer to Lamu. Its title was: "To be isolated on an island in detention is an unforgettable experience". Many detainees practised singing the song and within two days, everybody could sing it. Here it goes:

1. To be detained on an island is an unforgettable experience
   An unforgettable three-days journey from Kajiado to Lamu.

   Wherever they try to isolate us
   Whatever tribulations they put us through
   We will never give up our bid to regain our land.
   God is our guardian, we shall regain our freedom.

2. We boarded our transport at Maboko, at around 8 o'clock at night
   All our belongings borne on our shoulders, none of us trembled with fear.
3. When we arrived at Mariakani, we found multitudes waiting to see us
   They had been told we were a weird lot; our train journey ended here.
4. We cunningly discounted those rumours of our weirdness, spread to sow mutual hatred.
   Then we boarded trucks on our way to Malindi.
5. They packed us in cells like animals in a shed
   Thank God, the morning did come, after the sweat of the sweltering night heat.
6. We experienced the troubles of the road, hunger during the journey
   Confinement in trucks because of the rain and mud of July.
7. In the woodlands of Lango la Simba, we found our own people, taken prisoners.
   Their hospitality offered a respite, and they sang songs which instilled courage
8. They put us in rowing boats to cross onto Lamu island

> They put us in the main prison, where, a long time ago, slaves were locked up.
>
> *Thaai*

9 July 1953

We started making friends among the warders. Our cooks would clandestinely offer meals to them in the kitchen. There were no Gĩkũyũ warders at Lamu. Therefore the officer in charge of the prison, knowing how colonial propaganda had spread lies about how bad we were, would never have suspected that we could succeed in fraternising with prison personnel.

10 July 1953

Kagĩĩka Kũhũtha was released from hospital. His eye ailment had been successfully treated, and his eyesight was now quite good.

12 July 1953

We expressed our wish to go for a bath and a swim in the sea to the sergeant. The sergeant obtained permission for us from the British officer. We were given the escort of a few warders; the authorities had come to appreciate that we were men of good behaviour!

We marched to the beach in style, in line formation, two people abreast, singing our song "To be isolated on an island in detention is an unforgettable experience". The local women would pick up their babies and beat hasty retreat into their houses when they saw us, and we would bitterly reflect how wide colonialist lies had travelled.

We bathed and swam for about half an hour. Then we marched back in formation to the rhythm of our sweet song; to the show tune, some of us whistled in the manner of recorded music. The beat was so good that the warders, walking on either side of our formation, could not help joyfully marching with us to the rhythm of our song.

Our march back to the prison seemed to reveal that a good number of us were acquainted with the military march. The warders asked us where we had acquired this experience. And we informed them, quite truthfully, that some of us had seen the 1914 War while yet others had been in the 1939 War.

14 July 1953

We saw a copy of the newspaper *East Africa and Rhodesia* which carried a story on a debate in the British parliament on the arrest of Jomo Kenyatta and his associates. I, the author, was referred to in this story. One British M.P. had claimed during the debate that one of the detainees had been put in for publishing "The Creed". (See Appendix 8.) According to the story this M.P. had in his possession a copy of the Creed in English translation. He had held it up in Parliament and declared, "The opening words of this Creed are as follows: 'I believe in Ngai, the Almighty Father...', the second line declares: 'I believe in Gikũyũ and Mũmbi, our parents'. " The M.P. had wanted to know: "What crime has a man committed by declaring his faith in God and his faith in the values of the ancestors of his community?"

The other detainees commented that I had, unknown to me, acquired an advocate in England.

17 July 1953

The oath was administered to two people who had, like most of us, come from the Kajiado detention; they had not previously taken the oath. It is the convicted prisoners who brought the necessary tree branches and leaves for the ceremony, as well as preparing the oath-taking site in one of the prison cells. This was done secretly during the day; the warders were around, but they never suspected that this was happening.

18 July 1953

Gacuĩri Kĩarii was released from hospital. He came back to the prison with those people who had gone to the hospital at 1.00 p.m. to deliver food to the patients. He let us know that the Mũgĩkũyũ medical attendant had offered to be our link with the outside world; he would deliver our letters to the post office. This piece of news was cause for rejoicing.

22 July 1953

We were taken for a swim, but the elderly men among us didn't come along. This time the women residents of Lamu did not run away from us, for the bluff had been called: they knew we were normal people, just like them, and not cannibals We greeted them as we passed them standing leaning against the posts of their houses. Some boys followed us, watching curiously the long beards and hair worn by some of us. And when we got to the sea, two Abajuni men indicated their desire to join us in the water, but the guards wouldn't allow them. It was clear they wanted to demonstrate they no longer considered us objects of fear.

28 July 1953

Prisoners told us they had completed building four big dormitories, constructed with *makuti* reeds. They had also put up quarters for camp personnel as well as fenced off the camp on Manda island. They were now constructing an office block.

For some time now prisoners had been crossing on to Manda island by boat in the morning and then back at night.

31 July 1953

Our transfer to what we thought of as the disease-ridden Manda island now appeared frighteningly imminent. We found it necessary to write a petition to the Colonial Secretary in London, telling him we considered our lives threatened.

We elected a committee to draft the petition. We made a collection for buying paper, an envelope and stamps. Ng'ang'a wa Kanja contributed most of the money.

Eventually our petition to the British Colonial Secretary was posted by air. Copies of the petition were circulated to a number of sympathetic lawyers. We requested them to try and assist us in this matter.

August, 1953

1 August 1953

Our petition, and copies of it to lawyers, were taken to the Mũgĩkũyũ hospital attendant. He was instructed to post immediately the petition to the Colonial Secretary; he should then have the copies posted to lawyers three days later.

4 August 1953

Paulo Gĩcaana was taken sick; he was admitted at Lamu hospital.

9 August 1953

All patients who had been earlier admitted to the hospital in Lamu were brought back to prison, irrespective of their condition. We were informed that we would be transferred to Manda island—tomorrow morning.

10 August 1953

After we had finished eating at 1.00 p.m., we were ordered to collect our belongings.

Then under very heavy guard, 138 detainees were marched through Lamu town. Watched by large curious crowds, we marched on, singing hymns of political resistance.

We crossed onto Manda island in four boats. We arrived on the island at 4.00 p.m. Manda is fifteen miles away from Lamu. From the boat landing, we walked about 500 yards before getting to the detention camp. The camp was fenced off with barbed wire. There were four windowless dormitories constructed with *makuti reed* basketwork on all sides as well as the roof; each dormitory had two entrances, each on either side. We were put into two dormitories, 69 of us to each dormitory.

Some prisoners at the camp had prepared our meal. After eating, we spread our mats on the sandy floor, all the time keeping a wary lookout for the scorpions for which Manda was infamous. We slept lightly, fearing an attack from scorpions. But the dawn finally came—and none of us has been bitten by a scorpion.

11 August 1953

Prisoners brought foodstuffs in sacks, for tomorrow's meals, into the camp. Commander Stancey-Marks, the officer who had been in charge at Lamu and who was now in command here, issued orders that the sacks of foodstuffs should be returned to the boat landing where the boats from Lamu had first dropped them. We thought that the prisoners had brought in what was not meant for our camp.

In the evening we learned that the prisoners had been returned to Lamu, and we were supposed to collect the foodstuffs from the boat landing in the morning. And this was not all. We would from now on be required to gather our own firewood from the bush, fetch the water from the wells, cook for ourselves, and dispose of the camp night soil.

We held deliberations and decided to refuse to participate in certain kinds of labour. Many detainees argued that we had not been convicted in a court of law, we should, therefore, not be put into the kind of labour which virtually constituted punishment—like gathering firewood, drawing water and disposing of night soil. We would agree to cook our own meals, provided the foodstuffs were delivered into the camp. We had since our Kajiado detention been under orders not to leave the camp area on pain of being shot. Many of our people elsewhere had been shot, on the pretext that they were attempting to escape, after being allowed to leave the camp. We resolved we would not collect the food from the boat landing.

12 August 1953

At around 7.00 a.m. a Luo sergeant came to the camp and instructed Cege Kabogoro, our camp leader, to appoint a group of people who would go to the boat landing to collect our food provisions. Cege told him the detainees would not agree to this arrangement. The sergeant talked to us, but all of us refused to be party to these new arrangements.

The sergeant went to report to the officer in charge of the camp, who told him not to be bothered with us.

Joram Wawerũ became seriously ill. He had been taken from Lamu hospital before he was well. He was provided with a bed and isolated in dormitory No. 2, away from our sleeping quarters. Other detainees who were complaining of ailments were taken to the camp dispensary, situated near the camp gate, to be treated there under guard.

The rest of the detainees whiled away the time reading books and complaining about the treatment we were receiving from the colonialist officer. We waited in vain for his response to our rejection of the arrangements he had initiated. Nobody lit a fire that day. When it was dark we went to bed.

In his sick room, Joram Wawerũ was given bread and tea, which were prepared by the Mluyia medical attendant who had treated him.

13 August 1953

We got together for a meeting at around 9.00 a.m. People talked with much bitterness.

We had nothing for breakfast. Neither the sergeant, nor the officer-in-charge of the camp came to talk to us. There was an armed guard in the watch-tower, another at the entrance to the camp, and two guards patrolled the camp grounds.

At 10.00 a.m. we asked Cege to write a note to the officer in charge of the camp to remind him that we had not eaten since yesterday. Cege drafted this memo in English.*

To The Camp Officer,

I have the mandate of 138 detainees to remind you that we did not get any food yesterday and we have received nothing today. It is now 10.00 a.m., and we do not know what is happening.

Yours faithfully,
Cege—Camp leader:

*Much of the correspondence carried out in this chapter was originally in English and old copies, which we would have liked to reproduce photographically, had been preserved through the years by the author. Maina wa Kinyatti who assisted the author in editing the Gĩkũyũ diary, translated these original documents into Gĩkũyũ, and retained the original copies. Unfortunately Maina went to prison before making these documents available to Heinemann. The rendition here, therefore, is an English translation of the Gĩkũyũ, which, in its turn, was translated from the original English.

The note was given to the gate guard who had it delivered at the camp office. The British officer scribbled his reply on the same note:

Your food is available, and has been available since yesterday at 9.00 a.m. Go and take delivery.

(Signed)
N.S. Stancey Marks,
Camp Officer, 13.8.53

When this note was read to us our bitter anger increased. We complained about our affairs being placed in the hands of a settler who was motivated by great hatred for us, we who dared to demand back our land, part of which he had acquired for himself. We repeated our stand: detention regulations disallowed us to leave the confines of the camp; our food and wood fuel had always been delivered into the camp. Cege was instructed to write to the imperialist a second time and state our case. Cege wrote:

Manda Island
13.8.53

To the Camp Officer,

Further to your reply of this morning to our letter in which you stated that our food is available for collection at the boat landing, we would like to state that we will be willing to collect the food from the camp store. Wh n we were first detained, we were strictly ordered never to go beyond the precincts of the camp; we believe we must continue to adhere to this regulation.

Yours faithfully,
Cege—Camp Leader

Once again the officer scribbled his reply on our memo:

My orders are that the food be collected from the boat landing. I have nothing else to add on this matter.

(Signed)
Officer-in-Charge of the Camp.
13.8.53

Two detainees, Chokwe and Kali, had already made approaches to the gate guard, a Giriama man by the name Karisa, who had agreed to deliver a letter from us to the post office at Lamu. We made a contribution and made a little allowance to the guard, for his use before we started using his services. During the night we deliberated that we should not acquiesce to the things as they were. We would send a telegram to the Governor of the Kenya Colony the following day.

14 August 1953

On this third day of going without meals, people's faces reflected the gnawing hunger. They complained that the white officer meant to have us all exterminated—before the expiry of even a single week. The camp guards informed us that foodstuffs meant for us were dumped at the boat landing every day; they were going bad, and nobody would allow them to cook them.

We wrote a telegram to the Governor, for secret delivery to the post office, with a copy for hand delivery to the officer-in-charge of the camp.

On this day some of the detainees spent the day in bed. Those who walked around did so with an effort.

14 August 1953

TELEGRAM
VERY URGENT
GOVERNOR OF KENYA NAIROBI
THRO'

COMMISSIONER OF PRISONS NAIROBI

FOLLOWING OUR LETTER OF 1.8.1953 TO THE COLONIAL SECRETARY, 138 DETAINEES WERE TRANSFERRED FROM LAMU TO MANDA ON 10.8.53. AFTER STRONGLY REJECTING BEING TRICKED INTO GOING BEYOND CAMP PRECINCTS, BEEN DENIED FOOD, WOOD, FUEL, WATER AND REMOVAL OF NIGHT SOIL. WE REQUEST URGENT INVESTIGATION WITH VIEW TO GIVING DETAINEES ASSURANCE OF PROTECTION

TRULY 138 DETAINEES,
MANDA ISLAND CAMP

The officer sent the sergeant to know our mind. He found Babu Kamau seriously ill and ordered that he be taken to the dispensary for treatment. Babu didn't return, but was referred by the medical attendant to the sick room where Waweru was convalescing; he was provided with a bed.

When at 1.00 p.m. they were given two loaves of bread for their midday meal, they did not eat them, but saved them for us. Then they obtained six empty bottles and filled them with water. They wrapped the bread and the bottles of water with clothes into a bundle and gave this to a detainee who had gone for treatment, who brought it into our dormitory as if he was bringing in a bundle of clothes.

At around 3.00 p.m. we gathered in dormitory number one and agreed that we would share the four loaves of bread and six bottles of water. We took as our guide the creed of the Olenguruone community: "We shall all have a share, however small the portion is, even if it be a bean seed." The loaves of bread were broken into 136 tiny pieces in accordance with our number. Rev. Stefano Waciira was asked to offer prayers of thanksgiving. He stood up as he prayed. He asked God to bless the pieces of bread so that they would become like the two fish and five loaves which Jesus blessed so that five thousand people ate and were satisfied. May the pieces of bread have the strength to sustain our lives and may the drops of water cool and soothe our parched throats. May Ngai help us to overcome our enemies.

By this time the joints of our legs were loose with fatigue. At the end of the prayer, Kīhaato Kībuukū passed the pieces of bread on a plate; each person would take a piece and put it into his mouth. Cege Kīraka would in his turn pour some water into a spoon from which each person would sip to soothe his throat.

After this, we discussed our fate and affirmed that we would not quietly acquiesce to extermination by the imperialist officer. We therefore elected people to write a memorandum to him. From dormitory number one J.D. Kali and Kamawe Mwega were chosen; from dormitory number two Gakaara wa Wanjaū and Cege, the Camp Leader, were chosen. It was agreed the letter would be written and delivered the following day.

15 August 1953

On the fourth day of hunger, the camp officer and the sergeant came into our sleeping quarters at around 2.00 p.m. and found everybody in bed. The officer ordered us to wake up. But when he ordered us to get out and carry out work, nobody obeyed and nobody left the sleeping quarters.

He stormed out in annoyance.

While some people became ill and went to the dispensary for treatment, others faked illness in order to get an opportunity to get just a bit of water to soothe their burning thirst. The medical attendant, a Mluyia from Nyanza was aware of this and he would kindly give each person a small glass of water'

This is the letter which we wrote to the camp officer:

Manda Camp
15.8.53

To the Camp Officer,

1. Following my two letters to you, I have been authorised by 138 detainees to record our protest that you are subjecting us to penal punishment contrary to the law of Britain. You denied us our supply of meat on the following days: Thursday, Friday and Saturday; as well as other food and nature's own water (the Government doesn't buy supplies of it!) on the same days.

2. You are no doubt aware that among our number are five sick people who were literally put on a journey to this island straight from Lamu hospital, where they had been admitted as inpatients. These people require all-round care, attention and medical treatment if their lives are to be preserved.

3. We the detainees have subjected your attitude to close scrutiny and we have concluded that your aim is to create unnecessary disaffection in the minds of the detainees against the Government. Many of our people, men and women, are shot every day in different places on the pretext that they are found escaping. We would like to know the truth: does the Government empower you to kill all of us by way of denying us food and water? We are aware that on the day we arrived here, prisoners brought food for cooking right inside the camp, but you issued orders for the food to be returned to the boat landing.

4. As a consequence of all this we have written to the Government about our complaints; yesterday we also sent a telegram to the Governor, a copy of which was forwarded to you. We feel that you have failed to act towards us in accordance with Christian principles. In all fairness you should have allowed the Government to continue dealing with us in the old way instead of introducing your regulations designed solely to vex us and make our life intolerable.

Yours truly,
Cege—Camp Leader.

This time the officer sent back a reply on his own paper:

Manda Island Camp
15th August, 1953

To Cege,

1. I have received your letter of today and noted its contents.

2. There is no penal punishment whatsoever that I have designed for any detainee in this camp. And I have denied detainees neither food nor water.

3. Food for cooking has been made available and is available even now. When detainees decide to obey my orders, they may take delivery of this food. I have informed you so many times. Today, I expressly instructed some people to take delivery of the food, but they refused to do so.

4. Water has been available in plenty all the time. When detainees agree to fetch it they may draw as much of it as they like. I have asked people to come forward to carry out this work. My call has gone unanswered. Today those who were asked to perform this work refused.
5. I assigned people to the work of disposing of night soil. They refused to do so.
6. I am not prepared to offer any comments on the other matters raised in your letter. I am taking your letter to the Commissioner of Prisons right away. Your telegram was received when the boat had already left for Lamu; therefore, it will be delivered today.

(Signed)
N.S. Stancey-Marks
I/C Manda Camp.

It was the camp sergeant who brought the letter to our sleeping quarters and handed it over to Cege. He complained that the Government was angry with us for the letter we had written from Lamu Prison. Cege asked him, "Is that why you persist in denying us food?" The sergeant responded, "What do you people want me to do? Aren't you the ones who are punishing yourselves with all this suffering? Give me two men only, and you'll see what I'll do to help you." We told him none of us was prepared to leave these quarters. He left us.

When we talked among ourselves, we expressed our belief that the imperialist camp officer and the African sergeant were working hand-in-hand. They wanted us to voluntarily release two men from our number in order to achieve our virtual surrender. We felt convinced that we were being subjected to suffering not because orders had been handed down from higher circles in government but rather because this particular officer was venting his anger because we had dared to send out a memorandum over his head.

People spoke in anger in spite of their frail and fading voices. We would not be brought to submission by being denied the sustenance of food, they vowed. We were but one wing of a people engaged in a bitter struggle; some of our people were waging a hard armed struggle for land and freedom in the forest, while reprisal killings were being carried against innocent people in the villages. If we had been brought to this remote island for mass extermination, so be it! But we would not be party to surrender, which would be ignominious and shameful in the eyes of our people who were engaged in struggle for all of us.

16 August 1953

On the fifth day of our hunger, only a few people found it possible to leave their beds. Many people could hardly speak, so parched were their throats and dry their tongues. People's limbs were loose and had no coordination. Their eyes had sunk into their sockets. Bodily functions had been affected. Calls of nature hardly took place. One would urinate hardly once a day; the trickle of urine had a reddish colouration as if the urine was tinged with blood, so dehydrated had the body become. There were hardly any bowel movements; the stomach was virtually empty. Since we wanted to meet in dormitory no. 1, the elderly people from no. 2 found themselves physically unable to move themselves there.

After deliberations it was resolved that we send a cable to the supreme ruler in the British Government, Queen Elizabeth herself, and tell her of our grave plight. If there were ways of telling the world, they should be used. We made a collection, as had been our habit, and managed to get enough for having the cable dispatched.

CABLE

VERY URGENT
TO HER MAJESTY QUEEN ELIZABETH,
THRO' THE GOVERNOR OF KENYA
THRO' THE COMMISSIONER OF PRISONS, NAIROBI
THRO' THE OFFICER I/C MANDA ISLAND DETENTION CAMP
P.O. LAMU
FURTHER TO OUR LETTER OF 1ST AUGUST TO THE COLONIAL SECRETARY AND OUR TELEGRAM TO THE GOVERNOR ON 14 AUGUST, WE 20 OCTOBER DETAINEES REGISTER GRAVE COMPLAINT. ON JULY 2ND WE WERE TAKEN TO LAMU FROM KAJIADO AND ON 10TH AUGUST TO MANDA ISLAND. SINCE AUGUST 12 CAMP OFFICER HAS DENIED DETAINEES SUPPLY OF FOOD, WATER AND WOOD FUEL IN A PLAN TO STARVE THEM TO DEATH. OUR CONCERN IS HAVING OUR FATE LEFT SOLELY IN THE HATEFUL HANDS OF A SETTLER OFFICER WHO MAY KILL ALL OF US WITH THE GOVERNMENT IGNORANT OF HIS INTENTIONS. PLEASE TREAT OUR CABLE AS AN SOS.

TRULY
138 DETAINEES
MANDA ISLAND CAMP.

17 August 1953

George K. Ndegwa said the time had come for us to have a frank discussion of the turn things had taken. Some people, he said, had started to murmur behind their blankets that the time had come for us to define the extent of our struggle against the settler officer, for it was futile to keep despatching telegrams and cables which never received a reply. Each person should speak out his mind; the situation should not be allowed to develop where people felt forced to join in an action without being convinced about its rightness. Many detainees agreed wholeheartedly with Ndegwa. It was agreed that all people in dormitory No. 2 be asked to come so that all of us could confront this issue.

W.J. Wambũgũ Maina was asked to take the chair. Most people talked from a sitting position although a few managed to talk while standing. Benson Gatonye suggested we should obtain a written undertaking from the imperialist officer that we would not be shot if we left the precincts of the camp. Charles M. Wambaa and Henry Wambũgũ suggested we should accept all work except disposal of night soil; but Gĩcohi wa Gĩthua countered: how could we carry out manual labour when we had not been tried and convicted by any court of law? Daudi Wanyee advocated our acceptance of taking delivery of the food, which we would cook and eat to our fill before refusing to do anything else. Samuel Koina said he had in his day seen much suffering; it was necessary for people to learn to endure; we should at least wait for replies to our petitions. John Adala said he was the only Mluyia person among us; he would accept any resolution we would make. Joel Kuria Werehire reminisced that after he was arrested at Eldoret he had been transported in chains; he could never see himself ever compromising with the imperialists. J.D. Kali spoke in the same spirit, stating that we should keep in view that we had been arrested, not on a mundane issue like the food we were being denied, but on a vital cause. We should be ready to demonstrate to the imperialists that we were ready to seek victory even through death. We should each of us go back to our beds and cover ourselves up and wait for death. Prison personnel would collect bodies for burial as and when each of us died. Our children would in future come and see our graves.

Chairman Wambũgũ Maina cautioned us against talking easily about dying. We had not taken the oath with the objective of coming to die on this island. "It is we people here at Manda who will supply the brains to the leadership of our independence which we are fighting for. Deliberate on methods of achieving victory against this great fool of a white man, but by no means play into his plot to get rid of us over the matter of food. Should we allow ourselves to die, our children will laugh at our memory."

At that very moment something we would always remember happened. Nahashon Kang'aari spoke. So ill was Kang'aari that he could not sit up in bed. He raised his hand and said in a faint and croaking voice: "It is as we vowed."

When the chairman asked Kang'aari to clarify his meaning, he repeated his enigmatic words and would not say a word more.

The voice of somebody who was lying down said: "Let us wait until tomorrow." It was George Njue Kamŭmbŭ. Many voices assented, with some urging that we wait for replies to our petitions.

After we had finished the meeting, people said Kang'aari's words were like a curse; all the same we should heed the wisdom of chairman Wambŭgŭ's words.

J.D. Kali confirmed that our cable had been delivered by a warder to Lamu Post Office. It had been put into an envelope like a letter and was being posted to Kiburi House, Nairobi from where it would be despatched to England. A copy had been made and given to an Indian building contractor, who was on his way to India: he had been requested and he had agreed to despatch this cable to England from India. Another copy was put into a bottle; a note was attached asking whoever might recover this bottle to make the cable available to newspaper people. The bottle was tightly corked and given to dispensary-bound patients; it was to be thrown into the sea where night soil was being disposed of, so that it would ride on the waves to some foreign land.

When people went to bed, the only thing that could be heard were the faint voices of people from neighbouring beds talking to each other.

18 August 1953

We were woken up by the sudden burst of gunfire at around 5.30 o'clock in the morning. The firing had taken place somewhere outside between dormitory 1 and dormitory 2. We were frightened into wakefulness, convinced the hour had come for our extermination by mass shooting. Then we heard the shouted command of the imperialist officer: "*Simama!*"

We stood up wrapped up in our beddings, and heard this address made by a person we couldn't see.

"We have you properly surrounded in case any of you wants to cause trouble. If you don't show any violence, we shall not use force. We have not known you to be men of violence but we are ready for any eventualities. You shall stay in your sleeping quarters until 8.00 o'clock when a very important officer will come to address you: you may explain your grievances to him."

At that point somebody murmured that he would like to use the slop pail. But nobody waited to understand his request. An African police inspector burst into our sleeping quarters followed by two warders and demanded, "Who talked?" The officer who had been addressing us affirmed, "Yes, I heard him! Get him out of here fast, Inspector! He wants to heckle me! Get him locked up in a cell!"

The *askaris*, for no good reason, lighted on Waikwa Mwaniki, seized him and dragged him outside raining blows on him. He was locked up in a cell.

The officer who had been addressing us said, "That is a warning to all of you. No talking to each other in there!"

The darkness dissolved in the light of dawn. We could see that we were surrounded by prison guards and police on all sides.

At around 7.00 a.m. the officer came to the entrance and said, "You may elect two men from these quarters who will present your grievances to the very senior officer who is coming." He went to the other quarters and told them the same thing. The detainees said they did not need to appoint representatives other than the very people who had been elected to draft our petitions.

At 8.00 o'clock we were informed that it was the Commissioner of Prisons himself who was coming to address us. We were taken outside where we sat on the ground. Some elderly men, among them Mariko Kaambuĭ, Harrison Karŭme and Eongwe Icaŭ, had to be supported, so weak had they become.

The Commissioner of Prisons was escorted to us by the camp officer and other senior British prison officers; armed guards and police took up positions at a short distance to our rear. He made the following address:

"I will speak in Kiswahili so that every one of you may follow and understand well. After that your four representatives will speak.

"I have found it necessary to come here to make clear to you once and for all the conditions under which you are being kept here. I want to clarify the regulations and rules under which you are detained on Manda island. I expect you know I am the Commissioner of Prisons.

"The Governor has placed you under the administration of my office. You will therefore obey the rules and regulations of my office as these are handed down to you through the officer-in-charge of this camp. The camp officer is my representative here. Any regulations he gives derive from my office. For six days now you have refused to obey regulations issued by the camp officer who has been placed over you for your welfare. You have refused to:

(a) Cook your own food;
(b) Collect food from the boat landing;
(c) Remove slop pails;
(d) Draw water, and
(e) Gather wood fuel from the bush.

All these activities are written into the regulations of detention under the Emergency and you are required to carry them out.

"You have been brought here because investigations have unequivocally revealed you are very bad Mau Mau elements (*watu waovu kabisa*). When you were detained at Kajiado and Athi River, investigations were carried out which revealed that you were part of the inner core of the Mau Mau leadership you played a part in the formation of the movement and in the propagation of its programme. Many of you appeared before the Advisory Committee on Detainees, and it was recommended that you continue to be held in detention until this great enemy, Mau Mau, is annihilated for ever. There are some among you who have yet to face serious charges in court. And many among you are dangerous anti-social elements because you have taken Mau Mau oaths.

"You are going to be visited here by a committee led by Colonel La Fontaine and David Warũhiũ. Any of you who can convince this committee that he has changed and become a good person who is ready to cooperate with the Government may have his case reviewed; the committee may recommend his transfer to Athi River where he will be put in category 1 of those being rehabilitated. After that he would still have to be upgraded to categories 2 and 3 after which he may be released if the Governor recommends it. But before a detainee may attain those stages, he has to show willing cooperation to the Government, be prepared to reveal the secrets of the Mau Mau movement, and be ready to join the ranks of the loyalists who are taking care of the welfare of the community on every side.

"Now before you are two choices:

1. The road of light, that is the road of restoring peace to your people, and
2. Darkness and death in this uninhabited island. You have been brought here so that you may be effectively isolated from good law-abiding people in the country, for irrefutable proof has surfaced that you constitute the worst anti-social elements.

"It is your own people themselves who have put forward an irrefutable case against you, showing that you are leaders and organisers of a movement bent on bringing unrest and suffering in Kenya. Most unfortunately you have chosen the road of darkness and you have embraced a religion whose beliefs and prayers could only lead you and your country to eternal damnation. You have turned away from the way of truth and Christian faith.

"You have been writing petitions to me since your detention in the other camps until now. I have received copies of the telegram and cable which you addressed to the Governor and Her Majesty the Queen; they are right here in my pockets. But I would like to assure you that all these petitions are being sent in vain.

"The camp officer is empowered to punish you in accordance with prison regulations. If you do not obey his orders, I have empowered him to carry out punishment."

The Commissioner had finished.

Our four representatives now talked in turn. They talked faintly, without power and with parched throats.

The first to speak, Cege wa Kabogoro, requested that we be given a drink of water so that we may be able to speak, but the Commissioner angrily turned the request down.

So Cege spoke, and explained that in all detention camps where we had been, water was brought to us within the precincts of the camp, as was wood fuel, and we were under strict instructions never to go beyond, not even touch, the barbed wire that fenced in the camp. Many of our people elsewhere had been shot under the accusation that they were attempting to escape, when they had been ordered to go beyond the barbed wire of camps or even of communal villages. We had no objection to taking delivery of food from camp stores; this applied to water and wood fuel also.

Gakaara wa Wanjaũ (the author) stood up and said: "We have been assigned two different lines of work. One line of work is *domestic:* cooking, collecting fire wood and drawing water. The other line of work is *sanitary:* cleaning out the slop pails. The second line of work is normally part of the penal servitude of people who have been convicted in a court of law. We ourselves have not been tried in any court of law and we have previously not been required to carry out this kind of work. But we have always cooked for ourselves, and we are ready even now to do the same work."

Gakaara sat down.

J.D. Kali stood up and said: "We have been falsely accused of belonging to the Mau Mau movement. The tasks that are being assigned to us are the kind assigned to convicted criminals under punishment. We do not know for what we are being punished. We should be charged in a court of law so that a judgment based on justice may be arrived at, and so that any labour we perform is lawful. Some of us do not belong to that people who, according to you, have accused some of their people of being originators and leaders of Mau Mau."

The Commissioner asked Kali, "From where do you come?"

Kali answered, "I am a Mkamba."

The Commissioner told him, "There are also Mau Mau among your people.'

Kali sat down.

Kamawe stood up and said, "Malicious accusations (*fitina*) have led to our being brought here." He spoke about his own personal case. Before his detention he had worked as an officer of the Government, as a market master. Kamawe wanted to know whether a detainee could hire the services of a lawyer, to look after his legal rights in a court of law. The Commissioner replied that he was the final authority for receiving the grievances of detainees. Kamawe sat down.

After that the Commissioner said he would give us ten minutes to come to a final decision. He retired to the office.

We did not hold lengthy deliberations. A good number of people were willing to go with the Commissioner's argument that regulations requiring us to carry out work were in line with the law of the Emergency. Others urged us to heed the wisdom of Wambũgũ Maina's words, that we had not taken an oath to acquiesce to our being starved to death. We should carry out the work with the understanding that we were doing so under compulsion.

After a brief discussion the general view was that we agree to do all the work except cleaning out the slop pails. We sent three people to present our views to the Commissioner: Cege, Chokwe and Waiyaki. The Commissioner responded that before we could accept to do all the other work, we must first clean out the slop pails. Cege brought back this condition.

Hardly had Cege finished explaining this than a number of young men volunteered themselves for disposal of night soil and for collecting the food from the boat landing. They were led by Kĩhoro Mũrĩithi, Kĩbaara Gathũkũ, Mũtonga Karũri, Mwangi Kĩng'oora, Ndibũi Waweru, Kĩama Matũ and Gĩtahi Waciira. There was some fire wood left over by the prisoners in the kitchen. Some of the younger men who seemed to have retained some reserves of energy went out to draw water, while others got busy doing all kinds of chores.

The contents of each sack of foodstuffs would be divided into two, and each load would be carried by four men, such was the physical weakness to which men had been reduced by hunger. One pail of water would be carried by two men.

Cege Kĩraka and Paulo Njerũ suggested, and it was generally agreed, that to start with porridge would be cooked and allowed to cool before being drank slowly to soothingly open out our intestines.

At 11.00 a.m. all of us were sitting in the shade cast by the reed roof of our quarters drinking cooled porridge in a bid to redeem our lives.

19 August 1953

We collected more of the food that had been left at the boat landing. Some of it had gone bad and had to be thrown away. We prepared a long-term and short-term duty roster. The sergeant provided guards to escort each group to its place of work. The elderly men were left cleaning up the compound.

20 August 1953

I composed a song to commemorate the "Kang'aari Hunger". We gave this name to this period in honour of Kangaari's great endurance in spite of his ill-health and his steadfast faith to our vow that we would never capitulate. Here is the song:

1. From Lamu to Manda island
   A distance of fifteen miles across the waters
   We crossed by boat
   Under heavy guard

   Remember our vow
   A vow expressed in one word
   We shall never surrender!

2. Men have defiantly dared,
   We defied orders to go and work
   We neither ate nor drank
   For a full six days
3. We became awfully hungry and thirsty
   Our bodies became drained of blood
   But God came to our help
   And revealed a great secret
4. One hundred and thirty eight people
   Shared four loaves of bread in oneness
   Each of us shared a piece—
   That was God's secret
5. From six bottles of water
   Each of us had a spoonful
   And none of us grudged the others
6. When the Commissioner addressed us
   Who were locked up in our quarters
   He told us we were bad elements
   'Serve you right if you died!'
7. We whispered together
   Our wise men gave counsel
   Our God helped us
   To preserve ourselves, so our seed would live.

27 August 1953

Permission was granted for us to go bathing and swimming everyday at four
o'clock in the afternoon. Many detainees who hadn't known how to swim took
this opportunity to learn. But some people, notable examples being Chokwe,
Kali and Kibuchi, were very good swimmers: they could swim out to sea for
300 yards or more.

31 August 1953

A group of detainees who had received formal education met. We discussed the possibility of starting literacy classes for some of the detainees as well as enrolling ourselves for correspondence courses. The camp officer agreed to our request and even provided us with chalk, although each of us had contributed ten cents for buying chalk. We had only one blackboard which we had brought from Kajiado: Cege wa Kĩraka had personally been responsible for bringing this board. Learners felt beholden to him and expressed their gratitude to him at every turn.

Eventually the camp officer arranged to have a few more boards constructed at Lamu.

September, 1953

1 September 1953

Almost all the detainees, who had been taking part in classes, were asked to indicate the level they had attained. From this information, we organised six classes. Classes were conducted inside and outside quarters no. 4 during the morning and afternoon hours. Learners treated their teachers with due respect. If a learner came to class late, he would accept his punishment.

These were the teachers who had volunteered their services: John Cege (Head Teacher), J.D. Kali, Crispus Mwanĩki, John Mbũgua, Gakaara Wanjaũ, Rufus Kĩnũthia, Kamawe Mwega and P.C. Mulwa.

3

Serious Conflicts Over the Question of Work in the Camp

24 September 1953 to 20 February 1954

24 September 1953

We were informed that Col. La Fontaine had come to the Camp and wanted to talk to twelve detainees' representatives. We were to learn later that the old Camp Officer, N.S. Stancey-Marks, had been replaced by a new officer, by the name S.C. Martin.

Col. La Fontaine told the twelve detainees that new government regulations from henceforth required detainees to be involved in labour. What kinds of work? the detainees wanted to know. He gave this list: like growing our own vegetables, digging new roads, clearing bushland, building houses, and any other necessary work. He was asked how could we be expected to do heavy manual labour before we had been convicted in a court of law. He responded that these were regulations from the government; however, some kinds of work would carry their own pay. He was informed that we had been gathering our wood fuel, fetching water, cooking and disposing of the slops. He said such work could not be paid for. Before he left he threatened that if detainees did not accept the order to carry out work assigned to them they could be forced to do so.

28 September 1953

Officer Martin summoned us to quarters no. 4 and addressed us there. He was aware, he said, that we were hard hearted men; we had refused to cook our food when we came to Manda island, and the Commissioner of Prisons himself had had to intervene. The new regulations were from the Government. Although there was a stipulation that detainees should volunteer for work, he would require all of us to be involved in work. He asked those who wanted to volunteer themselves for work to come forward. Nobody moved. He informed us he had authority to deny us certain privileges if we failed to cooperate, but he would give us time to think things out.

We nicknamed him "The Naked One" since he was virtually naked most of the time, except for underwear shorts. Many of us also used to wear shorts only, so hot and humid was the weather at Manda.

51

October 1953

1 October, 1953

We received only 43 pounds of meat; the officer had ordered a cut on our ration. The officer said if we were not willing to accept the cut, he could allow the prison personnel to have *all* the meat. We accepted the reduced ration, but the officer had to add salt to the wound. He said this was his first act to demonstrate that he had authority to interfere with our privileges; if we wanted to eat vegetables we must be prepared to grow them.

8 October 1953

50 detainees were brought to Manda from Athi River. They told us they had travelled through Garissa. Most of them were known to us; they had been arrested with us and been detained in Kajiado before being transferred to Athi River in May 1953 before we ourselves were transferred from Kajiado to Manda. Some of these people were: Romano Njamumo, Solomon Meemia, Wamŭthenya Kang'eri, Rev. Arthur Gatŭng'ŭ, Henry Mulli, Simon Mbacia, James Waithaka, Kĩbuci Ndiang'ŭi, Maciira Kĩmarŭ, L. Kĩgume, and Job Mŭcucu.

13 October 1953

We were told that members of the Advisory Committee on Detainees had arrived in Lamu. A number of detainees were taken to Lamu to appear before this Committee.

14 October 1953

Officer Martin had a discussion with eight detainees, who could speak good English, on the question of detainees becoming involved in work. The plan, he explained, was to make Manda a "Special Camp" where self-sustaining labour would be the basic feature. For a start, detainees would take care of a herd of goats which had been brought recently to Manda. But the detainees were not agreeable. It would be dangerous to herd the goats in the bush, they said, for the detainees could be killed there. There were no objections to slaughtering animals for the kitchen.

The eight detainees who talked to Martin were: Joel Warŭĩ, Henry Mulli Cege Kabogoro, Babu Kamau, Maciira Mŭkenye, James Waithaka, J.D. Kalɟ and Kĩbuci Ndiang'ŭi.

16 October 1953

Martin gave a lengthy address to the detainees in a bid to persuade them to volunteer for work. When some detainees responded to Martin's address it did appear as if they were being won over to accepting participation in labour. Then he talked to a few people each in turn. If he could only have one volunteer, he said, he would be satisfied that he had established some measure of understanding with the detainees.

After everything he asked us to join him in prayers. He conducted a strange prayer session where he punctuated his words with the repeated action of raising his walking stick and hitting the ground with it. He prayed that God may help these fools to understand that the white man was placed in authority over us. We witnessed in dread Martin's gestures—of using a walking stick in prayer.

Three detainees—James Waithaka, Simon Mbacia and Henry Mulli— agreed to clear a field for use as a football field. There was bitter disagreement, for the first time, amongst us. For there were those who opposed this move and at the same time there were a number of people who backed these volunteers.

22 October 1953

The Camp Officer talked to the detainees one at a time. Six more detainees volunteered for work. These were: P.C. Mulwa, L. Kĩgume, James Njoroge, D. Wawerũ, D. Kũng'ũ and N. Mwaũra.

Martin reminded us that we were being held here because it had been proved that we belonged to the Mau Mau movement. He had the authority, he warned us, to deny us privileges and to subject us to punishment for defiance. He could refuse us the outings to the sea for a swim, or disallow our classes. He could order us to fold our beddings each morning or to stand at attention when he or the camp sergeant were passing; he could make us stand in the sun, refuse us permission to go beyond the barbed wire, or make us use green firewood.

Those people who had volunteered for work were given permission to go swimming and to go beyond the confines of the barbed wire without the supervision of camp guards.

23 October 1953

James Njoroge who had volunteered for work informed the Camp Officer that he had changed his mind; he did not want to volunteer, after all. He was returned to quarters no. 1, the place for the hardcore rejectors.

27 October 1953

We wrote a petition to the imperialist Governor of Kenya, expressing our rejection of participation in labour. We sent the petition through the Officer-in-charge, Manda Camp and through the Commissioner of Prisons, Nairobi. But we sent a copy of the petition directly to the Governor using our secret means.

29 October 1953

In the morning the Provincial Commissioner and the Commissioner of Prisons came to tour the Manda Camp. When the P.C. learned that most of us had refused to volunteer for work, he commented that the camp administration should work with those who freely volunteered. As for us we should be shown no consideration; it were better if we had never been born.

At around 2.00 p.m. the commissioner in charge of detainee affairs, Askwith, and his assistant, Col. La Fontaine, came and toured the camp, then left.

31 October 1953

Martin was furious about the petition which we had written to the Governor, expressing our opposition to work. He ordered Camp guards to shave our hair and beards. This should teach us that he had authority to punish us and deny us our pleasures.

November, 1953

2 November 1953

Martin had all of us assembled together in one block. He told us that if we persisted in refusing to volunteer for work, he would use powers given to him to force us to work. He would train his camp personnel to be more harsh than any prison personnel anywhere in Kenya. Our living area would be divided into three compounds to facilitate a separation of the good elements from the bad.

9 November 1953

Prisoners from Mombasa were brought in. They divided the area containing the detainee living quarters into three compounds using barbed wire, such that there were now three minor compounds within one large camp compound. They left a kind of roadway between each two neighbouring compounds along which guards would conduct their patrols. Compound 1 was on the side of the sea; compound 2 was in the middle and compound 3 on the other side. There were no other barriers except the barbed wire, and people in compound 1 could talk quite well with those in compound 2, while those in compound 2 could speak to people in compound 3. Each of these areas could contain fifty people and their belongings.

Convicted prisoners had their own separate quarters, away from the detainees' compound.

10 November 1953

Two more detainees volunteered for work. Inside our quarters, people were involved in bitter recriminations. Those who volunteered for work were accused by the rejectors of having ignominiously betrayed our vows to fight and defy the colonialists at every turn. They had sold out! An English word came in vogue for describing these people: "cooperators".

11 November 1953

The authorities slyly introduced the practice of throwing people into cells for minor misdemeanours. Johana Kĩraatũ was falsely accused of having used abusive words by a guard. He was thrown into a cell for four days and put on punishment diet—bread and water only.

14 November 1953

Since the division of the camp into three compounds the ten people who had volunteered for work were segregated in compound No. 3, where they were allowed to cook their own meals. They were expected to do all kinds of work, except cleaning out the slop pails, which work was done by convicted prisoners.

They kept compounds number 1 and 2 open so people could volunteer to join the "cooperators" in number 3.

The prison personnel grew in their cruel harshness.

16 November 1953

An elephant's skull was found somewhere on the island. The Naked One had it propped up on a tall pole near the office. When a detainee refused to volunteer for work, the Naked One would point at the dried out white skull and hint that those who followed the road of defiance would end up like the skull. He would tell people to look up at the skull in the same way the Israelites looked up at the Serpent of Bronze.

The rejectors composed a song which they would sing to debunk the whole idea of the elephant skull: "Don't allow yourself to be frightened by a little elephant's skull/Thereby compromising your honour/We are at the gateway of our destination!"

20 November 1953

The sergeant fired thrice into the air; guards claimed that about 20 or 30 people had touched the barbed wire that surrounded the camp. Martin burst on the scene breathing fury. He was ready to feed us with the bread of pain, he vowed. There and then Gĩtaũ Karani was seized and thrown into a cell for punishment for touching the barbed wire.

23 November 1953

The sergeant came into our compound and after some time one man followed him as a volunteer for work. Many of us felt this was a cunning way of giving the impression that the man had volunteered only after persuasion; either this man had himself made approaches to the authorities or the section 3 people had made approaches on his behalf.

December, 1953

10 December 1953

We were forced to shave our hair and beards yet again, for having refused to cooperate over the question of work. People would crack: "As if it is the hair and beards which have rejected work!"

20 December 1953

We were divided into two groups. 46 of us were put in compound no. 1, and 131 in compound 2. A guard was stationed at the barbed wire partition between the two compounds to see to it that these two groups would have no intercourse. We were ordered never to attempt any fraternisation with the African sergeant; any time we saw him we should stand at attention like soldiers. From now on we should collect our water from well number 3, and we should keep clear of the areas where the cooperators were when we went to gather fire wood. We should never sing, dance or participate in any games or play. If we contravened these rules we would be liable to corporal punishment—administered in the presence of all.

25 December 1953

The cooperators were given Christmas entertainment: they were bough beer at the canteen and invited to the houses of the camp personnel to eat with them.

27 December 1953

Two people, Mũcaai Karoobi of compound 2 and Joshua Njũgũna of compound 3, were caught talking across the barbed wire that separated compounds 2 and 3. Both were confined in punishment cells for seven days and put on punishment diet, bread and water. (After confinement, Mũcaai was taken to section 1.)

29 December 1953

Maina Njathi was summoned to the commandant's office and over tea advised to volunteer for work. He rejected the advice. The officer called a number of people individually without achieving any positive results. He gave up his attempt.

Kĩhaato Kĩbuukũ was transferred from compound 2 to compound 1. He had committed no offence. We suspected he had been falsely accused by the cooperators.

30 December 1953

Rev. Stefano Waciira was transferred from compound 1 to compound 2; but two people, Obadia Thuo and Paulo Njerũ, were transferred from compound 2 to compound 1.

January, 1954

1 January 1954

Two people from compound 2, Romano Njamumo and Karĩmanjaga, joined the work volunteers in compound 3. Romano bid farewell to the inmates of compound 2 at around 2.00 p.m. Karĩmanjaga was collected by guards; of course the cooperators had arranged it all.

On the same day, files of charges which had been drawn against us at Kajiado were brought to the Manda Camp office. People were instructed to obtain details of their cases from the office.

3 January 1954

Two detainees from compound 2, J. Njenga and E. Ndama, volunteered for work. Mwangi Thabuni from section 1 was put in a punishment cell, where he would eat bread with water, because he had talked to somebody in compound 2.

M. Kamau was made the compound 2 leader.

4 January 1954

The cooperators started construction work. They were building quarters for another camp, constructing enclosures for water wells as well as building stores. Maciira Kĩmarũ was thrown into a punishment cell for talking to Paulo Ndũrũ from compound 2. He would eat bread and water for four days and *ugali* for 3 days. Paulo Ndũrũ was not put under punishment.

6 January 1954

Two men, Wamũtĩ Mũhũngi from compound 2, and Mũcaai Karoobi, from compound 1, volunteered for work in compound 3 in the evening.

8 January 1954

I, Gakaara wa Wanjaũ, was given a severe beating on the charge that I had talked across the barbed wire to somebody in compound 2, although the person whom I was supposed to have talked to could not be identified. My right arm was dislocated and I was put in a punishment cell. The officer ordered that I was not to be given further punishment as the beating I had been given was enough. When I left the cell, Stanley Kagĩĩka bound my dislocated arm and secured it with two splints. Kagĩĩka had been a hospital assistant before his detention.

The act of subjecting me to physical assault was the cause of much anger among all the detainees.

Gideon Ngatirĩ from compound 2 volunteered for work.

11 January 1954

Joel Werehire direct from compound 1, the hardcore compound, volunteered for work. He was called to the camp office and asked how he had managed to soften so suddenly, having been one of the hardcores.

Meroni Guandarũ was transferred from compound 2 to compound 1.

At 2.00 o'clock in the afternoon three people, Duncan Wainaina, Peter Ng'ang'a and Godfrey Mwaũra, left compound 2 to work in compound 3.

At 7.00 p.m. detainees were brought on transfer from Athi River Detention Camp. They were brought by air. One of them, Henry Kahooya, immediately offered his cooperation and he was taken to compound 3 that very night. But Isaac Gathaanju, James Beauttah, Mwangi Mathu and Benjamin Mang'uurũ rejected work and they were quartered in compound 1. They told us that at Athi River detention camp only 250 detainees had opted for cooperation; more than 1,000 people had rejected cooperation. They told us five more detainees were being brought to Manda.

12 January 1954

The five detainees we had heard about arrived from Athi River. Two of them, Kagūnda Gĩkaria and Gĩtaũ Mũrĩmi, refused to volunteer for work, and they were put in compound 1. Three of them, Maranga Mbaria, Timothy Maina and Mwaũra Karanja, requested that they be given time to make up their minds; they were taken to compound 2.

Nehemia Kũiyaki was transferred from compound 2 to 1.

We wrote a petition protesting against the beating of detainees by camp guards.

17 January 1954

Four detainees, who had been arrested on 20th October 1952 and held in Marsabit, arrived at the camp. They were brought by air and put in compound 2. They were Waira Kamau, Fredrick Mbiyũ, Mbũrũ Njoroge and Paulo Thiong'o They told us eight more detainees from the same camp might arrive the following day. They expressed the view that the colonial authorities were now starting to realise that they had made a mistake in scattering the nationalist leadership into a multiplicity of detention centres. Now that the armed struggle in the countryside was in full flare, it appeared the authorities now wanted to concentrate this leadership in one place in order to determine how best to deal with it.

19 January 1954

Eight more detainees from Marsabit arrived. Of these, Mwai Koigi, Cege Kĩbũrũ, and Mwinga Chokwe refused to volunteer for work, and they were put in compound 1. Five of them—J. Mbiyũ Koinange, Mũrage Wokabi, Peter Gatabaki, Samuel Kĩragũ, and Onesmus Gacoka, asked for time to come to a decision; they were put in compound 2.

They told us they had left Ex-Senior Chief Koinange wa Mbiyũ, Dedan Mũgo and Jesse Kariũki at Marsabit. They told us about the verdict in the trial of Kenyatta and associates; it was only Achieng' Oneko who had been discharged: he might be brought to Manda.

20 January 1954

When the Marsabit detainees were brought to Manda, we began to look at the political implications of the move. Indeed, as the first four detainees who had arrived on 17th January had speculated, it appeared the colonial authorities were doubting the wisdom of keeping the nationalist leadership scattered all over. May be plans were under way to bring together all the "Jock Scott" detainees. In any case things appeared to have gone sour on the authorities. For arrests and detentions had failed to contain the growth and rebellion of the nationalist Mau Mau movement. The authorities would carry out arrests—and new political leaders would spring up to replace those arrested in the countryside; the authorities would be puzzled to hear new names in the military leadership in the forests.

The colonial authorities had, therefore, been driven into a frenzy of making blind arrests. When they had arrested those they learned were in the leadership, they would learn tomorrow that their positions had been filled. So they reverted to mass arrests which netted leaders and the led. They found the camp population growing uncontrollably; they had not even planned for this. Unable to feed the masses of camp inmates, the authorities had to introduce self-supporting labour in the camps. The detainees should grow their own food!

Waira Kamau commented that the colonial authorities had, by bringing us together, done us a favour. We could now in togetherness deliberate on the formation of our future nationalist government. For the nationalist government, which would be led by Jomo Kenyatta, would recruit its leadership from the Manda and other detention camps as well as the prisons and the persecuted areas of the countryside.

Onesmus Gacoka expressed support for Waira's sentiments. Indeed, he said, it was quite apparent that Manda camp would be an appropriate recruiting ground for ministers of the nationalist government.

Paulo Thiong'o and Samuel Kagotho commented that while they had been at Marsabit they had speculated that after nationalist victory had swept away the colonialist administration, Kenyatta would lead the new government while Dedan Kĩmathi, assisted by Mathenge wa Mĩrũgĩ, would lead the new nationalist army.

People now allowed their imagination to grow wings. People would suggest which individual would fit which particular government ministry or branch of administration. At the end we cautioned ourselves these were merely preliminary thoughts on the matter. We would allow our thinking on these matters to grow in response to the way things continued to develop. But on one thing we appeared to be adamant: Kenyatta would form his government assisted by a committee drawing membership from every district of Kenya; there would absolutely be no room for colonial collaborators in the new nationalist government. Kenyatta's council would also determine the policy of reallocating the land we had been fighting for, once the colonialist forces had been expelled from the country.

Solomon M'Mwĩricia ended our deliberation on a humorous note. He expressed a personal wish about the office he would want to hold in the nationalist government: he would want to head the rehabilitation department in the African government so that he could carry out the work of correcting the heads of the collaborators with the colonial administration.

21 January 1954

Kĩhoro Mũrĩithi was falsely accused of insulting a camp guard. He was brutally beaten by guards who said he was rudely unapologetic. His left arm was injured. The authorities did not intervene.

23 January 1954

Mũũgĩ Cege was transferred from compound 1 to compound 2 because he was caught talking across to somebody in compound 1. Mathenge Njari was subjected to a similar transfer without, however, being told why. We could only speculate that the cooperators were passing on information about the other detainees who had refused to cooperate to the imperialist authorities, probably suggesting which people were "hard" and which "soft".

26 January 1954

We complained about the reduction of the share of food given to compound 1, a reduction implemented from the store. Our leader, Cege, expressed our grievance to the camp sergeant, who said our grievance was no valid.

When the officer-in-charge of the camp learnt about our complaint, he responded in a very strange manner. He ordered that a thorough search be conducted in our quarters to make sure we had no hidden weapons. Detainees from compound 2 were ordered to remain there.

The guards invaded our compound and came out with all kinds of objects: any little stick, including any firewood we had kept indoors, gunny bags, clothes lines. Beddings and our clothing were left littered on the floor.

Two such operations were carried out—at 10.00 a.m. and at 2.00 p.m.

After this we were given two razor blades and ordered to shave our beards. Our leader, Cege, was condemned to a punishment cell for seven days on a punishment diet. Firewood was taken to a place outside the barbed wire, and we would be required to obtain our daily requirements from there.

In the course of the search Koina Gĩtĩbi's box for personal effects was broken apart, Musa Mũturi lost his fountain pen; and James Beauttah lost his spoon; many detainees also lost tin containers.

We had been expecting a visit from a British Parliamentary delegation which had come to familiarise itself with Emergency conditions in Kenya, and which was supposed to tour the Manda Camp today. As it was, this delegation never visited Manda, but we managed to have a memorandum smuggled to them before they left Nairobi for England.

27 January 1954

The Commissioner of Prisons and Mr. O'Hagen, the Coast Provincial Commissioner, came to the Camp. They were taken round the detainees' living quarters in compounds 2 and 3; they were also shown the well from which our water was drawn.

James Beauttah, who was acting as the leader in compound 1, had a discussion over the work question with these imperialist officers. They assured him that it was not intended to introduce forced labour, that is the kind where people would work under the explosions of guns or at the pain of being subjected to assault and torture. However, they restated the Camp Officer's position— that we would be denied privileges if we persisted in refusing to volunteer for work. When Mwai Koigi petitioned for the return of his correspondence course materials, which had been seized from him, his request was turned down on the grounds that he had refused to volunteer for work.

After the white officers had left we had some deliberations in compound 1. We wanted to know where our people, in compound 2, stood. Even the white officers had emphasised the need for people to make their stand clear. Did our people in compound 2 stand for noncooperation or for cooperation?

28 January 1954

One by one the detainees from compound 2 were subjected to interrogation by the Naked One. At the end of it 38 detainees were transferred to compound 1; not a single one of them went to compound 3. There were now 90 men in compound 2. Those who volunteered to join compound 1 would be beaten as they were chased into this compound.

Gacangi Gĩkaru and Mwenenia Mũgo were condemned to punishment cells for seven days; they would eat a diet of *ugali* without relish; in addition, Mwenenia would be given corporal punishment.

Achieng' Oneko was brought to Manda at around 12.30 p.m. He was put into compound 3 for the night, without being asked whether or not he would volunteer for work.

29 January 1954

Achieng' Oneko was taken to the office for interrogation by the Camp Officer. He accepted to volunteer for work.

February, 1954

4 February 1954

All the detainees from the Marsabit camp were summoned to the office and ordered to surrender receipts obtained after buying books and paying for correspondence course materials. Newspaper cuttings found in the possession of these people were torn to pieces. Mwai Koigi was assaulted by guards when he refused to sign a declaration that he had had correspondence papers in his possession. The Camp Officer ruled that Mwai had committed no offence and therefore no further punishment was meted to him. But people expressed great anger at his having been assaulted.

5 February 1954

Mwenenia Mũgo was given sixteen lashes of the whip. The camp dispensary dresser first gave medical sanction for this punishment. After this he was taken to compound 1.

Two detainees, Waigwa Rũcathi and Kamanũ Kĩnya, agreed to volunteer for work, and they were transferred to compound 3.

6 February 1954

Two other people, Thuũ Thagicũ and Nikolas Njaũ offered to cooperate and they, too, were transferred to compound 3.

8 February 1954

The Camp Officer, His Naked Excellency, came to compound 1. He did not talk to anybody. Then he pointed at 6 people—Gĩtahi Waciira, Kĩhoro Mũriithi, Mwangi Thabuni, Kamawe Mwega, Bongwe Icaũ and Ngure Gacũgũ—and ordered them to gather belongings and transfer themselves to compound 2.

Job Mũcucu was transferred from compound 2 to compound 1.

11 February 1954

Bedan Mũirũ willingly volunteered for work. He had been in compound 2.

12 February 1954

Two people from section 2—F. Kore Njenga and Samuel G. Gĩtiha—and Gacuĩrĩ Kĩariĩ from compound 1 obtained a transfer to section 3 after willingly volunteering for work. John Mbiyũ was ordered to transfer from compound 1 to 2.

Then the Camp Officer issued an order: we should select 40 people from our number in compound 1 who would be deployed in doing construction work at the new camp site at 7.00 a.m. on 15th February, 1954. None of us responded, and the officer left us.

We were not clear what the officer actually meant by asking us to select people from our number. We agreed among ourselves to send for the officer who should be asked to spell out the implications of his directive. A little note expressing our request was sent to him.

Our apprehension was real. Word had it that construction work at the second camp, in which the cooperators had been involved, must be completed by 16th February 1954. Rumours were rife that we would be subjected to forced labour. Rumour also had it that a number of us would be transferred to Takwa. It was not surprising, therefore, to see that a number of people from section 2 appeared willing to volunteer for work.

Wambũgũ Mbũya was condemned to a punishment cell and a punishment diet of *ugali* without relish for seven days.

13 February 1954

As requested the Camp Officer paid a visit to our section. He informed us that the law of Kenya had now made a provision for forced labour for detainees; all detainees would now work whether or not they volunteered for it. He answered several questions from detainees, but expressly refused to answer questions put to him by James Beauttah and Mwai Koigi. When I, Gakaara Wanjaũ, requested him to show us the written law pertaining to forced labour, he brushed this aside and vehemently assured everybody present that I would be the first person who would be forced to work.

The officer claimed he had received lawful authority by a confidential cable. to subject us to forced labour. Forty men from our number must join the cooperators on Monday to complete construction work at Manda detention camp no. 2, for this camp required to be used immediately to confine the "irredeemable" elements among the detainees. He was terribly angry at the fact that the Government had borrowed a sum of £11 million for running detention camps; we should not be allowed to live idle lives where all we did was consume things bought with Government money. We should realise, the officer warned us, that we had gone beyond the regard of the law courts of the British Government.

"You are great fools," the officer informed us, "because you have failed to realise that you were isolated in this remote island because the Government had given up on you, and you were now being left to your fate; it was your business if all of you died. Look on every side: you are surrounded by the sea.

Where could you escape to? We need not even keep a substantial num
guards on this island. A guard manning the watchtower would suffice—to pass
on information when any one of you drops dead so that his body could be
collected for dumping into the sea."

By the time he left, we had reached no agreement; his words had angered
us and poisoned the atmosphere.

But 11 people from our compound did volunteer for work. These were:
Stephen Mwaŭra, Mwangi Macaria, John Mbũgua, Fred Mbiyũ, Ng'ang'a
Kiboobo, Onesmus Gacoka, Nyamũ Marea, Maxwell Ndua, Ex-Chief Njiriri
Mũkoma, Mũtonga Karũri and Karũgi Kĩariĩ.

The same day we sent a telegram to the Governor of Kenya through the
Commissioner of Prisons protesting his bid to induct us into forced labour.

TELEGRAM—URGENT
T.M. 4
THE GOVERNOR OF KENYA
THRO' COMMISSIONER OF PRISONS
ADVOCATES DE-SOUZA & PATEL
AFRICAN MEMBERS OF LEGCO

ON 13TH FEBRUARY CAMP OFFICER INSISTS ON OUR ACCEPT-
ING SLAVERY. ON 15TH FEBRUARY SAYS IT IS PART OF NEW
LAW TO INVOLVE US IN FORCED LABOUR. WE REJECT FORCED
LABOUR. PLEASE CLARIFY.
STATE OF EMERGENCY DETAINEES
13.2.54

14 February 1954

We had the telegram posted to the Governor. We sent copies to African members
of the Legislative Council and to advocates De-Souza and Patel.

In the evening at around 6.00 p.m. our representative was summoned to
the office and, in spite of our telegram, ordered to oversee the selection of 40
people from section 1 who would be recruited for construction work. He was
warned that if he failed to do so, the camp officer himself would come to
compound 1.

We told Cege, our leader, that none of us would volunteer for work. We
were now 92 in compound 1.

But that evening we lost two people—J.D. Kali and Kĩbuci Ndiang'ũi—to
the camp of volunteers for work.

Ngatia Kangangi was confined in a punishment cell for allegedly going
outdoors in the dark to attend a call of nature.

15 February 1954

A corporal came to see Cege our leader at around 6.30 a.m. He had been sent by the camp officer to obtain our response to instructions that we line up 40 construction workers. He was told no one was ready to volunteer for the work.

The Camp Officer came to our quarters at around 7.30. He was furious. Since we had refused to work, he announced, he was going to deny us food.

Water which was boiling in the kitchen was poured out.

We were ordered to fold our beddings into a pack and stay close to our sleeping places. Then the searches started taking place every one hour.

Those who would back down and volunteer to work, we were told, would get their food—and a transfer to compound 3.

Two elderly men, Mariko Kaambuĩ and Paulo Gĩcaana, obtained an immediate transfer to compound 2. Compound 1 had now a total of 90 inmates—with two of them currently confined in cells. Compound 2 had 76 people—who had not made up their minds on the work question. And compound 3 harboured 45 cooperators.

At 2.00 p.m. colonialist officer Martin came to our compound. He read to us Emergency regulations pertaining to detainees. He warned us that we could be charged with conspiring to disobey the lawfully constituted Government and the penalty for this offence could involve our being deprived of blankets, beds, books, indeed everything except our barest underwear. He would institute such penalties the following day if we continued to be defiant.

Martin also ordered that food and water be kept outside the camp, just near the gate. If a person volunteered to go and work, Martin said, he could collect his food and water from there. As a last resort, Martin warned, he could get a person imprisoned at the main Lamu prison for two years on hard labour. He and the District Commissioner of Lamu were empowered to invoke such measures.

We let Martin rant on: none of us said a word to him.

On that day searches were conducted twelve times.

The Camp Officer issued instructions that good care be taken of two goats which were grazing in the camp grounds, so that they didn't find their way to compound 1, for we might feed on them.

People from compound 3 smuggled three loaves of bread to us, thanks to the initiative of Kali, Waigwa and Kamau. God, we felt, had given them the spirit of sympathy.

In the evening we received news from the compound 3 grapevine that Martin had already complained to his superior officers that it was impossible to complete construction work in camp number 2 on schedule because of the resistance offered by detainees who refused to volunteer to work.

From the overtures from people in compound 3 we got the strong impression that some of the people there held no grudge against us, but there were some who would have welcomed our surrender, so that the present bitter division between ourselves would be bridged in the eyes of the colonialist authorities.

Detainees from compound 1 felt the need to offer stiff resistance to the designs and trials of the colonial authorities. They found it necessary to carry on the struggle, which had led to our arrest and detention, until final victory.

Kahũgĩ wa Gĩturo was summoned into the office from compound 3—after which he obtained transfer to compound 1.

16 February 1954

When we woke up, we collected our belongings and put them into packs, and waited for the Officer to come and deprive us of everything as he had said he would. But Martin didn't come.

At 3.00 p.m. we drafted a telegram to the Governor, through the Camp Officer, and complained about our being systematically starved. Martin drafted a little note acknowledging receiving the telegram.

Peter Mũtahi was called to the office and attempts were made to persuade him to go and work. He didn't offer to cooperate, but asked for time to consider the matter, and so was taken to compound 2.

Njoroge Njui and John Ng'ang'a, from compound 2, voluntarily offered cooperation.

An interesting development was taking place. Cooperators from section 3 would have people from compounds 1 and 2, when these people were known to them well from home or in other camps, summoned to the office. A rejector of work who was so summoned would face a united pack of persuaders, made up of Martin as the pack leader and his friends from the camp of cooperators; they would preach to him to agree to volunteer for work.

On this day four detainees from compound 1 were summoned to the office to face the persuaders: James Wainaina, James Ng'irũ, John Gĩcũhĩ and Ng'ombe Gakũrũ. However, they neither opted to cooperate nor to stay in compound 2 like those who were in the process of making up their minds.

Those who would brush off the efforts of the persuaders would receive the taunts of the Naked Officer: rejectors would be detained until the end of the Emergency, Martin would warn, or even until the end of time. And the cooperators would insist that it was foolish and pointless for the rejectors to starve themselves in protest against a normal thing like work. Why condemn ourselves, they would ask, to an indefinite stay on this inhospitable island?

Many arguments would be marshalled. Some people would be reminded they had never, in the days before detention, assumed any prominent role in nationalist politics and agitation. Their ticket back home was acceptance of work—for the Advisory Committee on Detainees, which would be coming soon, would only look sympathetically on cases of people who had agreed to work.

But those people who believed in all way resistance to the designs of the colonialist authorities rejected the sugar-coated wooing of the cooperators.

Today was the second day we had gone without eating.

Some people from compound 2 who sympathised with us agreed to set aside their meat rations for us.

When darkness fell they made packs of meat and bread wrapped in sack cloth; water they put in bottles and wrapped in cloth. Then the exercise started, carried out by the younger and stronger men: hurling the packs across 12 yards of space to our compound. The packs would make a booming noise as they fell. The men from compound 2 who carried out the exercise were: Ndibũi Wawerũ, Mbũrũ Njoroge, Mwangi Wawerũ and Gîtahi Waciira. When the packs reached our compound, the following people were involved in their quick collection: Kĩhaato Kĩbuukũ, Ngũgĩ Gĩkũũma, Karĩnga Gakure, Njoroge Kĩronji and Paulo Njerũ.

In due course the guards were alerted by the noise of the falling packs. They managed to collect a substantial number of pieces of meat and bread, which they delivered to the office in the morning.

Those who collected the packs divided the meat, the bread and the water among the 88 inmates of compound 1; each of us got little pieces of bread and meat and a sip of water. A little life was restored to us as we went to sleep that night.

Searches were carried out eight times that day.

The Camp Officer was to receive news about the act of mercy from compound 2 with great annoyance. As a result of this act, we heard that compound 2 would be subjected to sub-division.

17 February 1954

At 8.00 a.m. we talked among ourselves about what awaited us in the near future. We decided that we should not give up our resistance, which would naturally mean our continuing to go hungry, until some higher authority should intervene. We were pinning our hopes on the possible intervention of the Advisory Committee on Detainees.

People's bodies had started to wilt with weakness. At 9.00 o'clock the guards poured down the water we had put on the fire with a view to cooking our breakfast.

The Naked Officer had gone to Lamu to consult with his superiors.

People from compound 2 sent a note to us commiserating with us but expressing their regret that they could not now send any help to us under the watchful gaze of the camp guards. In their view we had sufficiently expressed our resistance to the policies and designs of the colonialist authorities. We wrote back to them and told them we had agreed among ourselves that we would wait with the hope of seeing some intervention.

On that day six people from our compound agreed to volunteer for work: Babu Kamau, Maciira Mũkenye, Kĩbera Gathũkũ, Kĩhoro Mũrĩithi, Mũtahi Gathemia and Z. Mũigai.

We were subjected to six searches.

* * *

It was a group of the younger men, including Kagũnda Gĩkaria, Kĩhaato Kĩbuukũ, Mahuti Gĩcũkĩ, Paulo Njerũ and Njoroge Kironji, who hatched the idea of digging a well inside our living quarters—so thirsty and parched had people become. They reasoned that if wells on Manda island required virtually surface digging, there should be water near the surface right under our living quarters. When this idea was given to George Waiyaki, who had experience in prospecting for water, he took a forked stick and prospected for water all over our living quarters, and declared that there was water right under Njoroge Kĩronji's bed. This discovery was kept a secret until night fell. In the meanwhile all cunning was marshalled in collecting digging instruments and concealing them.

After the last search had been carried out, the digging started. It was around 7.00 p.m. People used metal plates to dig into the sandy ground. There was maximum cooperation among us. One would dig, put the sand in a *debe* and have the *debe* hauled out and the sand poured onto a sack. After enough sand had collected on the sack, two people would have the sand spread under the sleeping mat of one of the detainees. The sleeping mat and beddings would then be neatly arranged on the new sand.

The following people worked with admirable devotion: Kĩhaato Kĩbuukũ, Mahuti Gĩcũhĩ, Kagũnda Gĩkaria, Karĩnga Gakure, Maciira Kĩmarũ, Isaaka Gathanju, Paulo Njerũ, Maara Gatundu, Njoroge Kĩronji, Ngũgĩ Gĩkũũma, Gacago Gacerũ, Gacangi Gĩkaru, and Mwanĩki Rĩbuthi.

People would take quick turns in the well-hole. In the meanwhile the elderly men lying on their beds sang political hymns to the rhythm of the digging in-order to drown the noise and distract the attention of the guards standing outside from our carryings on. We had also appointed our own sentries to keep a look out; at any sign of trouble, the digging would stop.

My arm had not recovered from the injury inflicted on me; I was one of the sentries, keeping a watch on the guard in the sentry box.

Muddy soil was reached at eleven feet deep. Our hopes of reaching water grew.

At 11.30 p.m. we reached proper water.

The water was muddy. We collected it into tins and left it for the dirt to settle at the bottoms of the tins. A strict order was given that everybody should wait until the moment arrived when everybody would be given his share.

There was enough water for each of us to have a cup. Water was shared out first to those who had become weakened and to the elderly people. Among the elderly who got their early share were: Nehemia Kũiyaki, James Beauttah, Willie J. Wambũgũ Maina, Kĩrongothi Ndegwa and Job Mũcucu.

After everybody had had his share we covered our well with sticks and sack cloth and sprinkled sand on the sackcloth. I was personally asked to record the dimensions of this well. It had a depth of 12 feet, a length of 3 feet and a width of 1½ feet.

Very early next morning, at around 5.30 a.m. people woke up and each of us drank a cup of water, before covering the well as before. When dawn came, Njoroge placed his sleeping mat and beddings on the well site and positioned himself on the side.

When we were subjected to morning searches and inspection our guards did not discover a thing.

Compound 2 had not been subdivided as the colonialist officer had threatened it would be.

18 February 1954

The Naked Officer came to our quarters at around 10.00 a.m. and conducted an inspection. He called out to Cege, who refused to leave his bed; he was unable, he said, to interpret the camp officer's address.

The Naked Officer chose nine men whom he led to his office. These were: Kagĩĩka, Mwai, Cege, Mahuti, Kĩraka, Maciira, Beauttah, Mwangi Mathu and J. Wainaina. The cooperators from compound 3, he told these men, had complained to him that he had been too harsh to deny us our food. But, he boasted, he was eminently satisfied with the way he had handled the situation. He had proved he was a man of great astuteness and cunning. When he was being given the Manda camp assignment, the Government was not sure he would manage to push the cause of cooperation. What about today? There was cause for rejoicing: as many as 55 detainees had agreed to volunteer for work.

The officer was asked whether there was any written regulation requiring us political detainees to be put under labour. He required no such regulations, be asserted. And he warned that our circumstances had become quite different from circumstances in compound 3—where people had shown a cooperative spirit early enough.

The nine men were given a bucket of water. When they requested permission to bring water to the rest it was not granted. They were ordered back to our quarters.

After thirty minutes the officer came to our quarters in the company of his guards. He asked us to let him know what our position was. We asked him to allow us a supply of water, which he refused. We told him we were not ready to volunteer ourselves for camp labour. The officer left.

He returned at around 3.00 p.m. He called the nine men he had interviewed in the morning. He talked to them in the "no-man's-land" between compound 1 and 2. Which decision had they reached? he demanded. They told him they would only be able to respond to written regulations and orders. We had been misled by the colonial authorities before, they insisted, and this time we would want to see a written order to which we could append our signatures of assent. We could not, otherwise, depart from our position that it was unlawful to put us under labour in the absence of a sentence from a court of law.

When he saw he was not getting anywhere, the officer left. He would come back the following morning at 9.00 o'clock.

When we uncovered our well at around 7.30 p.m., we found that a lot of sand had fallen in and covered the water; this sand was removed. People had a drink of water at 8.00 p.m. and at 10.00 p.m. One could have two cups of water that night.

People from compound 2 had managed to throw in a few loaves of bread, which we divided among ourselves; about eight people shared one loaf. Therefore, people slept feeling slightly stronger than they had been the whole day. For people had manifestly weakened: some had been counted while lying on their sleeping mats, while others had sat down in a row as the count was being taken.

That day, the officer took punitive measures against people from compound 2 who were involved in throwing food to us. That night Gĩtahi Waciira and Reuben Wawerũ were thrown into punishment cells for throwing water and a loaf of bread to compound 1 inmates.

And when Wambũgũ Mbũya finished his term in punishment cell, he was taken to compound 2—on the reasoning that it would not be fair to return him to compound 1, since he had not been a party to the compound 1 act of going on a hunger strike.

19 February 1954

When we woke up to the fifth day of our hunger, we discovered that two of us were terribly ill: Mũrage Wokabi was afflicted with a blood-stained diarrhoea and N. Kũiyaki was unable to speak even a word. Our concern was aroused just after we had woken up, and Paulo Njerũ was feeding us with water from a 1½ pint tin. When guards came to conduct a search at 8.00 a.m., it was discovered many people had taken seriously ill. Mwaŭra Marite was taken out into the open and fanned when he fainted with hunger. When the doctor came he gave him fish oil, water and bread. Mŭŭgĩ Cege was also taken out into the open, fanned, and fed with fish oil.

The camp personnel were struck with pity and at the same time turned their anger upon us: "Do you people choose to die simply because one sole individual among you has misled you into striking against work? Please go out and work! God created people to work. See, we are people like you and we are working!"

They referred to the leadership of one individual because they had got the impression, from seeing Cege talking to the camp officer, that it was Cege who had engineered our strike against camp labour.

Many people started to moan with stomach pains, among them Kĩragŭ Kagotho, Johnson Rŭgĩo, Gacuuru Ngorano and Wahogo Njŭrŭri. Some of them were afflicted with blood-stained diarrhoea.

The atmosphere was tense and pregnant with anger and concern. People from compound 2 stood against the barbed wire looking with eyes of pity and anger at the goings-on in our compound. John Mbiyŭ and others mixed sugar and water in bottles which they threw to us, together with a loaf of bread, for the seriously afflicted. The guards clearly saw this happening. Some wanted to arrest Mbiyŭ and the others and have them punished; others prevented it. The guards got involved in arguments and mutual recriminations. A Mluyia guard complained to the people in compound 2: "You will only manage to make things worse for yourselves and in the process complicate things for us. How on earth do you expect to be able to offer any genuine help to these people?"

An emotion-packed voice demanded from compound 2: "Do you people desire our mass annihilation on this miserable island!"

And among ourselves, people became involved in bitter recriminations, in spite of attempts by some of us to prevent this from happening. A group of people were in favour of our asking the colonialist officer to give us food. Others opposed this: we could not succumb to this shameful compromise just when we were at the gateway of a final resolution. We should wait until 9.00 a.m. when the camp officer would come to address us.

But at 9.00 a.m. the officer did not turn up. We sent Kĩrongothi Ndegwa and Mwai Koigi to inform him that many detainees were ill.

At 9.45 it rained. Those people who still had some reserves of energy took tins to collect water flowing from the roofs. The guards made some token protest but hardly made any attempt to stop us; enough water for drinking was collected. We thanked God who had sent the rain to save us from death.

The camp officer came in at 10.35 a.m. and found everybody in bed inside the blankets. When he talked to Cege, Cege refused to answer him. He declared he was aware Cege and Beauttah were the ring leaders of the strike against work; he could have them charged in a court of law.

Everybody he approached refused to talk to him.

He was very angry. "All right!" he shouted. "It is up to you to die if you persist in upholding your odious Mau Mau ideals. I myself have resolved I'll yet make you go out to work!"

He summoned the dresser and instructed him to have Mwaũra carried to the guardroom where he should be fed with bread and maize gruel. Whichever one of us collapsed should be given this treatment.

At 11.20 a.m. the camp leader returned to compound 1 in the company of John Mbiyũ. Mbiyũ said he had come to inform us that the colonial authorities had decided to force us to go out and work. One of us, Mbiyũ said, had fainted with hunger and all that had been done was to pour cold water on him; when he recovered he would be returned to section 1, where his suffering would continue. We should decide to go to work and put a stop to our suffering.

Then the camp officer revealed the procedure he meant to use: he wanted to ask each of us in turn whether we would accept to go and work. He asked Maara Gatundu and Kagũre Mũriithi in turn—but they refused to respond.

At this juncture George K. Ndegwa said, "We are waiting for the officer himself to make a selection of the 40 people he needs for work." This elicited a lot of grumbling from people. Ndegwa sat down.

Henry Wambũgũ stood up and said, "We have not rejected forced labour. What we are not ready for is to offer ourselves in *cooperation* for camp labour."

The officer asked him, "Should I order you to go and work, would you obey?"

Wambũgũ answered, "Indeed, yes."

He was told to take his belongings and move to compound 2.

When he asked whether there were other people who were prepared to obey an order to work, nobody talked to him. The officer and Mbiyũ left.

Recriminations continued, with some people arguing it was the leaders who were misleading everybody else. But a counter-argument was offered that nobody had talked out of turn, or in conflict with our general stand: when Wambũgũ had talked about acceptance of *forced labour* and readiness to work if so "ordered", he had not departed from our stated stand on rejection of cooperation.

We received another note from compound 2 stating that our action to date had demonstrated sufficient resistance to cooperation: we could now still go to work while holding on to our principled stand against cooperation.

After lengthy deliberations we came to the conclusion that we and people from compound 2 were united in our stand against cooperation; after all these people had not volunteered to be where they were: they had been ordered to be there.

We made a decision which constituted a turning point: we would agree to clear the compound if ordered to do so, but not because we had volunteered for it.

Mūrage Wokabi fainted. The dresser ordered that he be taken to the dispensary at 1.00 p.m. Soon after Wahogo and Mũũgĩ reached a point of collapse, and they were carried to the guardroom.

The atmosphere was shot through with sadness, despair, and despondency. We sent a delegation made up of Wamũthenya and Chokwe to the camp officer.

At 1.45 p.m. Wamũthenya and Chokwe came back to section 1 and confirmed that they had informed imperialist Martin that detainees from compound 1 had agreed to clear the compound on orders but not through their voluntary will. The colonialist had agreed to the terms of our acceptance and had ordered that we be given food.

The camp officer soon made his entry carrying a bucket of water; following on his heels were his guards who came with their own buckets of water.

People from compound 2 offered to cook our food that day. We had our midday meal at 3.30 p.m.

Gĩtahi Waciira was taken from his punishment cell and brought to compound 1—his further punishment for throwing food to us bad elements.

Wambũgũ Mbũya personally asked that he be brought to compound 1 from compound 2.

That same day a number of people went to work: Waira, Gatabaki, Kamawe, Bongwe, Ng'ombe, Mĩnyarũ, P. Ngũgĩ and Kĩnũthia Mũgĩĩa.

Wahogo, Mũũgĩ and Mwaũra were taken from the guardroom and returned to compound 1. But Wokabi's condition worsened and he was taken to a proper bed in a sickroom in compound 2.

Three searches were conducted on that day.

20 February 1954

The colonial officer was requested to allow the emaciated people from compound 2 time to recover their strength before they would be sent to work. He agreed to let them have two days. However, people assigned the work of gathering firewood, fetching water and cooking were on duty.

Gĩtaũ Mũrĩmi and Kahũgĩ Gĩturo were requested by their friends from compound 3 to join the ranks of the cooperators, a request which they turned down.

A man called Mũriũki did become a volunteer for work.

4

Interrogations in Manda

21 February 1954 to 24 June 1954

21 February 1954

The David Warŭhiŭ Interrogation Committee arrived in Manda. Its membership included Warŭhiŭ, a British officer named Church and 6 Gĩkŭyŭ elders drawn from the ranks of the collaborators. Tents were erected to house them and to provide an office from which they would work.

The presence of these people created a great stir and agitation among the detainees. Rumour grew that they had come to take us home. Already, it was said, 480 people had been released from detention. A large number of people from compound 2 went to work on that day, among them: Mwai Thogo, Gakami, Rev. Arthur Gatŭng'ŭ, Rev. Ephantus Waithaka, Mbŭrŭ Njoroge, Njenga Thagicŭ, Ngarama Wagakura, Karŭrŭ Mŭrebu, Stephen Ngure, Peter Mŭtabi, Mwangi Wawerŭ, Arthur Mahiga, and Mwangi Mwea.

In compound 1 we met; after fierce debate, the resolution was passed that people were not restricted from going to work. But there was still a lot of misgiving over seeming to join the ranks of the cooperators: how could we collaborate with the enemy? people asked. Some said they would wait and see.

Even so Kahŭgĩ Gĩturo from compound 1 did go to work.

And a puzzling development: a sick and very old man, Paulo Gĩcaana, asked that he be transferred from compound 2 to compound 1. He was carried to compound 1 on his bed.

22 February 1954

The camp officer sent Corporal Muli to obtain the names of the 40 people who would go to work from compound 1. Wamŭthenya and Chokwe informed the corporal that many people were still unwell. When the officer was given this information he said he would himself come over to compound 1.

All our personal effects which had been taken from us were returned to us. In addition parcels which had been sent from home, containing things like clothing, shoes and letters, were released to us.

When the officer came to our section, he agreed to give us another two days to recover our strength. He took Wamŭthenya and Chokwe to see the grass he wanted slashed. When they returned, he informed us he had appointed Wamŭthenya and Chokwe to become camp captains. He would give orders and directives through them. He warned that those who would continue to refuse to go to work on the pretext that they were sick may be charged with the offence of malingering.

He, however, warned us that our avenue to offering voluntary cooperation was now closed. On no account would he allow people from compound 1 to embrace cooperation with a view to making a good impression on the inter- rogators.

Chokwe said he was ready for cooperation. Martin said he would on no account allow the bad elements from section 1 to mix with people who had shown obedience all along.

At around 6.00 p.m. people from compound 1 and 2 were able to talk to each other. There was no guard in the no-man's-land between the two sections. The camp officer had already declared that compound 1 and 2 would be re- combined. Many people from compound 2 now said they wanted to go back to section 1.

23 February 1954

People from compound 1 expressed a lot of curiosity about what the actual stand of people in compound 2 was. People exchanged notes as well as holding intense question-and-answer sessions. Martin had made this declaration: "A man who declares his clean intentions from the heart will receive acceptance in compound 3."

At 5.00 p.m. compound 2 was abolished. Fifteen people from this section expressly declared against cooperation. These were: J. Wandimbe, H. Karūme, J. Kĩraatũ, M. Mbaria, W. Waciira, H. Wambũgũ, V. Wokabi, M. Mũnene, M. Kambũĩ, M. Gacũgũ, K. Ngucune, K. Matu, Maregwa, M. Gatũndũ and Gĩitwa Ndimũ. All these people obtained transfer to compound 1. All those others never took a definitive stand and they obtained cooperator status. They remained where they were, but the barbed wire separating compounds 2 and 3 was removed and thus was created one cooperator quarters, accommod- ating 112 detainees; section 1 held 99 detainees.

A breakdown by district of origin of the inmates worked out something like this; "Cooperators'" quarters: Kĩambuu—63; Nyeri —23; Mũrang'a—17; Embu—3; Machakos—4; North Nyanza—1; South Nyanza—1; anti-cooper- ation quarters: Kĩambuu—27; Nyeri—52; Mũrang'a—18; Embu—2.

That night detainees in compound 1 prepared a duty roster: 40 people would cut grass and clear the compound; 12 would draw water; 5 people with disabilities would do sanitary work: the remaining 32 would be involved in cooking, preparing rice for cooking, peeling potatoes, and cleaning up our living quarters. Those who went for outdoor clearing would also bring in the

firewood. The information would be passed to the camp officer that we ~~~~~
ourselves allocate duties and shift people as necessary to different areas of
work. The officer should not interfere with our arrangements as long as he got
his 40 people for camp work.

We talked about the kind of relations we would want to maintain with
the other people in the camp. We would try as hard as possible to maintain
good relations with people in the cooperators' compound; we would not resort
to verbal abuse even if they became insulting and provocative. We would carry
out our resolution to obey the orders and directives of the authorities, and we
would endeavour to befriend the camp personnel with a view to learning
something about the intentions and methods of the interrogators, and also
with a view to getting to know whether those in the cooperators' camp would
seek to curry favour with the interrogators by bearing false witness against us.

24 February

All the detainees went to work in the morning. Those guards who would oversee
people doing forced labour were strictly enjoined not to use any violence. They
should take their position at 20 or 25 yards away from the work gang. Those
detainees who misbehaved should be reported to the camp officer.

People worked until 1.00 p.m. At 4.00 p.m. people were allowed to go and
bathe and swim in the open sea.

The cooperators started doing sanitary work. Previously their slop pails
had been cleaned out by ordinary prisoners.

Interrogations started for compound 3 detainees.

25 February 1954

A number of detainees were called in for interrogation. These were the kind
of questions asked: Have you taken the Mau Mau oath? Would you accept
undergoing a cleansing ceremony by taking a solemn vow? Your land: how
did you acquire your right to it, by paying for it or through inheritance? If you
didn't take the oath what are the reasons? And many more such questions.

40 people from compound 1 were taken to cut grass and construct a fence.

26 February 1954

Three British colonialist interrogation officers, two men and a woman, visited
the camp but they did not stay. Information had it they were from the C.I.D.

27 February 1954

We were granted permission to write letters home, and we went to watch a football match. The Naked Officer mentioned to Wamũthenya that he was satisfied with the way people were working; should people continue the same way they would considerably reform themselves.

Division and mutual distrust became evident among the cooperators; some of them were bearing witness against their fellows.

And it appeared the Warũhiũ Committee was not satisfied with those people they had already interrogated. "In three days' time you may have heard something from us," they said noncommittally to the detainees.

28 February 1954

There were rumours that the interrogators had asked Martin to permit the use of beatings to extract confessions about the Mau Mau oaths from the detainees. It was said Martin had refused to grant this permission and had in fact written a letter to the Commissioner of Prisons expressing his rejection of and opposition to the use of violence in interrogations.

March, 1954

1 March 1954

A meeting was held at the District Commissioner's Office, Lamu, between the Prison Officer, Lamu, the Manda Camp Officer, Martin and David Warũhiũ and his team of British C.I.D. officers who had come to Manda to conduct the interrogation of detainees. The interrogators wanted the facility of an interrogation site just next to the ocean where they would be able to subject detainees who failed to confess to taking the oath to certain punishments: beatings, being left outdoors where mosquitoes would torment the detainees, forcing detainees to spend the night with part of their bodies in the water. Martin, the District Commissioner, and the Lamu Prison Officer rejected this scheme. It was decided that Askwith, the Commissioner for Detainees' Rehabilitation, would be awaited to give his verdict in the dispute between the prison authorities and the district commissioner, on the one hand, and the Warũhiũ Interrogation committee on the other. From what we heard on the grapevine, Martin vowed he would resign his position in the camp administration if Warũhiũ were allowed to subject to physical torture detainees, some of whom had been tried and acquitted in courts of law for involvement in the murder of Warũhiũ's father.

The interrogators, so we heard, had also put a demand that Achieng'

Oneko be put in chains when he went to work outside the camp precincts. He could not be trusted, they insisted. Here too, the Naked Officer put his foot down: he reminded the interrogators that Achieng' Oneko had been working long before they set foot on Manda island. He had never required a guard when he went to work in the bush—and he would always bring himself back to camp.

That day no interrogations were carried out.

2 March 1954

Four Agĩkũyũ interrogators were escorted into compound 1 by Martin in the company of four camp guards, armed with heavy clubs and shields. David Warũhiũ and Permenus Kĩritũ addressed us, and detainees were not allowed to ask any questions.

They told us, "Confess the oaths you have taken. In the Gĩkũyũ country-side everybody else has confessed. We have come to take you home. An abomination has been committed: people have used womens' menstrual blood and the organs of manhood in oathing rituals. A delegation sent by the British Government has uncovered all these things and has reported back in England on them.

"You people are rejecting cooperation with the authorities in fear of the dark powers of the oath. In the meanwhile Mau Mau continues to carry out murders of women and children, while you continue writing ineffectual memoranda on land rights and workers' wages. The Agĩkũyũ people are dying on both sides, and our role is to save you and save the situation. He who confesses the oath, we will go back home with him.

"I can see many leaders here in Manda," Warũhiũ said, "you, Beauttah, for example, Mwai Koigi, Job Mũcucu and many others here who were well known to me. I direct my appeal to you. He who confesses the oath will not face prosecution; he will go home to cooperate with the authorities."

3 March 1954

Askwith, the Commissioner for Development and Rehabilitation, and his assistant, Allen, arrived by plane.* They went to the canteen which was very heavily guarded by armed soldiers. They never visited our living quarters. And in the afternoon we were not allowed to leave our quarters.

The interrogators summoned sixteen elderly men and asked them to counsel the other detainees on the wisdom of confessing the oath. The elders would have none of it.

*A helicopter used to land at Mukowe.

4 March 1954

There were rumours circulating in the morning that there were some detainees who would obtain immediate transfer to Jeanes School, Kabete. Some detainees with homes in Kĩambuu became agitated with hope. But nothing happened.

Two people, Gacuuru Ngorano and P. Ngũgĩ, were summoned for interrogation. When Gacuuru refused to confess the oath he was subjected to beatings and torture: they would make him bend and touch the floor with his index finger and turn round continuously. In the end he resorted to falsehoods; he claimed the oath had been administered to him by one Wanjohi wa Wanyĩrĩ. They ordered him to go to the cooperators' wing of the detainee quarters. He refused to obey.

Gacuuru wrote to the camp officer complaining that he had been tortured and forced to confess the oath; he asked for permission to have his complaint handled by his own lawyers.

Ngũgĩ was not interrogated. He was told to go back. He would be summoned tomorrow.

It appeared Warũhiũ was stirring misunderstanding at every turn. There was bitter recrimination between him and the camp sergeant for remarks that had been dropped since the arrival of Warũhiũ's committee to the effect that the detainees had made dishonourable liaisons with the wives of the camp personnel. This caused an uproar.

The camp officer ordered his guards not to beat the detainees during interrogation. All the same, our feeling—and this was expressed when all the 99 of us met in section 1—was that detainees from our section were being subjected to torture during interrogation because we had refused to cooperate over the labour question. We were getting caught between the hostility of the interrokators and the resentment of the camp officer over our seeming intransigence. Some people suggested we should offer an acceptance of cooperation to Martin, so that we could win him wholly to our side. But this idea was rejected: it must remain an individual decision whether or not one accepted voluntary labour.

Chokwe went to section 3 of his own free will.

We asked the following people to go and ask Martin to supply us with soap: Wamũthenya, Cege, Mwangi Mathu, and Mwai Koigi. Soap was not available at the moment, they were told, but it had been ordered from Nairobi.

Martin informed our delegation that he had already written to higher government authorities about beatings during interrogation; he had specifically complained about Gacuuru's case. He had expressly instructed his camp guards to refrain from beating people during interrogation. The standing policy from Nairobi was that a detainee should on no account be beaten unless he exhibited violent behaviour during interrogation.

All the same, Martin went on, he was not prepared to protect people who had taken the oath and who refused to make their confession. It was this same oath which inculcated unreasonable intransigence. Those who had taken the oath must make their confession.

In conclusion Martin cautioned against backbiting and scheming against one another.

5 March 1954

Gacuuru was summoned by the interrogators after they learnt that he had lodged a complaint with the camp officer. He retracted his earlier "confession". The beatings he had received, he stated, had induced him to falsely confess to having taken the oath.

Five other people were interrogated on that day. They were not beaten. They did not confess, and they were told they would stay in Manda for ever.

8 March 1954

Many detainees from compound 1 were taken for interrogation. The younger men were beaten up by the interrogators themselves. Gathee and Mwangi Kĩng'oora were so beaten before being ordered to be confined in cells without food.

The camp officer did not learn about this until about 4.00 p.m. when it was reported to him by the camp sergeant and other guards, who were angry and upset about the whole development. The officer ordered the release of Gathee and Mwangi from the cells. Dr. Shah was called to examine them. Gathee had been hit on the head with a mallet.

Martin instructed Wamũthenya to advise Gathee and Mwangi to write statements about having been assaulted.

9 March 1954

The young men who had been interrogated were summoned again. Warũhiũ himself slapped them on the cheeks as he put questions to them and scoffed at them: "Do you call yourselves leaders? Who on earth can you lead?"

He spoke with bitterness. He was angry because the beatings used by his committee had been the subject of a report to higher authorities.

He did not beat the older people; nor those people known to him.

I myself was called at 2.00 p.m. I was shown a batch of books, some written by myself, others by different authors. But the books were shown to me as if I had been the sole author. I picked out the books I had myself written and confessed that, indeed, I was the author. But I knew absolutely nothing about the Mau

Mau oath. I was ordered out, and told there was no hope for me ever leaving this island; my eyes would never see that national freedom I kept demanding in my songs.

Mwanĩki Rĩbuthi, a young man, was beaten up as they demanded to know from him what people from section 1 discussed in secret.

Warũhiũ confronted Crispus Mwanĩki with this story: a conspiracy had been hatched under the leadership of George Njue Kamũmbũ and Wamũthenya to have Mwanĩkĩ murdered. Warũhiũ had learned about this conspiracy from the camp officer himself.

When Wamũthenya heard about this, he wrote to the camp officer complaining about being made the subject of a malicious and false accusation; he copied his letter to Warũhiũ.

At other interrogation sessions Warũhiũ would complain that the Mau Mau conflict was becoming protracted because of the intransigence of people from Nyeri; people from Kĩambuu had accepted moderation and their wish was to see an end to the conflict; but people from Nyeri were extremists.

The statements made by the young men who had been beaten—Gathee, Mwangi, Kĩama and Mathenge Njari—were delivered to the camp officer, together with Wamũthenya's letter of complaint against Warũhiũ.

48 Somali recruits were brought to Manda and housed in barracks which had been constructed some time back. Their meals were prepared by detainees from section 3.

11 March 1954

David Warũhiũ sailed to Lamu. The Coast Provincial Commissioner visited the Manda camp in the company of the District Commissioner, Lamu and the Commissioner of Prisons. Then they left. Soon the camp officer left for Lamu.

Our conjecture was that there was to be a meeting in Lamu over cases of physical assault on detainees.

12 March 1954

Martin came to complain that in spite of his help and consideration for us, we had failed to reciprocate with a spirit of understanding; if it was not for him some of us would probably have been executed during our stay on Manda island. From now on the camp authority would not be prepared to treat rejectors of work with any consideration.

In the evening we discussed the implications of Martin's threat. We expressed our realisation that cooperation over the work question did not necessarily imply acceptance of the ultimate compromise—confession of the nationalist oath. In any case for practical purposes there was no difference between the rejectors of work and the cooperators: all of us ended working; the authorities were only incensed because they had not achieved the psychological surrender of the rejectors. We felt that Martin's meeting with the other officials had emphasised the need of this psychological surrender.

Only four of us talked, after which we resolved to go all the way and accept "cooperation", so that they would stop treating us with suspicion and posting guards almost round the clock to watch over us. We would then see which steps the authorities would take after the removal of this last bastion of our defiance.

Our representatives went to inform Martin about our new resolution. He said he would accept immediately our offer of cooperation and would not insist on maintaining his earlier stand that we should not opt for cooperation to take advantage of the presence of interrogators in the camp.

We were accepted as cooperators, volunteers for work, and all the doors were opened and all barbed wire barriers removed.

13 March 1954

The camp officer informed us that all ordinary prisoners would be removed from Manda. People from compound 1 would from now on dispose of slop from the camp personnel quarters. Compound 1 should make three people available each day for this work.

Our interpretation of this requirement was that we were being put to the test. We accepted this work.

But it did appear we had not been fully accepted as cooperators, for people from our section continued to be subjected to guard watch as they carried out work outdoors.

14 March 1954

D. Warũhiũ learned that we had accepted cooperation, but he appeared to deem this Martin's victory and not his own victory. There appeared to be a silent power struggle between the two—Warũhiũ and Martin: who could change the detainees' way of thinking? To support his stance that he had more powers than Martin, Warũhiũ read out to detainees from compounds 2 and 3 a document spelling out his authority. He said he was aware that some detainees had given certain information to the camp officer which they had withheld from the interrogation committee. Because of this he would order that all detainees from compounds 2 and 3 who had already been interrogated should be subjected to a repeat interrogation.

16 March 1954

The camp officer gave orders that every person from compound 1 should go to work the following day. He should be supplied with the names of all persons who had disabilities or who were otherwise sick, so that these people should be seen by the dresser.

17 March 1954

People from section 1 felt they had started cooperation in earnest as they went to work en masse. People from compounds 2 and 3 were likewise swept out to work in the morning. The last person to go out of the door of our quarters was Kagĩĩka Kũhũtha.

18 March 1954

Detainees from compounds 2 and 3 were supplied with work clothes: black shorts and black apron per person. We learned that this was the colour of clothing supplied to those detainees who had not yet made a confession to taking the oath. There were other colours up the scale: yellow, and ultimately white.

19 March 1954

Warũhiũ and Martin, under an escort of three guards armed with shields, came to address compound 3 in the evening. Warũhiũ warned us that this would be the last time he would come to offer us the opportunity to make a clean-breast confession, those of us who had not done so. Those who had not taken the oath should give a full explanation why not; they would be listened to. If a person knew he had been arrested because of mistaken identity he should indicate the person for whom he was mistaken. He would distribute writing paper on which people could give all the necessary information on themselves; alternatively, people would be welcome to make a repeat appearance before his committee. People could use fountain pens or pencils to write down their statements.

When Warũhiũ asked who would require writing paper, no one responded. Martin flared up. "You people are hardcore Mau Mau!" he declared. "Your own people, people of integrity and good will, have come to help you—but you respond by refusing to talk to them. How in the world are you to be helped if you respond with the same mulish stubbornness you have shown to me when your own people offer help!"

James Beauttah in a conciliatory manner explained that we had already accepted cooperation; we were now working voluntarily—and devotedly. Martin said he was yet to be convinced that we meant to offer whole-hearted cooperation: we had not yet shown genuine acceptance. We behaved like a herd of sheep, doing things in concert with heads sullenly bowed. This was not good enough: he wanted each of us individually to walk to his office and bow our heads in acceptance.

Thirty people registered their names for appearance before the interrogation committee tomorrow.

We were left pondering on Martin's words. Some people confessed that they hadn't wanted to accept voluntary work but they had allowed themselves to be dragged along by the general will. Everybody could now see to what shame we were now being put. Other people said there was no need to change the stand on voluntary labour; but they vowed they would never ever walk to the Naked Commandant's office to individually kneel before him.

20 March 1954

Each of us was given writing paper on which to make our statements. I wrote down that before my detention I was an author of books and a publisher of a newspaper called *Waigua Atīa?* Everything I had ever written was contained in my books and in the newspaper.

We were wary about what the authorities intended to do with our written statements. Some people wrote superfially non-committal stuff. When Wamŭthenya's statement had been read, he was advised to have it published in the *East African Standard* so that readers would be treated to the virtues of not taking the Mau Mau oath. And when they read Koina Gĩtibi's statement, they were so incensed they had Koina transferred from compound 3 to compound 1, although Koina had been one of the earlier work volunteers who had earned a work uniform for cooperation.

Our interpretation of these acts was that cooperation was of little consequence as far as the Warŭhiŭ interrogation committee was concerned.

23 March 1954

The Warŭhiŭ committee men gathered their belongings together ready for departure from Manda. Warŭhiŭ recommended that all those who had recorded statements of complaint against beatings by the committee should withdraw them. The detainees agreed to consider this recommendation. The record of Gacuuru Ngorano's "confesion", obtained under duress, was destroyed, torn up, in front of the following witnesses: Wamŭthenya, Rev. Arthur Gatŭng'ŭ. James Beauttah and Rev. Stefano Waciira.

24 March 1954

For the very first time, detainees played football against a team made up of the camp guards. It was a goalless draw.

26 March 1954

Kagŭnda's and Mŭibŭ's shoes were stolen when a work gang from compound 1 had gone into the bush to cut timber for construction. The matter was reported to the camp officer; it transpired that nobody had been asked to look after these shoes. When the guards who had escorted the workers into the bush were asked about the matter, they reacted with violent hostility. They claimed the detainees had threatened them with pangas.

Kagŭnda and Mŭibŭ, whose shoes had been stolen, cast suspicion on the camp guard, one Wilson, who had been in charge of the timber cutting work.

At 4.00 o'clock, two guards were seen entering the camp from the direction of the work site. They wore long overcoats. They went to their living quarters. This was reported to the camp office immediately. Nothing, however, was done.

28 March 1954

Detainees from compounds 2 and 3 started construction work for a new camp on the site which detainees from section 1 had cleared. They would also build a hospital for in-patients.

30 March 1954

From now on, we were told, people from section 1 would work the whole day; they had not wholly qualified to be cooperators. We felt that Martin was indulging a grudge against us. Already a rumour was rife that Martin would be leaving the camp in the near future. We resolved to bear the conditions as they were and to continue working while waiting for a change of guard.

Two Somali camp guards resigned their positions in the camp purportedly in protest against practices in the camp.

* * *

During the month of March, people started collecting coconut fibre, when they went out for bush clearing chores, and used it in crafting baskets, bags and hats. Simeon Nyaga pioneered in making nice baskets which many people admired.

During this month, there was an outbreak of an ailment whose symptoms were dysentry and vomiting. There were no drugs for this ailment. When a person suffered from an attack he would be advised to go and drink lots of water. The disease first attacked the recruits.

April, 1954

1 April 1954

Three people—Cege Kĩraka, Mwĩcĩgĩ Karanja, and Wahome Kĩĩhĩa—were reported for slacking at work. Our feeling was that the guards were nursing a grudge, because we had cast suspicion on them for the stolen shoes.

2 April 1954

T.F. Anderson, the Director of Medical Services, Kenya, the D.O. for Nyeri, one Lloyd and two other British officers J.C. Carothers and Captain Rodgers came on a tour to Manda Island Camp. They came to compound 1 and questioned us about several matters. Carothers showed a keen interest and would question individual detainees about the cause of their arrest and the nature of living conditions in detention. When he asked us why we had rejected "cooperation", we informed him our rejection had ceased on 12th March 1954; we were, however, concerned that the camp officer did not seem to accept our offer of cooperation.

Did we get an adequate supply of vegetables in our diet? they asked. We said no. The D.M.S. saw the sick: Paulo Gĩcaana, Joram Wawerũ and Ndegwa.

The team inspected the food we customarily ate, the tunnels that bore away waste water and the general cleanliness of the camp. The whole place was terribly dusty; there were frequent wind storms.

When they left, they took with them Joram Wawerũ, whose condition was bad, to have him taken to the Native Council Hospital, Lamu.

Word had it that these officers had been delegated to come by the British colonial office in its response to the petitions we had sent to England.

The camp officer and the sergeant were visibly angry and upset. The Naked Officer was heard to grumble: "I am sure one of my guards was bribed to smuggle a letter for posting to England by these sly and eternally degenerate men!"

5 April 1954

There was heavy rain from the morning hours. Those who had gone to work returned drenched wet. Nobody went out to work in the afternoon.

We concluded the long rains had come.

6 April 1954

Joram Wawerũ had died the previous day: this information was brought to the camp by the camp guard who had been detailed to look after Wawerũ at Lamu. According to this guard, a stomach operation had been carried out on Waweru. He was in excruciating pain and had to be tied to his hospital bed. We wondered how it was possible to need to tie up a man who had undergone stomach surgery.

This news cast a shadow of sadness and despondency on the camp. People did not go out to work in the afternoon, on account of the mourning situation. In the evening we had prayers. People from all the sections gathered together and we were led in prayer by Rev. Arthur Gatũng'ũ who read the relevant section of the Christian Prayer book. Mbacia, Achieng' and Meemia gave a eulogy on the departed. They praised Waweru's patriotic heroism; even in the hour of physical illness he lived by his convictions. Solomon Meemia informed us that Waweru had been survived by two wives and more than eight children. We should always pray for them.

At about 2.00 p.m. the new camp officer arrived. His name was John D. Russell.

Joram was buried in the Lamu Hospital cemetery. His personal effects were collected for delivery to his wives back home.

7 April 1954

Martin spent the whole day handing over to the new camp officer. Ten detainees who had embraced cooperation from the very beginning were introduced to Russell by Martin. It was people from compound 3, Martin declared, who had made his work in Manda worthwhile and rewarding.

There was a quarrel between Mwangi Thabuni and Waigwa Rũcathi over some ripe bananas.

8 April 1954

Because of yesterday's quarrel, Mwangi Thabuni was returned to compound 1 without being allowed a hearing. We suspected that a secret complaint had been made against him by Waigwa himself or by other champions of cooperation; Waigwa was a cooperator of long standing.

9 April 1954

Martin went to Lamu without, however, carrying away his belongings.

Uniforms were supplied to all people who hadn't yet received them in compounds 2 and 3. When we asked when similar uniforms would be supplied to people in compound 1, we were informed the matter was under consideration by both Martin and Russell; they would declare their decision in due course.

10 April 1954

The new officer witnessed a general inspection being carried out on the detainees by guards on the football field. He addressed the camp personnel and informed them he had been assigned from England to come and concern himself with the welfare of detainees. Political detainees were not convicted prisoners and should be treated differently; the guards had no authority to beat the detainees.

On the issue of work, Russell said it should be a genuinely voluntary matter; no one should be forced to work if he chose not to.

At 5.00 p.m. Russell inspected the camp dispensary and our living quarters. He saw Gīcaana and Ndegwa on their sick beds in compound 1. He was told they were getting their medicine as necessary. He issued instructions that our living quarters should be kept clean constantly; the water reservoir should be thoroughly cleaned.

12 April 1954

Kamanū Kīnya was beaten up by a guard because he had refused to gather greens for him as well as to cut his hair. Two people—Kīnyanjui and Mahuti—had earlier refused to gather greens for this guard. When the matter was reported to the camp sergeant he refused to take up the case.

13 April 1954

Colonialist officer Martin left Manda camp carried in a small car. Before he left he gave away to the camp personnel the chickens he had been raising, beds from his house and tables.

Russell was now in charge.

After he had gone detainees made caustic fun of Martin's characteristic utterances: "I am the way unto a return home!", or "I am your salvation: the white man does not tell lies".

Some people were unhappy, feeling terribly deceived by Naked Martin over the question of "cooperation".

Some guards confined Gathanju, Wambūgū, Gīthaiga and M. Kīng'oora in punishment cells for allegedly trying to escape from the working site where they had gone to cut construction timber. But the camp sergeant had them released; he complained that many guards were novices who did not know exactly what they were supposed to do.

14 April 1954

Elder Paulo Gīcaana died in his bed in compound 1 at around 7.00 a.m. This was immediately reported to the camp sergeant, in the absence of the camp officer who had gone to Lamu. The sergeant ordered that no one would go out to work, for there was a state of mourning.

A coffin was constructed. When the camp officer returned he said the burial would take place at 4.00 o'clock in the afternoon. But Commander Stancey-Marks, the prisons officer, said it was necessary before burial that a doctor conduct a post mortem and issue a burial certificate.

15 April 1954

An African hospital assistant carried out a post mortem on Gĩcaana's body. He gave Russell the burial certificate.

When people returned to their quarters at 3.00 p.m., they changed from the work uniforms into their own clothes. A funeral procession was led by the elderly men, with the young men following bearing the coffin; they took turns in carrying the coffin.

The guards walked at a distance from the procession, on either side of the road. The camp officer, the sergeant and dresser followed from a discreet distance. A few detainees carried spades and some carried flowers.

When we arrived at the grave Rev. Arthur Gatũng'ũ and Rev. Waithaka read the relevant section of the Christian Book of Prayers. George K. Ndegwa gave a eulogy on Gĩcaana. Mũibũ wa Mũkoma played the role of Gĩcaana's son, holding the part of the coffin where Gĩcaana's head was as we buried the elder with deeply felt respect.

The sergeant threw in the symbolic lump of earth. The camp officer stood at attention and saluted. We buried Gĩcaana.

Chokwe had prepared a board on which Gĩcaana's name was beautifully painted. It was used to mark Gĩcaana's grave.

We left the burial ground singing the hymn Gũthamĩrĩo Gĩcigĩrĩra—"To Be Detained on a Remote Island".

Gĩcaana's death brought people from all the compounds of the camp together, and after a long time of separation we mixed together. It was a new and refreshing thing.

Back in our compound Russell urged us to be good and he would reciprocate by being good to us. He asked us to construct beds like those used in compound 3. On Saturdays we would only work outside the camp until 10.00 a.m., after which we would only be required to clean up our quarters and the compound.

He reminded us that tomorrow was Good Friday.

16 April 1954

All Gĩcaana's belongings were gathered together and delivered to the officer who would make arrangements for getting them to Gĩcaana's family.

We learned that one of the camp guards had died at the Lamu hospital.

The camp officer made it a camp regulation that all detainees should have a hair cut and a shave every Saturday. Equipment should be obtained from his office on this day and returned after use.

17 April 1954

Russell came to inspect general cleanliness. He appeared to value cleanliness highly; his concern in this area was higher than Martin's had been. During his inspection he was informed that two people, Cege Kīraka and Mara Gatūndū, had been assaulted by guards while they were out cutting construction timber. They had been put in the guardroom and beaten with the butts of rifles. Russell said this complaint should be taken to him tomorrow.

At 4.00 o'clock a boat landed bearing with it, so we learned, things which Martin had dishonestly tried to take away with him—namely furniture like tables, chairs and beds which had been constructed by "cooperators", and which were considered Government property. This shocked us, badly—as we tried to match Martin's words and posturings and this his final act.

In the evening we met and decided that we should make joint representations to the camp officer about our problems and grievances and should not resort to individual approaches. We decided to choose people who would see the camp officer about our shared problems. Mwangi Mathu was chosen to represent people from Kīambuu, Mūrage Wokabi would represent people from Nyeri, Cege Kabogoro those from Mūrang'a and Wamūthenya would lead them as the chosen section 1 leader. The issues they would discuss were exhaustively discussed by all the detainees from compound 1. The colonial officer agreed to discuss these matters the following day.

18 April 1954

Detainees from compounds 2 and 3 elected a new representatives council, whose membership did not include the people who had made an early offer of cooperation. There was a split and a disagreement. The old representatives committee went to complain to the camp officer. Russell ruled that the new committee should handle the affairs of compounds 2 and 3 for a period of one month, after which the situation would be reviewed.

There was a lot of animosity between people in compounds 2 and 3 and some held others in disdain. Some detainees insisted on privileged treatment, shunning lowly jobs like cleaning up living quarters and compound, clearing the daily slop, cooking and drawing water. The old committee had, with the cooperation of Naked Martin, seized these privileges. But the new committee now refused to allow these people to continue to exercise the privilege of shunning certain kinds of work.

Our representatives were told they would have an audience with Russell tomorrow. It was clear he was less than happy about the dispute going on in compounds 2 and 3.

19 April 1954

Today was Easter Sunday.

Our representatives went to see the camp officer; with them went the people who had been beaten: Cege Kīraka and Maara Gatūndū.

Russell's first comment was: "If you are good, I will also be good." Then he addressed the points raised. He would make sure that the proper measure and ration was apportioned to us; however, he would not entrust one of us with seeing to the correctness of the measure since detained people should not be put in positions of trust. As we had actually been receiving 160 ripe bananas instead of the statutory 212, he had put investigations in the hands of the police to determine what was happening; at the same time he was checking the matter with the supplier. Four water buckets were unavailable since Officer Martin seemed to have carried them away with him.

An arrangement would immediately be put in hand for 12 people to work as permanent wood fuel gatherers.

As to the question of being treated with equality with people in the other sections—keeping the doors open and being permitted to maintain intercourse with people in the other sections—Russell said he needed time to give the matter due consideration. Time was all the more needed as it was necessary for him to determine why people had been segregated in three different sections in the first place.

He had issued instructions that guards should not beat detainees, who were not convicted prisoners. At the same time detainees should be obedient and cooperative and should not look down upon guards and prison personnel even if they sometimes had a lower education than themselves.

His role here was to look after the detainees; he was a soldier and not a rehabilitation officer.

In the near future we might be transferred from Manda to camps in Kisii or at Mackinnon Road. Our conditions might be improved and our wives may be allowed to come and pay occasional visist.

Russell issued instructions that people should go into the bush tomorrow to cut timber for constructing proper beds.

Rumours were rife that Elder Kenyatta would be brought to Manda.

20 April 1954

The camp officer warned that he did not have time to waste on solving pointless disputes. If a camp guard assaulted a detainee and injured him, Russell could invoke his powers to have the guard prosecuted and imprisoned for three years. Similarly if a detainee refused to obey orders given him or used insulting language towards a guard, Russell could recommend to the District Commissioner that the detainee be prosecuted and imprisoned, before being returned to detention. He would ask us all—detainees and guards—to cooperate in playing our different roles: after all, we were all Africans, and he was the only white man among us.

Russell's words seemed to have a positive effect on the guards—who started to treat the detainees with some consideration.

22 April 1954

Russell summoned the detainee representatives from all the sections, the work gang leaders, the camp sergeant and dresser and gave them the following instructions. No detainee should visit the living quarters of the camp personnel for this would put the wives of camp personnel in a compromising situation. If a detainee was assigned work that would require him to go there, he should refuse.

Russell would energetically oppose tendencies of people to malinger and to shirk physical labour. People should on the contrary welcome work as a means of exercising and maintaining physical fitness. People should grow vegetables for their own consumption: individual or communal plots would be encouraged; for communal cultivation people could organise around a row of beds, or around a section of the detainee living quarters, or even the whole camp. Meat had become unmanageably expensive; the D.C. had taken up the matter of meat prices with the suppliers.

People should treat the dresser with all respect.

An inventory should be taken of all the furniture items that the "cooperators" had made using Government materials. Camp personnel should surrender such items of furniture to his office.

An office where people could meet would be constructed in the near future.

Farmland for cabbage and other vegetable cultivation would be shown to the detainee representatives tomorrow. These representatives were: Mbiyū, Mulli, Waithaka, Kīgume, Wamūthenya, Mulwa and Romano. They should put the case for vegetable cultivation to the other detainees.

Lastly: Russell asked the Christian ministers among us—Reverend Arthur Gatūng'ū, Rev. Stefano Waciira, Rev. Waithaka, John Adala and others—to conduct religious services on Sunday in all compounds of the detainees' living quarters, including compound 1.

23 April 1954

After gathering firewood, the detainee workers refused to deliver some of it to the living quarters of the guards. In angry retaliation, some of these people were thrown into cells. Kagĩĩka and Kamau were badly beaten and it was falsely reported that they had insulted the guards. The sergeant listened to the case and agreed to have Kagĩĩka released from the cell; Kagĩĩka was taken to the dispensary where his hip injury, inflicted by a blow with a gun butt, was attended to. But the sergeant had Kamau appear before the camp officer, who condemned Kamau to a punishment cell for four days, to the chagrin of most of the detainees. Kagĩĩka wrote to the camp officer giving an explanation of the whole matter.

24 April 1954

All of us in section 1 met in the evening to deliberate on the proposed vegetable cultivation. We had adopted this policy: to have all matters that concerned us deliberated over by all of us.

A good number of people emphasised the fact that all through our stay in detention we had never taken on work as a voluntary undertaking. We were arrested and detained against our will on the authority and by the power of the Government which should not now abdicate its duty to keep us fed; we should not now be required to help the government out by growing food to feed ourselves. In any case the land here was very poor for cultivation; if the Government really wanted us to become farmers let them return us home to our highly cultivable land, or let them settle us on some other good agricultural land.

For us cultivation would be just like other work, such as clearing the bush and cutting timber—a mandatory requirement of official policy. None of us would offer to farm his individual plot; if we took on the work of cultivation we would all be involved in it as a group. We resolved that the colonialist officer be informed by Wamũthenya that people from section one had decided to work communally in vegetable cultivation, and they would do this in compliance with official policy.

28 April 1954

People from sections 2 and 3 held deliberations at night. They decided that the tenure of their new detainee representatives committee be terminated, so that the old committee, formed by the original band of cooperators with the blessings of Officer Martin, would resume its representative role. There was a general feeling that some conspiracy had triumphed, but people did not want to become involved in a situation of dispute and recrimination, so they accepted matters as they had developed.

From this date, a Saturday, there was no meat in the detainee meals. However, one goat was slaughtered from the camp herd each day for the camp personnel. Mbiyũ inspected the meat—he was the 'Health Officer'; the butchers were Gĩtahi Waciira, David Wanyee, Ndibũi Wawerũ and Ngatia Kangangi.

29 April 1954

Detainees from compound 1, it was decided, would be the first group to prepare a vegetable garden; people from compounds 2 and 3 would in the meanwhile continue with construction work.

We were told a livestock officer had gone in search of live cattle which would be supplied to the camp for slaughtering. On that day, we were given one goat from the camp herd. Those of us from section 1 complained about the inequitable distribution of meat—for the 109 people in compounds 2 and 3 had received two goats, while the 99 of us in compound 1 had received only one goat.

Some people from compound 1 grumbled that our leader was not making effective representations to the authorities; we went without soap; we hadn't been supplied with a working uniform; we were perpetually locked in; we never went to bathe and swim in the open sea. But others refused to countenance this way of thinking and staunchly defended our leader, who had, they argued, meerly given voice to our own general mood of defiance in solidarity. Those who were now raising cynical doubts about our united stand were playing into the hands of the colonialist authorities whose aim was to create bitter division among us. Those who were after easy pleasures should opt to transfer to compounds 2 and 3.

We decided to send a delegation to the officer to raise the following issues: Would we be paid for growing vegetables? When would we receive a working uniform? What was the authorities' response to the memoranda and petitions we had written expressing our opposition to camp labour? We wanted to ask this last question because we suspected that we continued to be denied certain privileges because of our expressed stand on camp labour.

May, 1954

2 May 1954

After the officer had heard our delegation out, he declared that he had not been able to make up his mind and required about two or three months to be able to decide on the status of detainees in section 1. We should consider ourselves lucky to have a good leader like Wamũthenya to represent our interests. We should channel matters through him; the situation should not arise where people should try to be given an individual hearing on each little grievance. At the same time we should not form political groups. He was aware we were holding meetings to frame our grievances; such meetings were not supposed to take place among detained people. It was precisely because we had been involved in political agitation that we had been isolated in detention. The Government's objective was to reform us and orient us towards correct methods of political expression. It was *not* correct to petition higher authority in Government, as we had been doing; this had been interpreted as an expression of our defiance and we would not receive any replies to our ill-intentioned petitions, which only served to annoy the authorities.

The Commissioner of Prisons would be coming shortly, and the Commissioner of Community Development and Welfare may soon be given charge over our affairs. The camp officer had been instructed that in the meanwhile he should not institute any major changes in the status of detainees, unless and until he was specifically so instructed by the Government. However, he was charged with the duty of improving day-to-day conditions in the camp, to the best of his ability. His introduction of vegetable growing among the detainees was meant to serve the purpose of improving the lot of detainees. People should grow their own cabbages; if they didn't they would neither eat cabbages nor get their supply of vitamin tablets.

From these words we got confirmed in our decision to go along with the idea of growing our own cabbages.

Some people on cooking duty in section three precipitated a dispute and breakfast porridge was not cooked. Later in the morning, the dispute was solved—and porridge was cooked.

3 May 1954

We cleared the bush over a two acre patch of land for our vegetable garden. The land was not very sandy and it was quite good farming land; on this very area in ancient times there had stood people's homesteads, which had been deserted for a long time. We could easily identify graves where people had been buried about 300 years ago, and there was evidence of the ruins of old stone houses.

People from compound 1 started to construct beds.

I wrote a letter to Owen, The Probation Officer, asking him to let me know how my family—my wife, children and my mother—were getting on.

4 May 1954

People in compounds 2 and 3 were allowed to start running classes. They would hold lessons in an empty hall. The following teachers conducted lessons: Achieng' Oneko (head teacher), Chokwe, T. Maina, Kali, Kagĩĩka, B. Kamau, R. Kinũthia, Kĩbuci, Warũũĩ, Fred Mbiyũ, Romano and Rev. Gatũng'ũ. Lessons would be given in the afternoon after people had finished camp work—from 3.15 p.m. until 6.30 p.m. Lessons were given in the following subjects: English language, Arithmetic, Agriculture, Traditional Culture, Reading and Writing in Gĩkũyũ, History and Geography. There were four classes, graded from 1 to 4.

In compound 1 we defied the ban on holding mutual education sessions. Classes were held for those who did not know how to read and write.

5 May 1954

The detainees who had been brought from Marsabit were called to the camp office. An inventory was taken of their personal effects. Rumours started to circulate that the "Jock Scott" detainees faced an imminent transfer to camps in Sakwa, Nyanza or in Mackinnon Road, to undergo rehabilitation there.

6 May 1954

Chokwe became the leader of a group of fishermen drawn from compound 3. They would supply fish to the whole camp. Many people developed a liking for fish; but a few people wouldn't touch them.

We got a reasonable supply of beef.

People from compound 3 were asked to go and look for wooden boards on the sea shore. They went as far as five miles away from the camp. They came back with plenty of boards and planed timber; they had also managed to collect unopened tins of food as well as canned beer—which they drank.

11 May 1954

Njoroge Njui refused to participate in cooking for the recruits. He was thrown into a punishment cell for three days; his diet would be *ugali* without relish.

A testimonial arrived from Nairobi certifying that John Mbiyũ was a qualified Veterinary Officer. He should be given charge of overseeing the care of the camp goat and cattle herds. He ordered that no more milking of the goats should take place; the kids should be allowed to suck to recover good health, which they had lost.

Mbiyũ would also inspect slaughtered carcasses.

Mbiyũ was allowed the privilege of receiving two newspapers for which he had taken out a subscription at Marsabit—*Colonial Times* and *East African Standard*. He was, however, warned not to allow the Mau Mau hardcore in section 1 to read these papers; for if they read the papers, it would only harden their stubbornness.

Some of the manure from the cattle and goat pens was carried to the vegetable garden, while some was taken to Russell's little garden, which he had prepared near his living quarters.

12 May 1954

Elder Gĩitwa wa Ndimũ developed a swelling just above the groin. Russell, the camp officer, sent to Lamu for Dr. Shah who arrived at the camp around 10.00 o'clock at night. After he had examined him, Dr. Shah said Gĩitwa should be hospitalised at Lamu to undergo a surgical operation. Gĩitwa was apprehensive, for he had had a not very pleasant brush with Dr. Shah a long time back at Nyeri; but he could not find it possible to refuse treatment under this doctor.

The authorities made assessments of the water levels in all wells in Manda.

13 May 1954

The camp officer told us he had had to spend 80 shillings of his personal money on Gĩitwa's hospital bills. This should show us he was out to help us, and we should reciprocate with our obedient cooperation. He said he would recommend that the authorities pay wages for the work we were doing.

He said we should collect pieces of rock, after finishing routine duties, for spreading around the camp wells, so that the sides of the wells would be nice and dry and didn't get muddy.

15 May 1954

The "cooperators" asked the camp officer to address them in compound 3, with a view to solving some disputes among them over work arrangements. He ordered that those people who had been allocated office duties should not at the same time be required to do other work, like cooking, gathering firewood or drawing water. He criticised the way his predecessor, Martin, seemed to have caused some confusion of expectations among the detainees, a confusion which was very difficult to clear.

Russell refused to answer any questions.

17 May 1954

People from compound 3 went out on a road construction exercise, far away from the camp. They were digging into rocky ground. Food for lunch was delivered to them by a motor car. They came back complaining of terrible fatigue, some of them grumbling that farming work assigned to compound 1 was far preferable.

18 May 1954

Five Abaluyia (Manyala) people were brought to the camp. Their names were Odoli Mudemi, Owino Omuya, Ouma Ochiyobo, Muchibi Ochieng' and Owanga Oninyani. We were to learn that they had been arrested in their Western Kenya homes, where they had gone on leave from their Nairobi jobs. They had been accused of having taken the Mau Mau oath in Nairobi. They had been brought all the way from Western Kenya for detention in Nairobi West camp, after which they had been transferred to Athi River. Eventually they had been flown to Manda island. They had undergone severe torture at Nairobi West camp, where they were accused of belonging to the Alego* faction.

For the night they were put in the quarters for convicted prisoners, which were currently empty. People from compound 2 cooked for them.

In the evening a number of people were instructed to appear at the camp office to endorse their identity cards: 34 people from compound 1, 13 from compound 2 and 3 from compound 3.

22 May 1954

The camp officer asked Wamũthenya whether there were people in compound 1 who would want to embrace "cooperation" wholly. Wamũthenya said he wouldn't know, but perhaps the officer could put the question directly to people in compound 1. Russell didn't accept this suggestion.

When Wamũthenya reported this matter to us, many people said they lived in ignorance of the meaning and implications of "cooperation" as a concept in official policy. Could Wamũthenya go back to the officer and ask to know what the ultimate purpose of "cooperation" was? "Cooperation" finally meant a detainee's complete confession and offer to work with the Government to destroy the Mau Mau movement; this was Russell's answer when Wamũthenya went back.

A similar concerned interest in the concept of "cooperation" was stirred up in compounds 2 and 3, who invited Russell to explain it to them. Russell said he would only be in a position to make a full statement on "cooperation" after making consultations with higher authorities.

*These people from Western Kenya had taken the equivalent of the Mau Mau oath in their cultural setting.

24 May 1954

At 3.00 p.m. after work section 1 detainees put their hoes and *pangas* outside the implements store. Then they retired to our living quarters. This did not please Kĩgume, the store keeper, who said these workers should be told to come back to put the implements inside the store. Njerũ answered back: Kĩgume was a detainee like everybody else, and he should take it upon himself to get the implements into the store. Kĩgume reported this to the camp officer. John Mũngai testified for Kĩgume. Njerũ was thrown into a punishment cell for four days.

Many people in the camp were very angry with Kĩgume, for being the first person to tell on a fellow detainee.

25 May 1954

Today was the "Empire Day" holiday. We didn't go out to work.

Elder Gĩitwa wa Ndimũ came back from hospital. He told us he had undergone a successful operation and he was now fully recovered. He had another story to tell. A young man named Waciira Gacĩthĩ had seen Gĩitwa at the hospital. He had himself been brought here from Lamu prison. He had asked a guard for permission to greet Gĩitwa, but Dr. Shah had found them having a conversation. Dr. Shah had reported this to the Lamu prison officer; the prison guard had wriggled out of the situation, claiming he hadn't been aware of the conversation. Waciira had been thrown into a punishment cell in Lamu prison. Gĩitwa had known Waciira at Nanyuki where Waciira was working as a farm hand on settler Dwelling's farm.

Simon Mbacia had an altercation with the guard in charge of the store; he accused the guard of stealing meat meant for detainees. The camp officer said that in future meat should be cut and shared outside; the detainees should get their share without the meat going into the store. The detainees were pleased with the way Mbacia had stood out for them and declared him a good cooperator. That day we had received only 48 pounds of meat—instead of our rightful share of 61 pounds.

26 May 1954

There was trouble in compound 3. In the morning the slop pails were not removed in time, and the camp sergeant refused to let them be removed. The section threes reported the matter to the camp officer. They also accused the sergeant of lending newspapers to people in compound 1. The sergeant said this was false: after reading his *Baraza*, he only made it available to his *askari* who were instructed to only read it in the secrecy of the guardroom. A search.

was ordered and a copy of *Baraza* was unearthed in compound 3! The officer ordered that in future the newspaper should come to him after it had been read by the guards; he would personally see to its burning.

People from compound 1 didn't have a quarrel with the sergeant.

A new arrangement came into force whereby doors of sections 2 and 3 quarters opened at 6.00 o'clock in the morning and closed at 6.00 o'clock in the evening. There was now a little more freedom for fraternising.

27 May 1954

It was a Saturday. After an inspection for cleanliness had been carried out, the cooperators were allowed to take a leisurely walk to the sea. The hardcores from compound 1 were only allowed to get out of their sleeping quarters, walk within the precincts of the camp, without, however, getting anywhere near the living quarters of the camp personnel.

But we noticed that they left the entrances to compound 1 open. And we felt they were slowly easing on the restrictions imposed upon us.

28 May 1954

We had planted cabbages, carrots, spinach and onions on the piece of garden we had completed preparing—but they hadn't sprouted yet. At the end of the month we completed preparing two acres of land.

I received a parcel from my brother, Isaac Hunja, who was teaching in Machakos; the parcel included a pair of half-length boots, underwear and sheets of cloth. I gave Kĩbuci 6 yards of cloth and one under-shirt.

June, 1954

1 June 1954

The Commissioner for Rehabilitation, the Coast Provincial Commissioner and the Lamu District Commissioner paid a visit to Manda camp at 4.00 p.m. We stood in two lines, and as these officers walked past as in an inspection they would put these questions to individual detainees: Where do you come from? When were you arrested? When were you brought to Manda?

They were given a memorandum that had been addressed to the Commissioner for Rehabilitation.

On that day a name register was prepared which classified people into five age-groups: 15 to 26 years, 27 to 40 years, 41 to 60, 61 to 70, and over 70 years.

3 June 1954

Consequent upon recommendations given by the Warũhiũ Interrogation Committee, four detainees were transferred by air to Athi River: Henry Mulli, Peter Kahũũra and Karĩmanjaga from compound 3 and Mũũgĩ Cege from compound 1.

Detainees were told they should complete construction work in the new detention camp; the Provincial Commissioner and Askwith had emphasised this point during their visit. Rumours were rife that new people would be brought to Manda, and some detainees currently in Manda were marked for transfer to other camps.

At 4.00 o'clock a new detainee joined our ranks. He was reputed to be a Mau Mau general who had been captured in action. He had been brought by an aeroplane, under the guard of two British officers, one from the C.I.D. and the other from the Kenya Police Reserve. His arrival caused a stir among us; we were eager to see him. They locked him up in a private cell. He was given a lamp to light his room, and a book for reading. He was given a smart sleeping mat and supplied with good clean blankets. Many camp guards came to see this man. They would ask us whether he was known to us, and we would tell them that the man was truly one of us, one of the many who were waging war in the forests. Had we not been unlucky to get arrested, we would say, we would have joined these people in waging war against the imperialist oppressors. Some of the guards, who had not travelled much, seemed to regard us with a new-found awe after they had seen this general.

We did not go to work in the afternoon as today was the Islamic holiday of Maulidi.

4 June 1954

They erected a tent for the general near the camp cell, and supplied him with a spring bed, nice mattress and pillows.

In the evening one Dr. Baker, a qualified psychologist, came to the camp. He visited every section of the detainees' living quarters and talked to a number of detainees in each section. He said he would want to have a discussion tomorrow with all people who spoke and understood the English language; he would see the others on a later date. He told us he was a writer for newspapers and showed us a card attesting to this.

5 June 1954

Dr. Baker met with 37 people who were conversant with the English language. These people were drawn from the 3 compounds. He told us he was a Rehabilitation Officer and his purpose was to learn about our needs so that he could help us. He was of German origin, but he had been in Kenya for the last 12 years; he owned a farm on the Karūri highlands. He had considerable education in matters of human society and psychology. He planned to introduce classes in history, geography, philosophy and economics; he would also start lessons for non-English speaking detainees.

We asked a number of questions, some of which Baker promised to answer in the course of giving lessons. He asked us to choose a committee which would assist him, and Achieng', Mbiyũ, Cege and Wokabi were chosen. These people went to see Baker at 2.00 o'clock; but when they came back they had nothing pleasing to say about that German.

The Mau Mau general attended the session of the English-speakers with Baker. His words to Dr. Baker had been hard and critical. People would later comment that the general held white men in no awe.

7 June 1954

Forty English-speaking detainees started their lessons in philosophy and economics at 8.00 o'clock. And at 2.00 o'clock in the afternoon peope from compound 1 were allowed to move to compound 3 to join classes 3, 4 and 5 which had earlier been organised.

Permission was granted from the camp office for people from compound 1 to fraternise with people in compounds 2 and 3. The guard who had been positioned between compound 1 and compounds 2 and 3 was removed. From now on, it was decided, people from compound 1 would not remain under close supervision. All the doors were opened.

It was the view of the compound ones that Baker had been sent by the Government to rectify the situation of division and barriers that had been created by Naked Martin.

Dr. Baker called the four committee men at 4.00 p.m. Since there was a lot of construction work needed to complete the new camp, he said, he proposed to terminate classes at the elementary levels. But the feeling of Baker's advisory committee was that the majority of the detainees were people in need of that elementary education, and these people should be helped. It would even be better for the advanced classes for English-speakers to come to an end; people from these classes could go on giving elementary classes to the majority as had been the case before Baker's coming.

8 June 1954

I received for the first time correspondence lessons in a short story writing course from England. Other people who had enrolled for correspondence courses were: John Cege Kabogoro, Mwinga Chogwe, Mwai Koigi and Victor Wokabi.

9 June 1954

Settler Baker set aside the recommendations of his advisory committee, and introduced his own study plan. According to this plan, the English-speakers would take lessons for three days a week, while the rest would have two days a week. He would himself appoint the teachers who would oversee the education of other detainees after assessing people's suitability. Only English language and arithmetic should be taught; he did not trust that other subjects would be properly taught. He wouldn't want history or geography to be taught, for such subjects could be improperly made the vehicles for teaching the politics of agitation, which was the cause of current troubles in Kenya. He himself would introduce the proper methods of teaching to the teachers.

Baker's attitude and acts did not please the education committee which voiced contrary arguments. Later the committee men complained bitterly that Baker had revealed himself for what he was—a narrow-minded and short-sighted dyed-in-the-wool colonialist.

The Chief Native Commissioner (C.N.C.), the P.C. and surveying officers arrived at the camp in the afternoon. They toured the place for a brief period including the recently prepared vegetable farm. After they had gone, Russel did reveal they were impressed with the work we had done; they had encouraged us to go on with the good work. Russell added that he was aware the Agĩkũyũ people make very good farmers; if we really meant to work nobody would go hungry on Manda island. Even so, some of us drew his attention to the fact that the soil here was not good for vegetable growing. He offered to consider having the farm fenced to keep out monkeys and porcupines.

10 June 1954

It was Coronation Day holiday and we did not go out to work. Some concerts were performed near the canteen by section threes; but not everybody got to see the concerts as they took place away from our quarters and in the early evening

Russell said we would no longer have four people permanently on water drawing duties and six on firewood gathering in compound 1; he argued that all of us were now allowed to go beyond the camp precincts.

12 June 1954

People from compound 3 performed concerts for all of us at night; the performance was done inside the camp shed where classes were held.

13 June 1954

The English-speaking detainees went for early-morning lessons with settler Baker. General sociological matters were discussed. Arguments arose between the pupils and the teacher. We told Baker that the Agĩkũyũ people alone did not constitute the "African" people of Kenya, and drew his attention to the fact that there were non-Agĩkũyũ people among us in detention, for example, Achieng', Chokwe and Kali. Baker instructed us that we should properly refer to ourselves as "Negroes".

A heated argument also arose when Baker asked us to outline the causes behind the war going on in our country. We told him we wouldn't know: we had no access to newspapers, we lived in the darkness of ignorance in a remote island. May be the Government authorities had seen our petitions, demanding, among other things, information on why we were arrested in the first place. We would admit, we argued, that we had made certain demands before we were arrested, and we had not given up those demands. If we had been arrested for making those demands then the Government was wrong. The correct response would have been to file a case against us and invite other nations to judge between us and the British.

After Baker had gone, we delegated Kali and Waiyaki to go after him and ask him, if he was in a position to, to make representations for us to the Government, on two matters: 1. to consider forming a political commission to study the case of detainees; 2. to consider a mass release of detainees, to allow a general amnesty so that our people could be reunited and allowed to regenerate itself in self-sufficient nationhood.

At 2.00 o'clock, imperialist Baker came to see us and informed us he would be leaving the camp for a short time. He was required by the Government to visit very many camps to carry out much-needed rehabilitation work.

We could not help feeling here was a white man who enjoyed giving his ego a boost; he probably misled the Government by creating the impression of doing great intellectual work among detainees, thereby collecting for himself fat payments from the masses of money that the Government had poured out during the Emergency.

14 June 1954

We started to put barbed wire around our vegetable garden. By this time some little carrots had sprouted; we had also started weeding around sprouts of the other vegetables.

The guards overseeing the fencing work reported that we were shirking work: we would carry one piece of fencing timber the whole day, they said. The camp officer took the complaint, all lies, seriously. We were terribly angry. Some of us grumbled it were even better to remain locked up and have the privilege of maintaining people on standby for supplying our water and our firewood. As it was now, we were expected to exert ourselves on farm work and later take care of self-maintenance work.

Russell imposed a restriction on sending or receiving letters as our punishment; this would go on until we were ready to work with greater devotion. When we sent for Russell to come and hear us out, he refused; we must first work better before he would reconsider.

We were given some copies of the Government newssheet *Kīhooto* ("Justice").

We collected branches and l aves for making a bonfire; the idea was that this should be lit if there was an emergency sickness and it would serve as an SOS signal to the doctor in Lamu Native Council Hospital to come over to attend the emergency.

18 June 1954

A committee comprising the camp leaders and the work gang leaders met. The camp officer explained that officer Martin had incurred a debt of 700 shillings: that is why the services of the canteen had been suspended. He was offering to obtain supplies for the canteen using his own personal money: the committee should make arrangements to repay Russell for the expenses, since the Government would not be prepared to incur a loss.

Russell said compound l doors would from now on remain closed. He would not allow compound l to have people permanently assigned to collection of water and firewood.

20 June 1954

At 11.00 a.m. we were all told to go and hunt for snakes. Russell's watchword was: "*Shauri ya nyoka!*" ("All on account of snakes!"). All of us trooped out, each of us armed with a stick. But after a big hunt and much ado, only Maciira Kīmarū killed one snake. He was rewarded with a bar of soap.

Baker came back from Lamu.

24 June 1954

It rained heavily, then it drizzled and it was very cold. People said Manda's weather had changed to the weather of Limuru or Nanyuki.

5

New Regulations on Detainee Status

1 July 1954 to 19th July 1955

July, 1954

1 July 1954

At 8.00 a.m. we were informed we would not be going out to work and we were instructed to pack our personal belongings and stay on standby like people who were just about to undergo an inspection. At 9.00 a.m. we were instructed to report to the school building in compound 3, the whole lot of us, including the sick people. We were subjected to a head count, after which Officer Russell addressed us. He told us:

1. New regulations on detainee status and detention regime would come into force with effect from today, 1st July 1954. Warūhiū's Interrogation Committee, which had recently done its work in Manda, had drawn up certain categories of detainees whose status would be different. A number of detainees had hindered positive developments towards rehabilitation by resorting to a hunger strike. At the same time the erstwhile camp officer had erred by making categories of detainees without due authorization from higher office. From now on compound 1 as a category was abolished, and all of Officer Martin's categories were no longer valid. New categories would now come into effect, in accordance with the recommendations of the Warūhiū Interrogation Committee.

2. From today, 1st July 1954, detainees would receive a revised rate of rations, slightly down-graded. People would continue to receive vitamin tablets. Loaves of bread would no longer be supplied, but people would get wheat flour from which to bake their bread. The meat ration had been reduced. The new rations were based on what good food was available in this part of Manda island.

The officer stressed that it was not he who was introducing a new regime; he had received instructions in writing.

"If you wish to dispute any matter," Russell concluded, "please wait for two weeks. I would not want you to resort to violent protest or to strikes of any kind. If you write any memorandum, I will be pleased to forward it."

Russell then called out our names.

Forty-five people, many of them elderly men as well as the detainees from Nyanza, were marked for transfer to the new camp whose construction had just

107

been completed. This camp was named camp no. 3. They carried away their personal belongings, sleeping mats and bedding. 130 people remained in what had been compounds 2 and 3; and 37 people were assigned to what had been compound 1.

There was much hustle and bustle as people carried away their belongings as they shifted to new living areas.

Many of those who were assigned to section 1 were young men, including many people who had opted early for "cooperation"; but there were a number of elderly men, a notable example being Bongwe Icaũ.

Russell explained that the detainees in compound 1 belonged to a higher category in the rehabilitation plan: they had made two steps towards rehabilitation. Those in compounds 2 and 3, on the other hand, had taken only one step. He asked people to accept this status without much ado.

People ate their lunch where they had been eating all along. However, in the evening food for supper was distributed in accordance with the new groupings.

New leaders were elected on instructions from Russell to meet the needs of the new arrangements: Romano and Cege became leaders in compounds 2 and 3; Fred Mbiyũ was elected in compound 1; and Achieng' Oneko was elected in the new camp. And Russell appointed Mulwa the work captain, in charge of all working arrangements.

According to the new regulations detainees would from now on receive payment for all non-domestic work; for example for digging roads, farm work, building construction, and fishing. Those who carried out such work in the past week had their wages computed.

As there were only 65 people now in either compound 2 or 3 there was ample room for each man and his personal belongings.

2 July 1954

The detainee representatives went for a meeting with the camp officer.

There were no boards on which we could knead the wheat flour and nor were there pans in which we could cook our *chapati*. The midday meal was a long time preparing and we became voraciously hungry. We had not gone out to work. People grumbled and talked with bitter sarcasm. "We should go hungry and take it nicely and quietly," they would say, remembering Russell's words. "Are we really enjoying the good food supplied in these parts of Manda island?" They were bitter with hunger.

After our representatives' meeting, Romano came and read out to us the new rations schedule:

No baked loaves of bread.

Meat: 6 oz. a week; 2 oz. three times a week (Tuesday, Thursday and Saturday).

Beans: 8 oz. per day, four days a week (Monday, Wednesday, Friday and Sunday) on no-meat diet days; 7 oz. 3 days a week on meat-diet days.
Wheat flour: 6 oz. a day.
Salt: ½ oz. a day.
Cooking oil: ½ oz. a day (They did not take into account we would need to fry our wheat-flour *chapati*)
Potatoes: 6 oz. a day.
Cabbages: 6 oz. a day.
Maize meal: 6 oz. a day.

If any of us were willing to bake our own bread, Romano said, the officer should be so informed so that he could make arrangements as necessary. Since there was now a great need to use charcoal to fry *chapati*, people should take the initiative to burn their own charcoal and to construct many little charcoal burners.

"If you burn your own charcoal, you may use some for camp purposes and sell the surplus at Lamu where a sack of charcoal costs 3 shillings and 50 cents. I would be willing to help you market the charcoal." These had been Russell's words.

We had only one meal during the day and for supper we made do with a little porridge per person. People grumbled throughout the night about this fare. The officer had said it was good to first face some difficulties over food preparation so that we would be able to write a complaint with substance.

3 July 1954

Two Probation Officers—Briton Montgomery and his man Kĩroga—visited Manda. The British officer explained he required to obtain the following information from detainees: each person should confess who oathed him and say where he took the oath. The African assistant added that apart from collecting that information, the probation officers would like to give the detainees a hearing on their problems; for example they could ask for information on the welfare of their families or on their bank accounts or on their land property, and so on.

7 July 1954

I went to see the Probation Officer about my box which the C.I.D. had seized from me on 27th March 1953 in Kajiado. I also complained to him about some of my books upon which the Government had imposed a ban irrespective of the fact that they were of a non-political nature. I requested him to trace the whereabouts of my mother, for rumours had it that she had been detained at Kamĩtĩ Women's Prison.

12 July 1954

We were informed that General Erskine, the British army officer in charge of the war effort against the Mau Mau forces, would tour the camp tomorrow. We spent most of the day cutting grass, tidying the compound and cleaning our living quarters.

In the meanwhile Montgomery continued to see detainees in the office. He would subject people to interrogation: where do you come from? Have you taken the Mau Mau oath? What is your educational background? What was your profession before your arrest? Were you a member of KAU? and so on.

But what really preoccupied us was the nagging hunger. We had only one full meal, a *chapati* and beans, during the day; in the evening each of us had a little porridge. And this had been going on for the last eleven days. There was general agreement that we would write a petition to the Government complaining about the inadequacy of food and everybody would sign the petition, although nobody would be forced to sign. We asked our representatives to make a rough draft of the petition.

14 July 1954

Imperialist General Erskine arrived in Manda after a boat journey. He was conducted around by the camp officer and the Lamu D.C. During his tour of our living quarters, he exchanged a few words with a number of people; he would ask one where one came from. When he went to the new camp he expressed open surprise at the fact that there was an ethnic mix of people here; he hadn't expected this, he confessed.

In the morning, section 2 detainees were addressed near the canteen by Probation Officer Montgomery. Kīroga translated Montgomery's English into Kiswahili. He had already talked to many people in sections 1 and 3, he told us. He was the detainees' good friend and was out to be of help to them. The detainees were also God's people. He was aware of our transgressions and he was aware that the Mau Mau oath had extracted from us certain vows and had invoked deeply believed in taboos; people held out against confessing the oath because of their great irrational fear.

"But I want to tell you this secret. The first step towards rehabilitation is to accept 'cooperation'. This must be followed by a confession of the oath, which should go hand-in-hand with a genuine willingness to cooperate with the camp officer and to help the Government. Only three people in this camp have convinced the authorities that they did not take the oath; it is believed all the others have."

Then Montgomery's tone changed to that of a preacher. A man may commit murder in secret, he told us, and walk away confident that no one has seen him.

But God is privy to his crime. But our crime was not committed in similar secret. Many people had confessed the oath and in doing so had mentioned the names of people who participated with them in the same ceremony, or of those who administered the oath to them. Some people among us had mentioned others in our midst who still refused to make a confession. He would mention no names. Let people come out themselves and make a voluntary confession. People who had recently been assigned to compound 1 were acknowledged as "cooperators". And yet they had failed to take an important step forward—by voluntarily confessing the Mau Mau oath.

We asked him some questions. Would he see to the release of those three people who had not taken the oath? He replied it might be risky to let these people go home at this stage because their lives might be threatened by Government collaborators who had all along stayed in the villages. Why had people who had not taken the oath been arrested in the first place and subjected to so much suffering? He replied that mistakes are always liable to be made; there were people in detention camps who had been arrested and detained because they were mistaken for other people.

Finally, he said he would be leaving Manda, but he would make a second visit soon. One of us asked him to report that we were being grossly starved to death. He said the camp officer would concern himself with that matter.

General Gatamŭki, the Mau Mau general, stole the show. He told Montgomery that an issue should not be made out of people having taken the oath. He was proud to announce openly that he had himself taken the oath in his commitment to wage a war for freedom; comrades-in-arms in their forest bases never made a secret of their unity through the oath.

Some detainees received the General's words in silent shock. But when we questioned him later, he was firm in his stand that there was no need to make a secret of our oathing, since we had purposely taken the oath to unite us in our struggle against the colonial oppressor. No one could move him from this stand. After this some people were heard to whisper that it did appear after all that the general was right.

15 July 1954

We received a visit from the assistant to the Commissioner of Prisons and a number of officers from the Department of Health at around 2.00 p.m. They took room measurements in our living quarters and the kitchens. We told them some of us were suffering from eye ailments, and they promised that an eye doctor would visit the camp in the near future. They ascertained that our drinking water had a high salt content.

Stanley Kagĩĩka took the form used for requisitioning supplies, addressed it to his wife back home, and filled out the following items for urgently needed supply: wheat flour, beans, sugar and tea leaves. There was a grave food shortage, he wrote. At 2.00 o'clock Kagĩĩka presented the form at the camp office for despatch to his wife. He was immediately condemned to lock-up in a punishment cell. He was told his impudent behaviour would be reported to the Commissioner for Prisons; furthermore he faced probable transfer to the new detention camp.

16 July 1955

Kagĩĩka was brought before the camp officer to answer charges. The officer told Kagĩĩka he had committed a very serious offence, for his act was calculated to bring the Government into disrepute. If Kagĩĩka's wife were to receive such a form she would show it around to other detainees' wives and the false alarm would be spread all over that the Government had failed to keep detainees fed; the criminally malicious impression would be created that the Government was starving the Manda island detainees to death. The doctor was satisfied that the ration being given to detainees was adequate. Kagĩĩka defended himself by reminding the officer that on 1st July 1954 he had authorised us to jointly or individually make a complaint about the food situation after we had reviewed it within a period of fourteen days. Instead of just lodging a complaint, Kagĩĩka had considered it wiser to make a request for food. Right now he would want to request that he receive food as payment for his work instead of money.

The officer said an exception could not be made for one man. He imposed a restriction against Kagĩĩka's sending of any letters home or receiving parcels for one month. As further punishment Kagĩĩka would collect soil and carry it to the vegetable farm for one hour each day for a whole week; this would be done in the afternoon after he had carried out routine work.

17 July 1954

Joel Warũĩ and Kang'aari were accused of climbing trees when they should have been working; they were gathering fruits to eat. They were condemned to punishment cells for four days.

Kali and myself were thrown into a cell for arguing with a guard when we had gone to draw water. But we were released not long after even before being reported to the camp officer.

The body weight of three people—Romano, Kariũki Mĩguĩ and Kamanũ Kĩnya—was taken. The idea was to assess the effect of the new food regime. It was decided that these three people would be weighed once every week. Njamumo had lost eight pounds.

20 July 1954

The Advisory Committee on Detainees arrived at 10.00 a.m. It was made up of four British officers and a Mũgĩkũyũ interpreter, one J. Kĩnũthia. Four detainees were informed immediately that their cases would be listened to.

The hearings were conducted at the canteen. People who were working near the canteen, including people who were fishing at the shore, were ordered to leave the area. The canteen had been given a face lift and sprayed with insecticide, to destroy flies and mosquitoes. It was guarded by four soldiers armed with guns, and a mortar gun had been positioned just outside the canteen. Those appearing before the Committee would wait in a mud hut close to the canteen, dressed in their best clothes. They would be subjected to a body search before being allowed into the canteen.

Seventeen people appeared before the Committee during its two day stay. The Committee men did their work during the day and retired to Lamu in the late afternoon.

24 July 1954

All detainees from sections 1 and 2 were called to the canteen by the camp officer. He had called us to express serious dissatisfaction with our attitude to work. We had adopted an attitude of shirking work, he charged. We had deliberately adopted the wrong attitude: he was aware that back home we used to work as devoted farmers and we were experienced in growing cabbages. For three full months 20 men had been working in farm preparation and cabbage cultivation, and yet all we had done was work on a tiny patch of land. At this rate we would require five full years to clear a reasonable and viable farm. And yet we were growing cabbages to feed ourselves not outsiders. Russell pointed out that he had noticed much difference between us and the fishermen, who worked devotedly to keep the whole camp adequately supplied with fish. But the so-called farmers? They were in essence cadging thieves—just like those shirkers who went out to collect coconut fibre for thatch and construction stakes. He had been forced to accept the view of former camp officers—that only forced labour could obtain results with us. But the Government would remain adamant on its stand: grow vegetables or do without them. Russel read a few lines from an official memorandum.

He had read the regulations on the new food rations; he knew how he could go about asking for an increase. But he could not do this when our negative attitude to work persisted. Recently he had asked the authorities to supply maizemeal.

He wanted to be of help to the detainees: he had recently requested the Government to send two teachers from Jeanes School, Kabete. But he could not be expected to pursue such arrangements in the face of our annoying non-cooperation. Some people had even failed to give in their names for vaccinations against diseases with which this island was endemic. We should understand that what was expected of us was to work with him, as the camp officer, the sergeant and the other camp personnel to form one communal team in this island. We should be like a local government in a town or district. The camp officer is the mayor; the sergeant is like the district police officer. Mulwa is the work officer; and the detainees' representatives or camp leaders are the eldermen or councillors.

"It is up to you to realise that you have made a step ahead in being involved in self sustaining labour," the officer concluded. "You should work willingly and voluntarily in full awareness that you work for your own good. You are not working for the Government: if you allow yourselves to go hungry the Government will not go hungry. Decide for yourselves: whether you will live on a diet of vitamin tablets, or whether you will grow vegetables for your diet."

25 July 1954

We had our memorandum on the food situation sent to the Commissioner of Development and Rehabilitation.

We received communication that our complaint about money lost at Kajiado had come too late to be looked into; we should desist from raising the issue any more.

26 July 1954

Imperialist Baker returned. He met with the English-speaking class at 11.00 a.m. He informed us that he had been assigned interrogation duties on top of his earlier work in rehabilitation of detainees. He was supposed to carry out a re-classification of detainees in Manda: the recent classification was not adequate. He would require our assistance in the form of advice.

He told us a little about what was going on in the countryside. He would soon bring his team of African interrogators; people should make confessions to this team. Four teachers would be brought to conduct classes and the better educated among us would be asked to assist them.

Baker was now in charge of rehabilitation work in Manda, Lamu and Lango la Simba.

We were vaccinated against small pox.

27 July 1954

Russell tore our memorandum complaining against the food situation. He gave two reason for doing so: 1. We should have waited until the end of

one month before putting our complaint in writing. 2. Our com
people had reduced weight should have been validated with weight
three or four weighings, which hadn't yet taken place.

The detainees responded to Russell's act with bitter anger. He had earlier
expressly asked us to wait for two weeks only before writing our complaint.
Again, three people had been weighed twice and all of them had lost weight.
We decided to send a copy of our memorandum using our own means.

28 July 1954

Imperialist Baker held counsel with four detainees: Waiyaki, Kali, Achieng'
and Beauttah. He asked them to give him advice on how to carry out a re-
classification of detainees, but their ideas were unacceptable to him. Baker
expressed his opinion that it appeared almost all the Agĩkũyũ people had taken
the oath. Arguments were exchanged and the four people parted with Baker in
bitter disagreement.

31 July 1954

Kĩhoro was thrown into a punishment cell for three days for insulting Waithaka.

Romano, Kariũki and Kamanũ, who had been put on a weighing schedule,
had their weight taken. They had added weight, since the last weighing, by 1, 1½
and ½ pounds respectively.

August, 1954
1 August 1954

Joel Warũũĩ organised four football teams from all the detention sections which
would compete with each other. Teams played each other.

G.P. Pinto was brought to Manda camp in the late afternoon. He was
taken to the convicted prisoners' quarters. From our quarters we waved at him
in greeting and he waved back.

2 August 1954

Those of us who were known to Pinto managed to snatch a brief conversation
with him. He had been arrested about a month ago, he told us.

6 August 1954

They drove Pinto away in a little car at around 3.00 p.m.; he was being transferred to Takwa Detention Camp.

We were vaccinated against typhoid. All of us remained in our living
quarters, sick and feverish and our wounds swollen.

I received a letter in reply to the letter I had written to Probation Officer Owen on 3rd July 1954 enquiring about my family. I was told my mother was being kept under arrest at the chiefs' camp on suspicion that she had acted as a treasurer to the Mau Mau. And my wife was in detention at Kamītī Women's Prison.

7 and 8 August 1954

Tests were given to "pupils" in classes 1, 2, and 3; those who passed would be allowed to move to the higher class. Pupils complained that the test was extremely hard. Many of those in class 1 were elderly men, like Gakami, Ex-Chief Njiriri Mūkoma, Ng'ombe Gakūrū, Ngatia Kangangi, Njue Kamūmbū, Maina Mūnene, Gĩitwa Ndimū, and others.

12 August 1954

The camp officer informed us that new regulations prohibited detainees from buying the following items: cigarettes, razor blades, hurricane lamps, cups and plates. He would, however, be going to Lamu to raise the matter with the authorities.

A list indicating the balance of money owed each of us in wages for work done was read to us. We were told the things we had requisitioned would be arriving soon.

There was a bizarre rumour that in future they would cut our hair and shave our beard with a gigantic blade, the size of the knife used for peeling potatoes.

14 August 1954

The fishermen made a record haul of more than 400 fish. People said this was God's way of telling us he had taken notice that we had been going hungry for a long time. The catch had also been quite good in the recent past and people had been eating better.

That night resembled a communal feast—this time organised around fish, and not the traditional Gĩkūyū goat meat.

We had not worked in the afternoon: we were celebrating imperialist Russell's birthday.

15 August 1954

At 2.00 p.m. all the students, their teachers and even detainees who had not enrolled for classes gathered outside compound 2. The results of the tests taken on 7th and 8th August were to be announced; as well other matters concerning education for detainees would be discussed.

Rev. Stefano Waciira read from the Bible from Paul's letter to the Corinthians where the Apostle exhorts both students and their teachers to pursue learning with devotion. There was happy satisfaction with the good work the teachers had done and the dedicated reciprocation from the students. Names of those who had topped their classes were read to general clapping: number 1 would receive three rounds of clapping, number 2, two, and number 3 one round. They would stand up when their names were called. All pupils who had passed and who were to be raised to the next higher class received their bit of enthusiastic praise and clapping.

Principal Cege passed a vote of thanks for the camp officer who had given us two more black-boards. We showed our appreciation to him. It was decided that from now on the following increased number of classes would be operative: 1A, 1B, 2, 3 and 4.

20 August 1954

At 2.00 p.m. there was a debating session. The motion was: "It is better to marry one than many wives".

After the debate some of us (myself, Kali, Mwangi, Waweru, Mulwa, Wamũũti, Kĩbuci and others) discussed a new idea: how we could organise a concert-performing group to be named "Manda Island Dramatic Society". For a start we could make a collection amongst ourselves, after we had received payment for work done, to buy a guitar to be used in musical performances by this group.

22 August 1954

In the morning there was a meeting between the teachers who were running classes in the camp.

In the afternoon Russell gave a general lecture to the detainees. Some of the things he said were that he had looked after Japanese prisoners of war during the 2nd World War. We ourselves deserved respect for our political stand on the need for self determination, but we were inexcusably wrong in resorting to oathing and murder. On the nature of women, Russell said women were people who forgot things easily. This was to be expected of them: they were preoccupied with domestic affairs, giving instructions to house servants and so on, and serving their husbands.

After the lecture there were cultural dances in the open field. We watched detainees performing for others. Mahuti wa Gĩcũhĩ had organised the most beautiful performance; his group performed the *mũcũng'wa* dance. The dancers were resplendent in colourful cloth; they wore strings of beads of cowrie shells collected from the sea shore; on their ankles they wore rattles made of tins containing pebbles which thundered in the rhythm of their energetic steps.

The camp guards brought their wives to watch the performance. Everybody enjoyed the entertainment greatly.

26 August 1954

Waigera Kĩmaathi and Gĩtaũ Mũrĩmi were thrown into punishment cells; the sergeant said he had found them sitting down when they should have been working.

The new regulation was introduced that at 10.00 p.m. a trumpet would be sounded to order people to put off lights and go to bed. There were many lamps in the sleeping quarters. People used them for reading and while doing their homework. Kerosene was supplied free. Were the authorities introducing this regulation to save on kerosene? Had they felt we were using too much kerosene? The detainees wondered. If so, it would be better to be required to buy our own kerosene.

30 August 1954

A cheque for 14,000 shillings arrived for making payments for work done. People were given their wages. They bought several items: sugar, cocoa, cigarrettes, cloth, lamps for night reading, exercise books, pencils and butter.

September, 1954

8 September 1954

We heard on the grapevine that 200 detainees had arrived at Takwa Camp on this same island of Manda.

16 September 1954

Gĩitwa Ndimũ was taken ill again with the swelling on the groin. He was taken to Lamu Hospital.

Clothing, blankets and rubber sandals were given to detainees.

21 September 1954

The camp officer took five days leave and went holidaying in Mombasa. Detainees made a list of things they would like him to buy for them: books for reading, fountain pens and watches.

Another officer, one Westlock, came from Takwa to act in Russell's absence. Even so, Russell had instructed Mbiyũ to take a look at his office every day. Detainees would joke it was Mbiyũ acting on Russell's behalf—and not the camp sergeant, or even Westlock.

24 September 1954

Ohanga, the Minister for Community Development and Rehabilitation, arrived in the camp at 2.00 p.m. We had written a memorandum, in anticipation of his coming, about our problems, and particularly about the food situation. The contents of this memorandum had been leaked to the camp officer and the sergeant by section 1 people assigned to office work, who were for some reasons unhappy that we had written that memorandum. The memorandum had been drafted by a team elected by the detainees: Chokwe, Wokabi, Cege, Warũũĩ, Kamau, Kagĩĩka and myself, the author.

When the motorboat bringing Ohanga was sighted, all the memorandum drafters were summoned by the sergeant who ordered that they be removed from the camp. They were taken away to a place we used to call Ka-mũnyongoro ("the place of many millipedes"), which was two miles away from the camp. They were kept under watch by two corporals, one of them with two decorations, the other with one, and four other guards. They were not to be allowed to leave this place until Ohanga had gone away from Manda.

Ochieng' informed Ohanga some of us had been removed from the camp to prevent them from seeing him and presenting him with a memorandum. Luckily the drafters had had the presence of mind to leave the memorandum with Mwai Koigi. Koigi gave the memorandum to the Lamu D.C. who handed it over to Ohanga, to the jubilation of many detainees. There was a spirit of daring defiance in many of us borne of the fact that our representatives had been spirited away to prevent them from presenting our case; at the same time there was anger at the betrayal by our own people.

Ohanga was conducted around the whole camp: he looked at our sleeping quarters, the kitchens, the dispensary, the wells and other facilities. He engaged in conversation with our representatives—Achieng', Mbiyũ and Mwai—whom we hastily asked to step forward in the place of those people who had been removed. They laid before him our grievances especially on the food situation and on the facilities for the sick.

26 September 1954

When officer Russell returned from leave he asked for a copy of the memorandum we had given to Ohanga. He would make two copies of this memorandum and would have them delivered officially in accordance with regulations.

Russell asked those who had requested him to obtain some things for them from Mombasa to report to his office. They obtained a good number of books. A good number of people had asked for books to use in learning English; for example, *Oxford English*, Books 1, 2, 3 and 4 and English dictionaries. Others had asked for books in mathematics and book-keeping. People thanked Russell warmly. He said his major interest was to see people further their education. There and then he allocated space in section three for study sessions.

27 September 1954

Those of us who had signed the memorandum to Ohanga on behalf of all the other detainees in Manda were called to the camp office. We were as follows: Chokwe, Warũũĩ, Cege, myself, Romano, Babu, Wokabi and Mwai. The officer rebuked us for failing to send the memorandum through the camp office. He showed us the memorandum which we had given to Ohanga: it had been referred to him for his comments. He let us know that as many as 34 people from section 1 had written a letter disassociating themselves from our memorandum which was full of lies.

Russell said he must mete out punishment. From now on, Cege and Romano would no longer be camp leaders; those of us on correspondence courses would no longer be allowed to receive our lessons. We would no longer be allowed to receive letters and parcels. Should we write a similar memorandum we could be transferred to the new camp. Baker was instructed to stop giving any assistance whatsoever to detainee education.

Detainees refused to elect new representatives in place of those who had been rejected by the officer: the colonial officer, they argued, should make his own appointments.

28 September 1954

I received a letter from the Minister for Defence. It was written in English.* Here it is:

Sir,

18 September 1954

I am directed to inform you that His Excellency the Governor has given careful consideration to your application, which was referred to the Advisory Committee on Detainees, but has decided that you must continue to be detained.

(Signed) Secretary of Defence.

*This letter is in English in the original Gikuyu version of this book.

29 September 1954

Elder Gĩitwa came back from hospital. He had undergone, for the second time, a successful surgical operation.

October, 1954

1 October 1954

The ban on receiving letters and parcels was lifted. Russell appointed Ex-Chief Njiriri Mũkoma acting camp leader. He ordered that two more detainee representatives must be elected by the detainees. When people still did not come up with their choices, Russell banned all classes in compounds 2A and 2B*.

3 October 1954

All people from compounds 2A and 2B were called to the camp office. The officer berated us for our defiance, now being manifested in our refusal to elect new detainee representatives. We should realise that he was empowered to impose the following punishments: we could be denied our food and our recreational facilities; we could lose the privilege of sending and receiving letters and other parcels; he could close down the canteen, stop fishing for the camp kitchen, put a stop to vegetable cultivation. He was aware there were a few individuals who were leading everybody else astray; he was slowly but surely getting to know who those individuals were and in good time would know them all. Eight people only, he charged, were responsible for the memorandum to Ohanga. The memorandum told lies about arrangements for detainee clothing and made false insinuations about the deaths of two detainees in Manda. We should appreciate that as far as the Government was concerned we were placed below the most worthless of the land and in fact we were below the law: nobody would deign to take us to a court of law, and we had no right to accuse anybody in a court of law.

He had been given the Manda assignment in order to have us taken care of, but for him to take good care of us we must first obey him. If we refused to obey his directives he would invoke his powers to enforce obedience.

At the end of the lecture he said he would give us time to go and elect the new detainee representatives. There was bitter grumbling: the officer should not have removed Cege and Romano who had written a memorandum as an

*Compounds 2A and 2B were what had originally been compounds 2 and 3. The "better" elements had been transferred to former compound 1 from compound 3; most of the other detainees had been assigned to compounds 2A and 2B, while a new camp, a new compound 3 had been created.

expression of the general will. The officer had added insult to injury by appointing his own camp leader.

Amidst this grumbling, we elected Kĩbuci Ndiang'ũi and Isaac Gathaanju. They were immediately escorted to the camp office by Njiriri Mũkoma.

8 October 1954

In the morning when nine detainees were being escorted to work, there was a bitter exchange of words between them and the guards; the sergeant uttered the threat that he could shoot detainees who were a worthless lot. The detainees involved were: B. Mang'uurũ, Kamau Macaria, Ngatia Kangangi, Mburati Njogu, Gĩtaũ Karanũ, Kĩama Matu, Kĩragũ Kagotho, Mbũgua Njoroge and Kariũki Karanja. They were taken to the camp officer and accused of disobedience. They presented a lengthy and energetic defence, and if justice had been allowed to prevail it would have been evident they had been subjected to a provocation by the guards. But in camp justice it could not be allowed to appear that the sergeant had lost a case. Therefore, the nine people were condemned to punishment cells for three days, after which each of them would be required to carry a wheelbarrow of soil to the vegetable garden before they would be allowed back to the normal life of the camp.

16 October 1954

There was a dispute between Babu and Kĩgume over some clothes. The camp officre appointed elders Wambũgũ Maina and James Beauttah to listen to this case. The two elders ruled that Babu had freely made a gift of a shirt and a pair of trousers to Kĩgume; he should not, therefore, demand these things back. Kĩgume's argument to the effect that he had taken the clothes to offste a loan of 35 shillings he had given to Babu before detention was, however, rejected. Here was not the place to settle pre-detention debts: he should demand repayment in other ways, at other times, in other places.

This was the first dispute among detainees to be solved among the detainees themselves, with the express permission of the camp officer. Russell was putting into effect his argument that we considered ourselves our community's leaders; we were even demanding self-rule; we should therefore be able to sort out little disputes among ourselves, without asking for the intervention of his office.

Russell used to say, "You have amongst you people who used to be community leaders, people who acted as judges in community tribunals, people who chaired different kinds of committees. Settle problems amongst yourselves."

20 October 1954

Those of us who spoke English were invited to listen to a radio speech by Leakey at 8.00 p.m. Back in our sleeping quarters, detainees sang hymns in remembrance of our arrest—for we were arrested on October 20 some years back. People in each section joined to sing the hymn, "*Ūtukū mweri mĩrongo ĩĩrĩ, mweri wa ikũmi*" ("During the night of 20th October"). After this prayers were led by the church ministers in each section.

Our hearts were full to the brim with grief and anger, as we remembered this fateful day.

22 October 1954

The sergeant and a group of guards swooped on the "domestic" workers—kitchen workers, sanitary workers, collectors of water, cleaners and people carrying out construction around the camp—and accused them of reading when they should have been at work. Eleven people were picked out for punishment by being assigned out-of-camp work; after work they would return to punishment cells. In addition, they would lose pay for all work done in the last four months.

After a head count had been taken at 6.00 p.m. the sergeant ordered the eleven people to retire to the cells. These people were: G. Mwaŭra, Kihaato. Chokwe, myself, Gathee, Mwangi Wawerŭ, Wamũtĩ Mũhũngi, Mwaŭra Karanja, Romano, Nyamũ Marea and M. Marite. However, the cells couldn't accommodate all of them—and Nyamũ and Romano were returned to the ordinary sleeping quarters.

23 October 1954

The work gang leaders were delegated by the detainees to raise the matter of loss of pay for eleven people. The camp officer agreed to reverse this decision. Everybody would be paid in accordance with recorded hours of work. In any case there were only 30 people who were eligible for payments—those who had been carrying out road construction.

About 100 Athi River detainees were driven past our camp on their way to Takwa Detention Camp. We waved to them from a distance.

We learned that a Nandi camp guard had lost five bullets the previous day. In the morning of 23rd October 30 detainees were assigned the work of searching for these bullets. By 11.00 a.m. their search had yielded nothing.

Then the emergency trumpet was sounded and all the detainees and all the camp guards gathered at the camp office. A mass search was conducted from the place where the Nandi guard had been overseeing work. By twelve o'clock, nothing had been recovered.

We resumed the search at 2.00 p.m. We poked into the sand with sticks, poked into the grass, searched in the bushes. The sun was scorchingly hot, but we searched with keen devotion, for we considered this young Nandi guard our friend. He had just recently come to Manda and he treated people with decency. Already there were rumours another guard had stolen the bullets in a bid to foul up things for the young guard.

But when the trumpet sounded at 4.00 p.m. the bullets had not been recovered.

24 October 1954

The trumpet was sounded at around 11.00 a.m. All of us left our work and went to our living quarters. We were ordered to go to the camp office. We were made to form four lines which faced each other. The officer ordered us to strip. The guards shook out each person's clothes—and found no bullets. Other guards made a minute search in our sleeping quarters but to no avail.

It was a terribly humiliating experience, all people being made to strip in front of each other irrespective of age. This engendered deep resentment—since we had not been responsible for the loss in the first place.

On this same day the search was on for a knife that had been made by Paulo Thiong'o and then had got lost. For this loss all construction workers were locked in. Paulo Thiong'o himself would be put on trial. During the search they took away all the knives used in peeling potatoes, and nails and timber for constructing beds and chairs. These were, however, returned to the owners.

The bullets were not recovered. We were allowed to retire to our living quarters.

25 October 1954

40 detainees spent the whole day in a vain search for bullets.

Rumours had it that there was a mass strike against work in Takwa Detention Camp, which was on another part of Manda island; as a punishment the detainees were being denied food.

27 October 1954

Detainees from the new camp—camp no. 3—were deployed in the search for the five bullets. The ' recovered nothing.

People from compounds 1, 2A and 2B went to do routine work.

28 October 1954

Another day was spent by people from the new camp in a fruitless search for the bullets.

30 October 1954

All the detainees were called to the camp office at 11.00 a.m. The officer informed us there were strict written instructions from Nairobi that we must find those lost bullets.

Another mass search was conducted. We poked everywhere the guard said he had been on the fateful day. We searched along the length of the camp roads, searched near the hospital, went right up to the shores of the sea; we even searched in our own living quarters. We searched until 12.00 noon—and found nothing.

We heard on the grapevine that they were bringing another British officer to the camp on the 14th of November. We did not know in which capacity he would come.

* * * *

During the month of October detainees engaged in carpentry were assigned the work of making desks for use in a Lamu school. Very good desks were made. Favourably impressed, the D.C. said the Manda camp detainees had a rich variety of skills and they would be very useful to society if it were not for the fact they had taken Mau Mau oaths.

The carpenters took on other work: making sitting forms, chairs, beds, boxes and cupboards. Carpentry in Manda became a reputable occupation.

During the same month, camp personnel had been impressed by our study sessions and had requested the camp officer to allow them to enrol in classes run by the better educated detainees. The officer refused to grant permission for this. They had bought exercise books and elementary readers. When we went out of the camp, we would give lessons to these people under the shade of trees. Three Luo and three Somali guards acquired an acceptable level of literacy under this kind of arrangement. A teacher was assigned to each guard.

During the same month, George Waiyaki introduced simple pulley system in the camp wells to replace the earlier system where water was drawn out by bucket attached to a rope. The detainees and the wives of the camp personnel found this system pleasing and convenient.

We had also learned how to carry water using *mkoko* poles. Two people would carry five buckets hanging from this pole whose two ends rested on the shoulders of the two people, one in front and the other behind. People would walk between 100 and 150 yards to make one delivery of water, depending on the location of the well. One person would be required to make a delivery of 10 or 12 buckets per day.

October was characterised by scorching heat. One could not walk on the burning sands without shoes or tyre sandals (*nyamŭga*). We requested the officer to reduce afternoon working hours, so oppressively hot did it get, but he refused to accede to this request. People would go out, find it impossible to work in the heat, and retire under the shade of trees; the guards, feeling as oppressed as everybody else, would be indulgent. And the bush did provide something else which made the weather bearable: a fruit eaten by monkeys which we named *hŭrihŭri*. Detainees and guards alike would crush a fruit in their mouths, their mouths would soften, their thirst would be assuaged, and they would find it possible to put in more work.

We would sometimes carry unripe *hŭrihŭri* into our living quarters and leave them for a period to ripen.

November, 1954

1 November 1954

Some drastic changes were introduced in the camp regime. From now on it was ordered detainees from the new camp, camp no. 3, would no longer be allowed to talk to detainees living in the quarters of the old camp. Lockable gates were constructed at every outlet of the camp.

We did not know why they imposed this ban on intercourse between the new and the old camps. Those people in the old camp had done nothing wrong as far as we knew; and we were not aware that *we* had done anything to benefit them in the course of our social interaction. Most detainees from Nyanza were accommodated in the new camp; for example, Achieng' Oneko, John Adala and the Abaluyia detainees who were alleged to have taken the "Alego" oath.

General Gatamŭki·was also in the new camp.

4 November 1954

In a discussion between the camp officer and the detainee representatives and the work gang leaders, the officer revealed that there was a strike against work at Takwa Detention Camp; as a punishment detainees were being made to go without food. He hoped people here had outgrown such foolishness. We had learnt about the benefits of working willingly. The time had come for us to increase the acreage of our vegetable farm, to five acres; he had already acquired a variety of vegetable seeds.

Russell suggested we should start cooking unpeeled potatoes. The idea received resistance among the detainees.

8 November 1954

Seven people offered to go to Takwa to talk the detainees there back to work; they made this offer to the camp officer in writing. Many detainees couldn't remotely guess at the motives of these seven people and there was general resentment against them. On the grapevine we had obtained some names of people we knew, who were among the Takwa detainees currently on strike against camp labour.

Some food was diverted from Takwa to section 3 in Manda camp. People refused to eat this food which was obtained through the deprivation of others.

Detainee carpenters and craftsmen, under the leadership of Mũcaai, started to construct woodboard and iron sheet enclosures around the wells, It was a beautiful job.

12 November 1954

The camp officer informed us that the Governor of Colonial Kenya would tour Manda camp on 19th November 1954, in the company of senior prison officers. We could draft a memorandum to him.

Each camp section elected two people to work on drafting the memorandum; the three sections elected six representatives. Before the memorandum was drafted there was a disagreement on whether or not the best thing was to give the Governor the very same memorandum that had been given to Ohanga. Some people argued for using the Ohanga memorandum, while others argued the idea wouldn't work since a group of people had already disassociated themselves from its contents and the camp officer had gone as far as discrediting its veracity.

These were the people elected to the drafting committee: from section 1: John Mbiyũ and James Waithaka; from section 2A: Mũrage Wokabi and Cege Kabogoro; and from section 2B: Babu Kamau and Kĩbuci Ndiang'ũi.

The effect of the disagreement on whether or not to write a new memorandum was that the section 1 preresentatives opted out of the exercise claiming that they were neither authorized to draft the memorandum nor to sign it by people in their section. The drafting and signing of the memorandum ended up as an affair of sections 2A and 2B, with the following people doing the drafting: B. Kamau, J.D. Kali, Mwai Koigi, Kĩbuci Ndiang'ũi and Mwangi Mathu. Everybody from sections 2A and 2B put their signature to the memorandum.

17 November 1954

The Commissioner of Prisons toured Manda in advance of the visit from the Governor. He inspected all the facilities on the camp to make sure they were in the right condition before the Governor's visit.

The motor road was carpeted with a layer of grass, cut for this purpose, to keep the dust in check.

19 November 1954

Our memorandum to the Governor was taken to the camp officer who would give it to the Governor when he arrived.

The Governor arrived by ship at 11.30 a.m. He was shown around the new camp and around the camp personnel quarters; a guard of honour was mounted for him near the guardroom. He never managed to visit sections 1 and 2. He was given a memorandum drafted by the detainees of the new camp.

When the Governor had left, the officer informed us he had been impressed by the cleanliness of Manda camp and had been generally happy about things.

30 November 1954

We experienced a rainstorm such as we had not seen in recent times. We concluded this marked the advent of the short rains. The rain soaked through the thick layers of dust.

December, 1954

4 December 1954

A camp guard failed to report that he had sighted a ship sailing at a distance in the sea. As a punishment for this failure he was put under a drill where he would jump up and down with his gun held high, for three days. Mohamed, for that was the name of the Somali guard, refused to accept his punishment. Even when he was warned he would face a prison term for his disobedience—he was no detainee but a government worker although he seemed to have learnt disobedient and defiant behaviour from the detainees!—he persisted in his refusal to take his punishment.

Mohamed was thrown into a cell for three days. He was then tried again and dismissed from his work for good.

5 December 1954

Mohamed collected all his belongings at around 11.00 a.m. Before he left he bid farewell to the detainees.

In Mohamed we had witnessed a transformation. To begin with, he was a cruel guard who would subject detainees to beatings. But the detainees had talked to him and in the process reeducated him—and recently he had been treating people decently.

9 December 1954

The Commissioner in charge of Rehabilitation, Askwith, came to the camp. A number of detainees went to see him. He stayed at the office and never visited the detainee living quarters. For a brief period he held discussions with Baker and the camp officer, Russell.

Mwai Koigi tried to see Askwith at the office. However, he was not allowed in since, he was told, he had not given advance notice of his intention to see Askwith.

14 December 1954

James Waithaka reported Mwai Koigi for alleging that it was he, Waithaka, who had been instrumental in having Mwai barred from seeing Askwith. The camp sergeant, Mũcaai, Kĩhoro and Waikwa presented themselves as Waithaka's witnesses. Mwai was found in the wrong and was condemned to a punishment cell for four days on a diet of *ugali* without relish. Further he would not be allowed to receive correspondence course lessons for one month. His lesson papers were confiscated and kept under the custody of the officer.

17 December 1954

Paulo Thiong'o was admitted to Native Council Hospital, Lamu. Earlier on, Dr. Shah had examined him at the camp.

It was terribly windy. People constructed "tents" around their beds using sheets of cloth to shelter themselves from the sand-laden winds. Without this shelter it would have been impossible to sleep.

18 December 1954

Six detainees sought and obtained audience with Baker. Baker subjected them to questioning. Had they signed the memorandum sent to the Governor? Were they aware that letters had recently been exchanged between Manda and Takwa detainees? Who were the prison personnel go-betweens in these transactions? The six detainees could not answer these questions satisfactorily, and Baker declared they were incorrigible Mau Mau and he would not find it possible to help them.

In the evening there was a tea party organised by Kagĩĩka to celebrate his daughter's tenth birthday. 50 people were invited to the party. Rev. Arthur Gatũng'ũ led us in prayers and thanksgiving. Kamau and Karanũ made speeches.

Then all of us spat on our chests and chanted in invocation of God's blessings: "May the child grow in wholeness."

24 December 1954

The camp officer distributed goats to all the sections—a goat each for every section of the camp. In addition each section got a sack of rice and its daily ration of other foodstuffs was doubled. This was done on account of tomorrow being Christmas day.

Prayers were held in section 2 at around 9.00 p.m.; people from section 1 were allowed to attend. Rev. Arthur Gatŭng'ŭ conducted the service. We sung Christmas carols. Kagĭĭka and Kali sung hymns from the Anglican hymn book and P.C. Mulwa, Mwangi Mathu and Romano Njamumo sang Catholic hymns, the *Misere nobe*. Peter Karanŭ and Simon Mbacia treated us to tea. Speeches were given in celebration of Christmas. The doors of our sleeping quarters remained open until 10.00 p.m.

25 December 1954

People were in a joyful festive mood. Nobody went out to work. We expected there would be a football match between our camp and Takwa—but this did not take place (we heard that Baker had been attacked at Takwa and they would not, therefore, be allowed to come to Manda). The doors of all sections remained open and we exchanged visits. In the morning I treated people from Nyeri district to tea; and Rev. Stefano Waciira treated us to tea in the afternoon. James Njoroge organised a tea party for people from Mŭrang'a district. People talked to each other with genuine friendliness. Prayers were held for everybody in compound 2.

A large number of people, about 150 of them, went to tour a small island we had baptised "Manda Toto", Infant Manda. This island lay just a few metres from the main-island. As it was low tide they were able to cross on foot to the "infant" island. This was a new experience: these people had left the camp five miles away on their own—unguarded and unescorted by prison personnel. Those people who didn't visit Manda Toto went to listen to the radio at the camp office.

The sergeant also entertained detainees. He invited them to drink with him and his *askari:* he had brewed liquor using maize flour. Detainees bought beer from the canteen and enjoyed themselves.

At 4.00 p.m. football was played by teams made of a mixture of detainees and camp personnel. After supper, detainees held traditional dances—*mŭcŭngwa, ngurŭ* and *kamanŭ*.

It was a day of festivities and goodwill, with people jumping around and dancing in childlike abandon. The doors of our living quarters remained open until 9.00 p.m.

Our joy would have been pure and unalloyed if it were not for one event that took place at 7.00 p.m., knowledge about which gradually grew into a cloud of sadness spreading throughout the camp. Mwangi wa Wamwea suddenly died. He hadn't been unwell and had in fact been one of the *kamanũ* dancers. But as he left the playing field he suddenly fell. Kĩbeera went to his aid and raised him up. When he was asked what was wrong, he joked, "I jumped!"* He never said another word. Kagĩĩka tried hard but in vain to revive Mwangi. He died on his bed.

The camp officer and *dresser* tried to get to the cause of this death by asking questions, but nobody could offer any clues. Mwangi's body was kept at the dispensary.

26 December 1954

Dr. Shah carried out an autopsy on Mwangi at around 4.30 p.m. It transpired that Mwangi had died of heart failure; Mwangi had also suffered from T.B. for a long time. It was decided Mwangi would be buried the following day. We went to bed in dejection and sorrow.

Dr. Shah also examined two patients—Mũngai and Owanga—who had been seized by a strange illness, whereby they found it difficult to walk, on 25th December. We couldn't understand this sorrowful turn of things, which ruined the kind of joy we had experienced for the first time in our Manda exile.

27 December 1954

A grave had been dug and a coffin had been made by Mũcaai and Njenga and other carpenters. At 10.00 a.m. people dressed in their best and marched in formation of three side-by-side. Wokabi led the procession; he was carrying a board with Mwangi's name painted on it. The coffin followed. It changed hands several times before we got to the burial ground where earlier on we had put Elder Gĩcaana to rest.

Mwangi belonged to the Catholic church. Prayers were conducted by Russell and Rev. Arthur Gatũng'ũ. Kagĩĩka and Wokabi then said a few words. Michael Njai told us about Mwangi's life. Mwangi belonged to the Agacikũ clan. His parents had died some time back. He was born in Mũrang'a, but he had spent most of his life in Nairobi where he had worked as a laundry man. Mwangi

---

*In Gikuyu when a child falls down and is about to cry, an adult dissuades him from crying by pointing out that the child did not in fact fall, but rather "jumped"

had been a hard working man, and had a developed sense of communal and patriotic duty.

After we had laid many flowers on Mwangi's grave, we left the burial ground singing our hymn, "Gũthamĩrio Gĩcigĩrĩra nĩ Ũhoro Ũtangĩriganĩra"— "To be exiled on an island is an unforgettable experience."

Examinations which had been scheduled for today were cancelled because of the funeral.

28 December 1954

Baker arrived from Lamu in the company of his wife. He called the English-speaking class to the canteen. He talked about the memorandum that the detainees had presented to the Governor of Kenya during his recent visit to Manda. He said he had purposely come to talk about the matters raised in that memorandum, which had been drafted by section 3; he had been detailed to do so. A discussion ensued in which many people participated. Baker said he would be coming back to Manda in the near future.

31 December 1954

At 2.00 p.m. we were instructed to deliver all tin cans to the office, so that marks could be painted on them. However, marks were only put on 1½ pint tin cans. We were thus deprived of our drinking utensils—for we had no proper cups. Our leaders complained about this to the camp officer to no avail.

At midnight we were still awake although they wouldn't allow us to go out. People exchanged new year greetings. And within our quarters we conducted prayers in thanksgiving to God for blessing our passage to the new year of 1955.

January, 1955

1 January 1955

I organised traditional dances for the afternoon. The camp officer, the sergeant, the camp personnel and their wives all came to watch and they enjoyed the performances tremendously.

The dancers were resplendent in ceremonial dress; they wore necklaces of cowrie shells around their necks, and rattles of tin and pebbles collected from the sea shore. They wore pieces of paper shaped to look like feathers in their hair. They had painted their faces and arms with white, red and blue chalk. Most of the dancers wore sheets of cloth—but ngurũ dancers wore only a pair of brief shorts. Among them all the following stood out: Cege wa Kĩraka, Mwaŭra Marite, Mũirũ Kĩmanjara and Karũru Mũreebu.

The following Gĩkũyũ dances were performed: *ngurũ, njukia, mũcũng'wa, kamanũ, muthuũ, ngũcũ,* and *mukuogo.* People from Nyanza performed the *kuoro* dance. A procession of all these dancers, led by the *njaama* dance conducted by Kahũgĩ wa Gĩturo, started at section 2 and performed its way to the field.

These were the people who led the individual dances: *ngurũ*—Cege Kĩraka and Kahũgĩ Gĩturo; *mũcũng'wa*—Mahuti Gĩcukĩ, Mwĩcĩgĩ Karanja and Mbũrũ Njoroge; *kamanũ*—Gĩcoohi Gĩthua, Gacangi Gĩkaru and Mũirũ Kĩnogu; *njukia*—Ngatia Kangangi and Karĩnga Gakure; *mũthuũ*—Kamanũ Kĩnya and Mwanĩki Rĩbuthi; *ngũcũ*—Cege Kĩraka, Gĩcohi Gĩthua and Gacangi Gĩkaru; *mũkuogo*—Gatimũ Ngiinga and Wahome Karĩmi; *kuoro*—John Adala and Oduoli Mudema.

Prizes were given by the sergeant for the best dances as follows: first position: *mũthuu*; second position: *mũcũng'wa*; third position: *mũkuogo.*

We wound up the ceremonies by all of us joining in the singing of the Kiswahili anthem, *Mungu Ibariki Afrika.*

2 January 1955

Sections 1 and 2 classes started taking final exams for the year just ended. Section 3 had conducted their examinations on 31st December 1954. All our living quarters were made into examination venues. Teachers treated these examinations with the utmost seriousness.

Those people who were neither sitting tests nor conducting them helped out with domestic chores—cooking, collecting water and so on.

8 January 1955

At 10.00 o'clock in the morning Gathanju Mwangi was called to the office. A letter he had secretly posted to Nairobi had, unfortunately, been returned to Manda after the addressee could not be traced. Gathanju defended himself by pointing out that he had tried to use the correct procedure but the camp officer had turned down his request for the letter to be posted from the camp office.

At 1.00 o'clock all detainees from sections 1 and 2 were called to the Office. We were told to reveal the names of the camp warders who assisted us in smuggling letters out of the camp. None of us said a word. The camp officer complained that the real culprits were those members of the camp personnel who agreed to be deceived into sending out letters secretly. But he found it necessary, he said, to impose this punishment: to cut off 3 ounces from our individual food rations; and to deny us facilities of receiving or sending letters and parcels.

Gathanju spent the night confined in a cell in the prisoners' block; he did not have anything to eat throughout that day and night.

9 January 1955

Gathanju was taken to the office early in the morning. All the camp *askaris* were paraded in line formation. Gathauju was ordered to identify the warder who had posted his letter. Gathanju refused to point out any person, and insisted he had given the letter to the office.

The camp officer gave the warders a lecture about our evil cunning: we were inclined always to do unlawful things, and to sow disruption, he said. If the camp personnel were tempted to be misled by us they would end up losing their jobs. They were warned that we were the same people who had fanned fires of war and conflict in the country; they should always be aware that our minds were full of hatred and we derived our motivation from anarchic political notions.

Gathanju was returned to the cell in the prisoners' block. He was given a little food.

At 9.00 o'clock in the morning we held a ceremony to close Manda Island Detention School for a two-week holiday. The secretary to the school board read out the marks awarded in the end-of-year examinations. The school principal gave a vote of thanks to the teachers and the students. Rev. Stefano Waciira read from the Bible a verse to the effect that many people may compete but only one of them reaches the end of the race first. Rev. Arthur Gatũng'ũ conducted closing prayers.

At the end of it all, we sang "*Mungu Ibariki Afrika*"

10 January 1955

Gathanju was released from his punishment cell. No further punishment was given. No discovery was made about who had posted Gathanju's letter.

But there was a reorganisation affecting the *askaris*. A group of warders was transferred from Manda to Takwa, and was replaced by warders from Takwa. The idea was that familiarity between detainees and camp personnel had grown to an unacceptable level. As they prepared to leave some of the warders said we would continue to meet when they paid visits to Manda.

15 January 1955

Joel Warũi organised four football teams for league clubs. They were given the following names: Simba, Chui, Faru and Ndovu. Each league club had 18 players, including a few camp askaris. The camp officer was not happy with the inclusion of camp personnel in the club teams, but he allowed it to be, warning however, that he could withdraw his men if he considered it expedient.

16 January 1955

16 detainees arrived from Athi River. They were housed in the prisoners' block, pending transfer to Takwa where they should have been taken in the first place if it were not for a mistake that had been made. *Ugali* was cooked for them. Some of these detainees were: Kīana Gīkuhī, James Njogu, Mwangi Gakumo, L. Karugo and Samuel Njatha. They complained about the bad conditions obtaining at Athi River. But they had encouraging things to say: in the Gīkũyũ countryside there was plenty of food and the armed conflict had abated; but we were winning the war for there was now a diplomatic war effort being waged by all the nations of the world on our behalf against the British imperialists.

25 January 1955

Gīteru was condemned to four days of confinement in a punishment cell. He had swum near the fishing traps against regulations. The camp officer himself saw Gīteru and imposed the punishment.

26 January 1955

A Catholic priest, Father Calton, arrived in Manda. Addressing the detainees he declared he had not come carrying the key to the detention blocks; but he did carry the key to Heaven. He had come to preach and administer the sacraments to Catholics, those who had gone through Catholic baptism. A considerable number of Catholics gathered in compound 3 for the mass and to receive the sacraments.

February 1955

2 February 1955

Twenty six cattle were brought to Manda. They should cater for the kitchens of three camps—Manda, Takwa and Mwana. However, they would be slaughtered at Manda camp before distribution so that the only health officer available, John Mbiyū, could easily inspect the meat within Manda.

6 February 1955

It was a Sunday. At around 2.00 an S.O.S. alarm was sounded. Ng'ang'a wa Kanja was the first man to catch the alarm, sounded on a whistle; it appeared to come from the bush beyond the camp precincts. Ng'ang'a alerted the guard manning the compound 3 watchtower.

It turned out that a camp guard had drowned in the sea. Three of them—Mulwa, Mwathi and Muita—had gone for a walk to Manda Toto. As they crossed the strip of sea separating the tiny island from Manda, the area had filled up with high-tide water, and Muita, a Mutende, drowned. Mwathi managed to swim across and blew the alarm. Mulwa would have drowned if it were not for the quick intervention of a Somali guard, Abdi, who rescued him from the sea waters. Abdi and a number of guards had come running to the scene when they heard the alarm.

Twenty good swimmers, including camp guards and detainees, dived into the sea in search of Muita's body. They didn't find it. Muita had joined the camp only recently, in fact just a few days back. His disappearance cast a cloud of sorrow over the whole camp. A number of guards kept vigil on the seashore, hoping to retrieve Muita's body if it surfaced. But it did not surface.

7 February 1955

At 2.00 o'clock a number of police officers came to see the place where Muita had drowned.

A bush fire broke out in the night. Section 1 detainees were detailed to put it out. They came back to the camp at 11.00 p.m., terribly tired.

9 February 1955

The Commissioner of Prisons visited Manda. When he toured compound 3, people complained that they ate only one meal per day; they showed the Commissioner a rotten orange that had come with the fruit allocation. Things took too long to arrive, they complained. They raised the issue of parcels and letters: why were we being denied the right to receive them? The Commissioner said he himself had authorised the restriction on letters and parcels. The detainees asked why they should continue to be punished when they had been cooperating with the authorities by doing voluntary work. The Commissioner promised to review the matter.

12 February 1955

During the night, the cattle broke out of the shed. The alarm was sounded. From our sleeping quarters we imagined that a lion had been sighted—there had been rumours that there were some lurking somewhere on Manda island. A motor vehicle was used to chase the cattle, which were rounded up at the football field. Twenty detainees worked at repairing the cattle shed during the night; they completed the repairs at 11.00 p.m.

14 February 1955

A restriction was imposed on receiving correspondence course lessons. We were told this was a temporary measure. The Government suspected that people on correspondence courses were exploiting their privilege to post out unauthorized letters.

15 February 1955

Imperialist Baker returned to me a story I had written for publication by the *Baraza* newspaper. I informed Baker that *Baraza* had not only previously published several of my stories, but they had also paid me for them. Baker said he would take the story and make enquiries at the *Baraza* offices in Nairobi. He would also make enquiries about the closure of our correspondence courses.

25 February 1955

We started making benches to stop soil erosion on our farm. We had already cleared up to six acres. The benches were not really necessary since the ground was hardly sloping. It was as if we were taking on the work to pass time. The plan for the benches was drawn by people who were experienced in this kind of work, for example Mang'uurũ, Kĩragũ, Gacuuru and Gathanju. They also showed us how to dig.

26 February 1955

Baker read to us the official reply to our memorandum to the Governor. The reply acknowledged receipt of our memorandum by the Governor. Our expressed desire to be released from detention corresponded to the ultimate desire of the Government. But before the Government could translate this desire to reality detainees should individually undergo a transformation by renouncing their allegiance to the Mau Mau movement. Once the Rehabilitation Department was satisfied with this renunciation, it would release the detainee.

After this reading, we delegated Achieng', Beauttah and Wamũthenya to go and read this letter with their own eyes. The letter had been signed by an officer working under the Chief Secretary. We came to the conclusion that it did not serve much purpose to write to the Governor since the Governor invariably referred our problems to officers of the Rehabilitation Department, people who were not ready to consider anything in the absence of confessions to taking the oath.

On the same day Baker came with two detainees from Hindi camp, in the Mukowe region. They told us that there were 37 Mau Mau detainees at Hindi, and all of them had confessed the oath. Although they had been detained on account of taking the oath, they argued, oath or no oath they would still persist in demanding back the land and national independence.

Finally a very elderly Briton, of about 90 years, from the Anglican church delivered a sermon. He had arrived a long time back in Kenya but he had never seen the situation as grimly disruptive as it was today. We should pray to God to restore peace to the land. On our part we should make peace with the Government. If we persisted in our antagonism to the Government we would continue to place the welfare of our own children in jeopardy. The elderly man confessed he was not quite sure what the Mau Mau movement was all about, although he was fully aware such a movement did exist.

On the same day, Baker allowed people to resume receiving their correspondence course lessons. There was one exception, however: Cege Kabogoro would not be allowed to receive his lessons from South Africa because his correspondence school did not appear genuine—Cege always received a "good" comment even when his performance wasn't good.

March, 1955

4 March 1955

Baker, Munro of the C.I.D., Daudi Warũhiũ and two other Gĩkũyũ collaborators arrived at the camp. They saw and talked to eight detainees: Achieng', Waithaka, Meemia, Beauttah, Mulwa, Mbacia, J. Mũngai and Waiyaki. From their questions it was clear that they sought to achieve the following objectives: to get people to confess the oath, to divulge the names of people who administered oaths to them as well as those of the Mau Mau leaders from their home ridges, and to reveal the source and hideaway of the firearms used by the Mau Mau insurgents.

5 March 1955

Gacangi Gĩkaru was condemned to a punishment cell for losing the water bucket and for shouting at the sergeant-major. Gacangi pleaded that a camp warder had taken away with the bucket, but they wouldn't listen to him. He was even subjected to a beating when he demanded to know what possible benefit he was expected to obtain from spiriting a bucket away.

9 March 1955

Two Ministers from the Legislative Council, Briton Hartwell and Ibrahim Nathu, arrived in the company of one Dotton. Arriving at around 4.00 p.m., they found many of the detainees having classes in the camp school. They were taken round by the camp officer and the Lamu D.C., after which they went away.

Many detainees learned about the ministerial visit only after the ministers had already left. They regretted that they hadn't learnt about the visit in advance since they would have wanted to lay grievances and problems in front of these people. But we suspected that it had all been deliberate—sneaking the ministers in and out so that people wouldn't get the opportunity to say anything to them.

10 March 1955

Russell, the camp commandant, proceeded on a short leave. Detainees gave him a list of books and other items which they requested Russell to buy for them either in Mombasa or Nairobi.

19 March 1955

Imperialist Baker issued instructions that the names be listed of all people who had in the past worked for the Public Works Department and the East African Railways and Harbours. He never disclosed why he needed the names. People could only conjecture that there was a plan to have these people re-instated in their earlier jobs.

21 March 1955

Russell returned from leave. He asked those who had sent for things by him to collect books and other items from his office.

L. Kigume was condemned to a punishment cell. He was replaced from his job as a storekeeper by Nyamŭ Marea.

In the evening Manda was deluged by a heavy rain storm.

23 March 1955

The camp farm was planted with beans, njŭgŭ*, pawpaws, and all kinds of vegetables, including English potatoes.

Twenty-five head of cattle were added to the camp herd at 4.00 o'clock.

28 March 1955

About 100 detainees were called to the office to be told how much money they had earned for work done in the period July to October, 1954. Many people complained about discrepancies: people who had worked for lengthy periods

* A kind of pea.

were down for payment of a pittance like two or four shillings; others who hadn't put in any substantial number of work hours were down for substantial payments like 60 shillings. I myself received Shs. 15.20 for the very first time since the system of making payments was introduced.

Suspicion of unfairness fell on the work supervisors and the office clerks who kept the records of hours worked. The sergeant-major said it was fair and just for people to complain—but they should provide evidence of having been defrauded. Mwai wa Koigi wrote a letter of complaint. But C. Mulwa, the work captain, explained to the camp officer that Mwai was not eligible for payment since the nature of his work was domestic.

April, 1955

1 April 1955

On receiving payment the group of people who had earlier hatched the idea of forming a concert troupe made a contribution which realised Shs. 200.00. They wanted to use this to buy a guitar. However, the camp officer said the rains couldn't allow vehicles to travel to Nairobi or Mombasa, from where a guitar would have to be bought. People could see he did not support the idea.

6 April 1955

Mahuti Gĩcũhĩ had a quarrel with the people working in the kitchen in his block. He resolved to isolate himself from everybody else and start preparing porridge for himself alone. This was rejected, however. When people from his section, block 2B, deliberated over the matter, they failed to reach a compromise with Mahuti. When the matter got to the camp commandant, Mahuti was questioned and condemned to a punishment cell for four days. He would be required after his release to eat with the other detainees on pain of being put to corporal punishment. It was a serious offence, the commandant warned, for a detainee to either strike against food or isolate himself from the others.

8 April 1955

Today was Good Friday. Peter Karanũ treated the teachers of the camp school to a tea party. He told us the parable of the Good Shepherd. The man in charge of the camp school, John Cege, thanked Karanũ on behalf of all the teachers. The secretary to the school, Babu Kamau, stressed the need for selfless devotion on the part of teachers for the good of those people who had joined the school.

George Waiyaki disclosed to us the death of his father—he had died on 12th March 1955. People talked with sadness and sorrow. But Waiyaki's words that his own grandfather had been detained, just like us, in the coastal region and that he had in fact died in that detention on the dawn of British imperialism in Kenya, were a source of strength and some joy.

18 April 1955

A wild pig was killed, slaughtered and eaten in the bush by detainees who had gone to gather firewood. This greatly angered Moslem warders, who reported the matter to the camp officer. The camp officer ordered the warders who had overseen the wood fuel gathering exercise to be punished. They would make jumps in the compound for three days for allowing 35 detainees to slaughter and eat a pig. The 35 pig-eaters caused punishment to be visited on all the other detainees; correspondence course lessons and the receiving and sending out of letters and parcels were stopped for two weeks. From now on warders were instructed to keep a close watch over people at work. Detainees were instructed to draw water from wells numbers 1 and 2 only; well number 3 would henceforth be reserved for camp personnel. All lights should go out at 9.00 p.m. instead of the usual 10.00 p.m. for two whole weeks.

The warders never adhered to the instruction on wells because well no. 3 was far away from their quarters. In any case most of them were not Moslems, and they continued to draw water from the same wells we were using—wells nos 1 and 2. They would remark sarcastically that they hadn't been aware that wild pigs were as "illegitimate" as domestic swine.

19 April 1955

Baker came for Kĩgume at 1.00 p.m. When Kĩgume had been replaced as storekeeper he had been heard to vow that one day he would say something. The time had now come for him to say his piece, people remarked.

Before he left, he returned the camp blankets, the sleeping mat, his working clothes and the utensils he had been using. People waited expectantly for a follow up but nothing else happened throughout that day.

20 April 1955

Imperialist Baker arrived with two police officers. They took statements from four detainees: Mulwa, Waithaka, Mbacia and Meemia. It transpired that Kĩgume had reported to Baker the following crimes. That on 25th December 1954, on Christmas Day, two people—the sergeant-major and a warder named Mbũrũ—had been oathed in the sergeant-major's house by John Mbiyũ,

Fredrick Mbiyū and James Waithaka. On the same day, a group of people who were drinking beer, had taken the oath at the camp office.

There were other allegations involving 11 detainees who were accused of either taking the oath, administering the oath or propagating ideas about the oath. Cege, Achieng', Gathanju and Beauttah were accused of having propagated ideas about the Mau Mau oath. Mulwa, Waithaka, Mbacia, Kĩbuci and Fred Mbiyū were accused of having taken the oath right inside the camp commandant's office. Yet other detainees were accused of performing Mau Mau hymns and dances organised by myself, Gakaara wa Wanjaũ, on 1st January 1955. The sergeant-major and the warder who was overseeing work at the office, one Karicha, were instructed to put in writing everything they had said on that day.

21 April 1955

The Liwali of Lamu came to visit the camp at 1.00 p.m. Only two detainees went to have audience with him: Mariko Kaambuĩ went to greet him; and I went to inquire how I could obtain a copy of the Holy Quran. The Liwali promised to have a word with the Sheikh in authority with a view to obtaining for me a copy of the Quran in the Kiswahili language.

24 April 1955

General Gatamũki was condemned to three days in a punishment cell. During a quarrel with a warder when planting was being carried out, Gatamũki had threatened to cut up the warder into small pieces, like those you make out of a banana stem. The camp officer, however, emphasised the general was being punished for refusing to obey a warder's instructions during work, and not for making the threat. For the charge of making the threat was a very serious one and he had no authority to listen to it; he could only refer it to the authority of the Liwali or the D.C. of Lamu. If found guilty of the offence of making the threat, the general would be liable to many years imprisonment under the current Emergency laws.

25 April 1955

There was no food and we went hungry. The camp officer explained that food supplies had failed to arrive because the roads had been rendered impassable by the onset of the rains. Our only meals consisted of *chapati* eaten with thin potato soup; in the morning we had had three-quarters of a pint each of thin porridge.

During the night, however, the camp fishermen managed to catch 500 big fish. The fish were brought in at around 2.00 a.m. the following morning.

People woke up and started preparing the fish; they did the cooking until 6.00 a.m. on 26th April. There was a lot of fish soup—half a drum of it, in fact. People drank to their fill and yet couldn't finish it. We felt that God had had pity on us and had come to our rescue.

On the following day and on subsequent days we supplemented our food by gathering edible wild greens, which Chokwe had introduced to us. We called these greens *gītuhia*. The camp officer instructed that *gītuhia*-gathering gangs be formed. *Gītuhia* would be brought to the camp and rations of it would be distributed.

We had also made it our habit to eat any fruits which made ready food for monkeys and birds.

27 April 1955

Two sackfuls of beans arrived on loan from Takwa Detention Camp and Lamu Prison. People ate to their fill at 1.00 p.m.

28 April 1955

The camp officer summoned the camp leader and the work captains. He let them know that there was a serious charge to the effect that some people were giving political education to others in the camp school. He warned that should this charge be proved the authorities would close the camp school for good; we should therefore take care to keep the work of the school free from political influence. There was also a charge that people were using warders, and books borrowed from the East Africa Library, to smuggle out letters from the camp. There was good evidence that this was going on since illegal letters had been intercepted in the process of being smuggled out of Takwa; right here, Gathanju's letter had been intercepted. The officer warned that the offence of one individual would make everybody liable to the following punishments: confiscation of beds, Government-issue uniforms, boxes used for storing personal effects, and so on. The guilty individual would be liable for trial under the Liwali, who was authorized to impose an imprisonment term to be served by the individual after his release from his current detention.

30 April 1955

For the first time since we arrived in Manda, we were supplied with maize meal instead of wheat flour. We cooked *ugali* which we ate with meat stew. Many people from sections 1 and 2 would have preferred porridge to *ugali* but people from "camp 3" welcomed this chance to eat *ugali:* many of them were from western Kenya where *ugali* is very popular.

May, 1955

1 May 1955

After a doctor had carried out examinations on Tadeo Mwaŭra and Mwangi Wawerŭ during the previous night, Tadeo was admitted at Lamu Native Council Hospital.

The very elderly British church minister came to preach to the detainees. He put up in a tent erected for him for the night. The following morning he gave another sermon, then departed. He lived in Lamu, we were told.

12 May 1955

A third batch of cattle, comprising 17 head, was brought to the camp. Only five head of cattle remained in the camp herd. A white bird used to follow the herd as it grazed; people said this bird was similar to *ndĩithi* (the "shepherd bird") from Gĩkŭyŭland.

A warning came from the camp officer that people who had at any time disagreed with Kĩgume should be on the alert. For Kĩgume had prepared a lengthy list of alleged Mau Mau leaders in Manda camp. It appeared he had made allegations against people he had quarrelled with when he was a store-keeper as well as people who had insisted that he should be involved in domestic work like cooking, fetching water and cleaning the latrine.

24 May 1955

It was the Empire Day Holiday. We planted a tree in the camp to comme-morate this day.

25 May 1955

The imperialist Chief Native Commissioner (C.N.C.), Windley, announced the surrender terms for Mau Mau. It had been in the air that the C.N.C. would make an important announcement, and Kagĩĩka and myself had made a bet. Kagĩĩka had bet that the end of the Emergency would be announced, and I had bet him no such announcement would be made. He had to pay me two exercise books.

26 May 1955

We were keenly eager to know which party would emerge victorious in the British General Elections—Labour or Conservative. However, no information was forthcoming on that day.

27 May 1955

At 9.00 a.m. we learned Labour was ahead with three candidates. But at 2.00 o'clock in the afternoon the Conservatives had not only overtaken Labour but were now ahead with a comfortable 17 candidates. At 8.00 p.m. Labour trailed the Conservatives by 72 candidates! Russell predicted a Conservative victory; he would let us know the final position tomorrow morning.

30 May 1955

In a gesture of honour to Cege Kabogoro, the Principal of the Camp school, people from section 2A agreed to exempt Cege from cooking duties and replaced him in the kitchen with Paulo Njerũ. Paulo Njerũ refused to stand in for Cege, arguing that it had not been found necessary to extend the same gesture to the other teachers in the camp school. Consequently, he was told that he would from now on be given his share of raw food so that he could cook it for himself. He rejected this suggestion.

31 May 1955

Njerũ went to the kitchen carrying a heavy club, and forcibly scooped out his share of porridge from the communal pot. He threatened to hit Johnson Rũgĩo, one of the cooks in the kitchen. During the parade count, camp leader Gathanju revealed what Njerũ had done. While out at work, some teachers from section 2A—Mang'uurũ, Gathanju, Warũĩ and Cege—came up with the suggestion that teachers should withold their services, in protest against Njerũ's insulting behaviour towards the head of the camp school. At 4.00 o'clock a discussion of the matter was held between all the school teachers. They came to the conclusion that this matter did not really concern the school administration, but rather the dispute was essentially between two individuals. Cege had just relinquished his post as principal, and G. Waiyaki, who had been Cege's assistant, had replaced him in that post.

There were no lessons on that day. And the whole affair really upset the pupils, leaving a bad aftertaste.

June, 1955

1 June 1955

In the morning Gathanju withdrew his name from the committee of teachers in protest against Njerũ's insulting behaviour.

At 4.00 o'clock Cege called all the pupils. He did it on his sole initiative without first agreeing with the committee of teachers. He announced that he had resigned his post as principal in protest against the insulting behaviour of one of the pupils, Njerū. He was like the proverbial young girl who came to grief because of her goodhearted and outgoing generosity, Cege complained. The teachers were not pleased by Cege's words, since it is not the pupils but they who had elected Cege the school principal. After he had spoken, the teachers instructed the pupils to go to their respective classes. Teaching immediately resumed. Those classes which had previously been taken by Cege and Gathanju were taught by Waiyaki, Kali, Mwangi Mathu and Mwai Koigi.

In the evening people from section 2A reviewed the whole matter in the light of what the whole camp, and especially the teachers, felt and thought. They decided that Njerū should be allowed to eat with everybody else, since the ban on him had hardly worked—he had all along been eating with his friends Ndiabūi, Kīhaato, Ngūgĩ, Mwai and Wambūgū. Since Cege had already relinquished his teaching duties, he was reassigned to work in the kitchen.

11 June 1955

Another batch of 15 head of cattle, plus a cow in calf, were delivered. Officer Russell had promised to add a milking cow to the camp herd; the milk it would supply would come in handy for sick people like Stephen Ngure.

Everyday they would assign two detainees, and a warder with a firearm, to the farm; their work was to scare off monkeys from the crops.

15 June 1955

Imperialist Baker came to inform us that the deadline for complying with the Surrender Terms would be 10th July 1955. All Mau Mau leaders who would not by that date have confessed everything or have left their forest hideouts, or have offered to cooperate fully with the Government would have all their land confiscated.

Baker had arrived in the company of two detainees and one Rehabilitation officer. He said it was up to each individual to make his forthright confession. He would be bringing a committee of interrogators in the near future.

17 June 1955

16 detainees, many of them from the group which worked on the farm, were called to the office. The officer said he had learned these people were instrumental in making others shirk work. As a punishment, they would not be allowed to go to classes for two months; neither would they play football for the same period.

We had no idea who had made allegations about the sixteen—detainees or warders.

18 June 1955

The camp officer held a demonstration of the measures that should be taken in the emergency of a fire outbreak. The trumpet would be blown to give the fire alarm. Each person should exit from the building wrapped in a blanket and carrying just the few personal belongings he would be able to grab quickly; he shouldn't attempt to get out with his personal box.

We heard that a man from Takwa Camp who had gone to dispose the night slop had drowned. We couldn't understand how a man could drown from the security of standing on the seashore.

Teachers met to discuss the case of two other teachers, Kagīīka and Mwai, who were now on the list of people who had been banned from participating in classes. It was agreed that camp leader Kībuci would be sent to the camp authorities to determine whether the ban extended to the teaching activities of these two people.

22 June 1955

A Mau Mau general, one Gīcūkī, was brought to the camp. He had been flown from Nyeri to Mwana Camp the previous day, and he was driven to the camp in the morning. He told us he hailed from Othaya in Nyeri. He had been fighting in the Nyandarwa forests, from where he was captured during the month of December 1954. Since then he had been involved in a lengthy court trial which he had recently won.

He told people about the fighting and about life back home. They took him to section 3 to join General Gatamūki.

25 June 1955

One judge from the Advisory Committee on Detainees, assisted by an interpreter, one Noah, spent the whole day interviewing 15 detainees from the Manda camp and 16 from Takwa. We never got an opportunity to talk to the people from Takwa: they were housed in the prisoners' block which was guarded by warders armed with guns. They departed at 6.00 o'clock in the evening. We waved to each other as they left.

27 June 1955

10 detainees from Manda were transported to Mwana Camp to appear for interrogation before the Advisory Committee. They found that Baker had

spread the mis-information here that all detainees from Manda had become good collaborators and they had confessed the oath. Our people from Manda said there was no truth in what Baker had said.

July, 1955

1 July 1955

Three detainees, Kagĩĩka, Warũĩ and Gacangi, were reported by the warder for shirking work, when they went to the farm, and sowing misunderstanding in working relations. They were condemned to isolation in the prisoners' block. The officer said they would live in this block and work from there, until they reformed. He would also report the behaviour of these people to Baker's interrogation committee which was expected to arrive soon.

Russell had instructed the warders to maintain a record of the names of people who shirked work and generally disobeyed instructions at work. Kagĩĩka, Warũĩ and Gacangi were among twenty people whose names had been so listed two months ago.

Those who were being isolated in the prisoners' block were instructed to carry their personal belongings but by no means to take books with them. The officer was very well aware that detainees from Manda valued books and enjoyed reading more than anything else; to punish detainees he often resorted to deprivation of books and banning of reading.

2 July 1955

Gathee was condemned to isolation in the prisoners' block when he insistently demanded back his pen which the warders had taken from him.

Russell called us to his office to announce an increase in rations for wheat flour and maize meal.

The four people in the prisoners' block, however, would continue to have the old rations—which they would cook for themselves—until they reformed.

In an address, Russell warned us against hoping for an early release. He had in many different places been put in charge of prisoners-of-war. Prisoners-of-war, and that was what we were, were never released as long as hostilities continued. We should, therefore, aim at improving conditions of our detention as much as possible. We should work hard on the farm and grow crops for our own good food. We should consider ourselves lucky for being allowed to work for ourselves. "You are farming for your own benefit," Russell said. "Nobody else receives the food that you grow."

"You are the brains behind the current conflict in Kenya. Before you were brought here you had kindled and fanned the fires of hatred against the legally constituted Government. The Government cannot therefore allow you to go back before it is fully satisfied that you have been reformed and pacified. Many of you carry the kind of crimes that qualify you for the hangman's noose; the Government is aware of the kind of cunning machinations you are capable of. If you are allowed back you might outwit those who have collaborated with the Government; you may organise a fund-raising purportedly to thank those homeguards who remained at home and looked after your wives and children, only to turn right round and inflict harm on these people. It is necessary before you are released, therefore, that you confess the oath, purge all evil from your minds and souls and make a solemn vow that you are ready to cooperate with the Government."

He himself was not a Rehabilitation Officer, but if anybody wanted to make a confession, he could discreetly go and see him. Russell would help such a person. Alternatively a detainee could write down his confession and pass it on secretly through the sergeant-major or any other warder.

3 July 1955

Most of the day was taken up with school examinations. After these, we went out to play football. An accident happened: Cege Kiraka, Kagunda and Mwangi Baru collided in play, and Cege's leg had a dislocation. Officer Russell carried out first aid on Cege, after which Cege was taken to Lamu hospital by boat.

6 July 1955

Baker came to talk to General Gicuki. He asked him whether he had been telling us how the actual war was being fought; for example, had he already told us that there were three firearm factories in the forests? Gicuki said he had been telling us about ordinary things back home. But were detainees to ask him about the actual fighting in the forest, he would gladly talk about that for he had stayed in the forest for a long time.

Asked about the oath, Gicuki said he was aware it had been taken; there had been mass cleansing ceremonies in the whole of Gikuyu land which in effect amounted to confessions by all the people. When he was asked what was the objective of taking the oath, Gicuki answered Baker himself knew: it was to demand back the people's lost land and freedom. Would he exhort other detainees to confess the oath? But he did not know whether or not the others had taken the oath.

Apart from Gicuki, who was obviously the main object of interest, Baker also talked to six other detainees, among them George K. Ndegwa. He would ask them if they were now willing to work with the Government; had they taken the oath? he would ask.

7 July 1955

The sergeant-major appeared at 6.00 p.m. From a slip of paper he read out the names of twelve people who were ordered to take their personal belongings and move to the prisoners' block. We had already nicknamed this block, 'Little Block 4'. It could house 18 inmates. It appeared people who were outspoken in detainee affairs became likely candidates for the Little Block. But people did not take condemnation to this Block very seriously—they could endure it and they laughed it off. Warders would comment that they would never understand detainees; we did not appear to take seriously what was quite serious.

10 July 1955

For the very first time detainees from Takwa came over to Manda for a football game. Eleven people came under the escort of three warders. It was a good friendly game. Achieng' Oneko was the referee. Pinto was in the Takwa team. Manda beat Takwa 2-1.

The camp officer then treated the Takwa team to tea.

We were very happy with this opportunity to talk to people from Takwa—whom we hadn't seen for two whole years. We discussed a little the expiry of the deadline for acceptance of the Surrender Terms—for the deadline was today! We would comment that we would be hearing in the near future that our lands had been confiscated. But somehow nobody was in a panic about this prospect.

12 July 1955

A building in camp no. 3 collapsed with the people who were thatching the roof The people involved were Achieng', J. Kĩhara, Kainja, Kũng'ũ Mũgekenyi, Mũcibi and John Mbũgua. Mbũgua sprained his arm, but no one else was hurt.

14 July 1955

Nahashon Kang'aari received a letter from home informing him that there was already a notice of sale displayed on his land. Kangaari's family wanted to know whether he had mortgaged his land at some time in the past. Kang'aari said he was not aware of any encumbrances. We could only assume that they had started to apply the penalties for failure to meet the Surrender Terms.

Information reached the camp that "Naked" Martin, our erstwhile camp commandant, had died on Lake Victoria. He had been working at Mageta Camp, where he had taken charge as commandant, after leaving Manda. In the boat that capsized causing Martin's drowning were the following people:

Martin's Ugandan wife and two children; eleven detainees and seven warders. But none of the others drowned: they were helped ashore by warders and detainees who were very good swimmers. Some people argued that more people than Martin alone must have died. And there were rumours that Martin's death had not been accidental: that he had tried to swim ashore but some detainees had wilfully pushed his head under the water until he drowned.

At 3.00 p.m. we were allowed the rest of the day off work to mark Martin's death. People would recall Martins' strange manner of conducting prayers—the way he would raise his walking stick and strike the ground with it as he prayed. And people recalled what he used to say: that the white man does not tell lies.

16 July 1955

All of us were told to gather outside the camp canteen. The camp officer addressed us for about one hour. He told us that from today all the camp sections had been merged into one—and the categories 1, 2 and 3 had been abolished. A detainee could now choose to live anywhere in the camp quarters. In about three weeks' time there would be a major reorganisation, for some detainees would be transferred out of Manda. Many things would have been reorganised earlier for our benefit if it were not for the misdeeds of the detainees in Manda who had gone as far as writing a letter to detainees in Takwa exhorting them to persist in their strike against work. That was why the authorities had put a stop to sending out and receiving letters—and this restriction would only be lifted when people in Takwa renounced their strike and went back to work. The Government had its own clever ways of knowing what kind of things we said and did in the detention camps.

Russell informed us that Takwa Detention Camp had recently received 90 more detainees, who had been transferred from the Manyani and Mackinnon Road Detention camps. They had contracted a skin disease which did not allow them to wear clothes—they had to make do with blankets wrapped around their bodies. They were all, of course, followers of our movement; we had left them sowing disruption when we were arrested and detained.

Russell commented on the relationship between work in the camps and the concept of "cooperation with the Government". The kind of work we did could not be equated to "cooperation" since the work we did was for our own support. Before the Government could consider releasing a detainee he must first confess the oath and then demonstrate with concrete acts that he was ready to help the Government. Far from all the people in Manda indicating they were ready to cooperate, there was a good number of work shirkers and bad elements among the detainees, and he had the names of these people; he had ways and means of establishing which detainees were responsible for inciting defiance and resistance to confessing the oath. We should not harbour hopes and expectations of an early release, especially those of us who had been in the leadership of the movement.

On the same day imperialist Baker had come in the morning and his coming had fanned rumours that six people were just about to leave Manda. There appeared to be grounds for this rumour: for Achieng' Oneko had aready been informed by the camp officer that he would be replacing Nyamũ Marea as storekeeper.

On this day all the people who had been isolated in the little prisoners' block were allowed to join the other detainees; they should prepare their minds for the coming re-organisation. Their old privileges which had been withdrawn—attending classes, sending and receiving letters, playing football, borrowing books from the E.A. Library—were reinstated.

And so we waited for the big re-organisation, which we heard had been in the offing for one whole year. From what we heard all Government officials who came singly and in committees to Manda in the course of one whole year had been making their recommendations on the individual detainees and, as it were, establishing a ladder grading people in accordance with their cooperation or lack of cooperation. The big re-organisation would be based on these recommendations.

17 July 1955

As people took their work assignments for the day, it became fully established that six people were in fact due for transfer. Six work captains were replaced by Chokwe, Kali, Wamũtĩ, Mburu, Cege Kabogoro and Achieng'. These new work captains were asked to report early to work to receive instructions from the old leaders who were due for transfer.

People who were working on digging roads were instructed to stop this work for a period. We were informed that more categories of work would now carry their pay—that is in addition to the old categories of fishing, building construction, fencing and office work.

Some very thin cattle which were actually the size of immature calves, were brought to the camp. People welcomed the chance of getting rations of meat, for the beans which they had been supplying lately were mouldy.

19 July 1955

The camp school teachers met to discuss the possibility of merging the same classes from the erstwhile different sections, now that the category of sections had been abolished. We decided to wait until the big reorganisation had been carried out.

We discussed whether or not it was in fact a good idea to merge classes from the different sections. It did appear the benefits of this would outweigh the disadvantages. But there was no need to make a decision right away: we had ample time to work out a new constitution to govern the running of the camp school. The question of which language to use was discussed and it was decided we should adopt Kiswahili in order to accommodate the non-Gĩkũyũ speakers from Nyanza. Final decisions were deferred to three weeks hence.

6

The Merger between Manda and Takwa Camps

24 July 1956 to55 5 April 1956

24 July 1955

At 9.30 a.m. all of us were instructed to assemble outside the camp canteen. The camp officer informed us that in three days time the camp would be re-organised: the majority of detainees would be transferred from Manda to Takwa, and all those detainees from Takwa who had persisted in their strike against work would be transferred to Manda. Takwa was a far larger camp and could accommodate many of us; furthermore, water was available in plenty in Takwa. A small number of detainees would remain in Manda. This, Russell assured the detainees, did not mean that the administration had judged them in any way wanting.

We were instructed to prepare our luggage in readiness for moving, so that there would be no problem when short notice was given. We would be transported by lorry on the material day.

In the afternoon many people went to record hours worked, for pay-assessment, to return books borrowed from E.A. Library, and to buy letter writing materials. People also started to return their work uniforms to the camp office.

Some of the people who would remain in Manda already knew: Achieng' Oneko, James Beauttah, George K. Ndegwa and John Mbiyũ had been called to an audience with officer Russell, who had asked them if they would be in a position to persuade the Takwa strikers to renounce their strike and start working. These people told Russell they wouldn't expect to have the confidence of Baker, who never lost an opportunity to accuse them of being Mau Mau leaders. Russell assured them Baker himself would be seeing them to talk about talking the Takwa detainees back to work. They, therefore, understood that they were purposely being left in Manda to induce the cooperation of the strikers from Takwa; the authorities' reasoning was that the Takwa detainees would respect the voice of these people.

25 July 1955

The day of the great shift! A lorry load of 30 people left Manda—and the same lorry returned from Takwa with 30 people. When the lorry arrived in Manda, thirty detainees would disembark at the football field; they would then walk to camp block no. 3 which was vacant.

Detainees from Manda would leave their sleeping mats, blankets and plates in the camp; they were to be issued with new items at Takwa.

Today would have been the camp-school opening day, but because of the shift nothing could be done. However, a small group of teachers and students who hadn't yet left for Takwa held a hurried ceremony to *close* Manda School. School Principal Waiyaki addressed the students; Babu did the same. And I assured the students that all those teachers who would transfer to Takwa would endeavour to start a school in Takwa. This was joyfully received.

The detainees who arrived in Manda from Takwa slept in the beds that had been vacated by those who had already transferred to Takwa. Throughout the night, people talked to those they had not seen for at least two years; and those who had come to detention more recently had news about home.

26 July 1955

There were standing instructions that the shifting should be completed today. Four trips left from Manda, and four lorry loads returned from Takwa. At 7.00 p.m. the exchange of people between Manda and Takwa was completed. At Takwa camp, the Manda detainees were housed in blocks 1 and 3; they joined detainees who had been transferred to Takwa from Mackinnon Road. And the Takwa detainees were housed in blocks 2A and 2B in Manda.

They did not lift their strike.

190 detainees were shifted from Manda to Takwa; of the original Manda detainees only 22 remained in Manda. These included: Achieng' Oneko, George K. Ndegwa, J. Beauttah, Samuel Koina, General Gatamŭki (Mŭthaamo), General Gĭcŭkĭ, Waira Kamau, J.D. Kali, Babu Kamau, Fred Mbiyŭ, Cege Kabogoro, Mwinga Chokwe, George Waiyaki, Gĭtahi Waciira and John Mbiyŭ, as well as six men whose names were associated with Baker—Baker's favourites, people would call them: Simon Mbacia, James Waithaka, Fews Kore, Solomon Meemia, P.C. Mulwa and John Mŭngai. And Mwangi Macaria was left to cook for Russell.

27 July 1955

The Takwa camp commandant Westrop said people were at liberty to choose which block to live in and which people they would like to stay with. People spent the day shifting. Then they constructed beds; they were helped with timber by the people we had found in Takwa. There was no assignment of camp work on this day.

28 July 1955

There was a difference between Takwa and Manda in working methods: warders allocated work assignments in Takwa while detainee work captains carried out this role in Manda; however, kitchen work was the same —detainees organised it and carried it out. We asked Wamũthenya to act as our leader—to take our grievances and our problems to the camp commandant, to oversee work in the kitchen including cooking, cleaning, peeling potatoes, and so on.

The things we had left in Manda—beds, chairs, black boards—were brought by lorry. Some detainees had gone back to Manda to see to the loading of these things onto the lorry.

29 July 1955

We asked what the position was on starting classes for detainees. The commandant said he would allow it, although the Government's regulations if strictly followed required that classes should be run by Government-appointed teachers. He would inform Baker that we wanted to start a school in Takwa, along the same lines as the school in Manda.

The doors of the different blocks were kept open. After work, people would get together to hold mutual help classes and people would visit each other without being escorted by warders. This was a new development, the Takwa inmates informed us; previously nobody would go outside the detainee living quarters, not even to the office, unescorted.

August, 1955

9 August 1955

Fourteen people went to Manda to complete construction work started earlier, on a guardroom, as well as to build a barbed wire barrier around the guardroom.

11 August 1955

Three Mau Mau generals—Mwangi Njoroge, Chui and Nyiingĩ—were transferred from Takwa to Manda, there to join the other generals.

The 14 construction workers returned from Manda. There was plenty of meat to eat there, they enthused.

18 August 1955

We opened a school in Takwa. It had 240 pupils and 22 teachers. There were 8 classes.

19 August 1955

A committee of interrogators, sent by Baker, arrived at Takwa. The chairman of the committee was one John Kahara, from Kĩambuu. There were three Nyeri committee men—Ndegwa Gĩkuhĩ, Wilson Gĩtumbũ and Mũkumbũ. These people gave me the information that my paternal uncle Isaac Hunja had been killed by the Mau Mau insurgents in 1953; and that my mother Rahel Warigia and my wife Shifira Wairire had been detained in Kamĩtĩ women's prison in the Kĩambuu countryside.

22 August 1955

Since there was a recommendation that the school be closed while the interrogations were going on, a number of teachers had a meeting with the assistant Rehabilitation Officer, John Kahara. He ruled that we could go on with our classes. Further he promised to assist by supplying certain things to the school—blackboards, chalk, library books and balls for games.

September, 1955

7 September 1955

The camp commandant, Westrop, informed the camp leaders that the monthly wages for each detainee would be fixed at Shs. 8.00 irrespective of the kind of work done. Henceforth people would only be required to work in the mornings, but work quotas would be allocated. The level of wages had been determined after deducting our expenses on food and Government-issue uniforms. People were not satisfied with these low wages; detainees who had come to Takwa from Mackinnon Road had already declined to accept the wages of Shs. 8.00. A group of people argued for accepting the money while at the same time writing to the authorities to complain about the inadequacy of these wages; we would point out that while we were in Manda we used to receive more money and nobody talked about deducting clothing and food expenses. Another group argued there was no point in accepting the Shs. 8.00 and then writing a complaint. We should reject this offer and show the just reasons for doing so. We decided to send back our leaders to the commandant requesting him to show us the regulations governing wage payments; we would make a final stand after studying those regulations.

8 September 1955

The commandant said he didn't have written wage regulations; he had received instructions by telephone. Those people who were ready to accept Sh. 8.00 should register themselves with Joel Warũũĩ, who had been appointed work record clerk. When our leaders reported back to us, people couldn't reach a consensus. In fact some people had already started registering their names, even before a united stand could be taken. And there were those who appeared to be sitting on the fence, studying which way the current was going.

9 September 1955

In the morning 29 people had already registered their names; it was said some had done so secretly, in the night. People commented it did not make sense for a person to register his name secretly, since the truth must come out; in any case it must be an individual's choice—whether to accept this pay or to decide to work and take no payment.

10 September 1955

Already more than 50 people had had their names registered. Block no. 1 housed many Governor's Detention Order detainees (those arrested on 20th October 1952) and one characteristic of the GDO detainees was their belief in consensus in matters affecting their life in the camp. They met during the night to decide between two choices: 1. to accept the Shs. 8.00 and then write a complaint; or (2) write a complaint about the proposed wages without accepting it. A consensus, however, became impossible because there were a number of people in Block 1 who had already given in their names at the office. In fear of creating grounds for accusations that some people were inciting others to reject the proposed wages, it was finally agreed that each individual should decide whether or not to accept the wages.

11 September 1955

In the morning there were already 124 people who had their names registered. I was one of the people who finally decided to have their names registered on 11th September, after seeing that a consensus had escaped us; I reasoned that it was not just to continue working without receiving some kind of pay however little.

Everybody was entitled to these wages, with the exception of a Singh prisoner who had been condemned to life imprisonment. There were three detainees of Asian origin at Takwa. Pio Gama Pinto, who was one of these, had been detained for political activities. The Singh and the other Indian detainee had been arrested for selling firearms to Mau Mau.

12 September 1955

20 detainees left for Manda to receive payment for work done there during the month of July. They brought back a supply of Gĩkũyũ sweet potatoes from our Manda farm. We enjoyed eating them after they had been boiled. Some of the potatoes were extremely thick—they had actually ripened in the last three months only. It appeared to us that the soil here was very good for Gĩkũyũ potatoes.

17 September 1955

I was one of the detainees who underwent interrogation. When they asked me about the Mau Mau oath, I said I knew nothing about this oath. They told me they knew exactly where in Nairobi I had taken the oath and they even had the names of the people who took me to be oathed. All my actions, they said, affirmed my Mau Mau convictions: composing Mau Mau hymns and creating a Mau Mau creed. Had I not taken the oath I wouldn't have done those things. Three members of the interrogation committee, I was told, came from my very own location, Kĩrĩmũkũyũ, and they had been able to carry out grassroot investigations about myself, my mother and my wife. They had established that false witness had been borne against us that we had been instrumental in the murder of my Father. Those who had actually perpetrated the crime had been arrested and they were being held at the detention camp at Kangũbiri, Nyeri. I should also be aware that some of my close associates like Mwanĩki Mũgwerũ and Stanley Kĩĩnga had already confessed everything at Athi River, and they were now waiting to go home.

They were offering me a chance—to be in the group of people they would take home with them. Why, they asked, did I persist in hardening my heart when my record was not as bad as that of other people right in this camp?

I answered that I had not changed in the least since I was detained and I had offered my cooperation to the authorities by voluntarily going to work. They asked me, "Do you long for home?" I answered, "Yes, I do, but they keep telling us that we 'Jock Scott' detainees will be released when the camps have been emptied of all other categories of detainees." I was asked: "And do you believe in such a thing?" In my turn I asked them whether any Jock Scott detainees had ever been released. Kahara answered that at times it took quite long to have the Governor's Detention Order or the District Commissioner's

Detention Order repealed after a detainee's confession had been accepted. Furthermore, a detainee's local home community must indicate its readiness to accept him back. In our case, the local communities had expressly asked the interrogators to come and take us home. It was in my own interests, they exhorted me before dismissing me, to do some heart searching before the committee left Takwa Camp.

18 September 1955

We went to play football with Manda camp. We beat them 3-0. It was a good enjoyable game. But for reasons known only to them the authorities did not allow the warders to play.

22 September 1955

We were informed that the Minister for Defence, Cussack, would tour Takwa Camp in the company of settler Blundell. Many detainees were for drafting a memorandum but detainees from blocks 1 and 2 felt we should not do this hurriedly. It was therefore agreed that we should let Cussack's delegation to come and go. Later we should write a detailed memorandum about all the problems in this camp, including the low monthly wages, availability of soap and problems affecting the camp school. And before writing this memorandum a consensus should be reached with people in block 3.

27 September 1955

Only the Minister for Defence came. He was shown around the whole camp. He saw people cooking *chapati* in the kitchen and he inspected the camp dispensary. In Block 4, where the Indian detainees were quartered, he was engaged in fairly long conversation by Pio Gama Pinto.

29 September 1955

British intelligence officers from the Criminal Investigation Department came to interview people who had already confessed the oath. After they had been in the camp office for some time they were shown to our quarters by assistant Rehabilitation Officer Kahara. They engaged people in conversation especially those who had come to Takwa from Manda. When they got to me, Kahara told them I was the author of Mau Mau hymns. They immediately subjected me to questioning: where did I print my materials? How did I gather materials for publishing? Who handled the distribution of published materials? One officer asked me why I had written the "Creed of Gĩkũyũ and Mũmbi"? I replied that it was just an idea that had possessed me; and the idea had occurred to me it would enjoy popular reception because of its deep nationalist content.

After the intelligence officers had gone, I learnt that among them was a literary expert who had a lot of interest in my writing activities. However, we did not see this team again.

October, 1955

1 October 1955

A detainee named Kamũtoto was asked to get his belongings ready, his Detention Oeder had been suspended because it had been found he had not taken the oath, and he would be going home. The C.I.D. officers who had visited the camp had recommended his release. We bid him farewell and people from his home area gave him messages to take home. He took his belongings and went to wait at the camp office. He stayed there the whole day. In the evening he returned to the living quarters and told us he had been informed that his transport had failed to arrive. He was to wait until transport was available.

7 October 1955

The warders provoked a problem by locking doors at 4.00 p.m. thus preventing people from going to attend classes. There were also incidents of physical assault on detainees during work. The detainees wrote a memorandum of complaint to the commandant.

9 October 1955

The new regulation was introduced that people should hold classes in their respective living quarters. But the teachers did not consider this practicable since there weren't enough teachers to go round leave alone things like blackboards and chalk. So we decided that the regular school should cease operation until things were sorted out. All the same pupils were advised to go on with self-learning; teachers should assist as much as possible. The chairman and secretary of the school committee were delegated to see the camp commandant as well as the Rehabilitation Officer over the school issue.

Detainees felt that the warders had sabotaged our school activities out of jealousy for the detainees' achievements in literacy. One warder had been heard to comment that all detainees now could speak English. The truth of the matter is that up to this time many of the detainees who had enrolled for classes had made good progress. Those who hadn't known how to read and write had learnt how to read and write in both Gĩkũyũ and Kiswahili. Those who had been literate in the mother tongue had learnt to read and write in English adequately. Most detainees were happy and proud of our achievements. Some of the things students used to say were: "We do not know what we shall give our teachers when we get home to show our gratitude!" Or a student may comment: "A great transformation has been wrought in my life, for I had lived a large part of my life in ignorance." Or: "I didn't know the ABC, but now I can make sense out of something written in English; I can read the *East African Standard* for myself!" Or yet again: "I used to transact my business in the darkness of ignorance; I did not know how to assess my profit or loss."

13 October 1955

I started working in the office. With me were Pio Gama Pinto and a warder. I was assigned the work of maintaining the store inventory. Pinto combined the duties of a typist and filing clerk and he also made the payroll. The warder assisted the Camp Commandant in filing and keeping confidential letters and correspondence.

17 October 1955

The school was reopened after the commandant and John Kahara had been seen by the school committee chairman and secretary. When our delegation was presenting its case Pinto and I also joined in; we showed Kahara how things actually stood contrary to the way they had been misrepresented by the warders.

They issued white uniforms to the detainees who had come from Manda. We had found the detainees who had been transferred from Mackinnon Road wearing yellow uniforms. People would comment sarcastically that detainees had become "white"—acceptable to the colonial government.

21 October 1955

Romano Njamuno and Ndibũi were assigned work at the dispensary where they would assist Kĩana Gĩkuhĩ, who had been in Takwa all along. Mohamed, the Government dresser, used to collect medicine from the district hospital in Lamu; he would also have the seriously sick taken under the escort of a warder to this hospital.

30 October 1955

The people who had gone to the bush to gather firewood saw a big python coiled upon itself in a thicket. It had white and black spots and it was swollen and distended with a huge prey it had swallowed. It was shot dead and skinned. The skin was displayed in the office.

November, 1955

5 November 1955

Warũũi and Pinto had organised four football clubs—Haraka, Chui, Simba and Sungura—which drew their membership from the whole camp, detainees and warders. Knock-out and league competitions would be held between the clubs. Competitions started on this day.

7 November 1955

There was a meeting between the teachers and the students to discuss how we could start using the same books used in the Kenya school system. A number of students offered to use their monthly wages to obtain copies of the syllabuses operative in the Government schools. A list was compiled of the operative textbooks for the different classes.

12 November 1955

Ten people were assigned to Block 4. Reports had it that they had already made their confession of the oath; however, they had been brought to Takwa for continued detention for other reasons. Most of them had been transferred from Athi River and Mackinnon Road. The committee of interrogators which had recently visited Manda had picked them out.

18 November 1955

A team of tailors was put under Maina Haruni's supervision. They would receive materials from the camp personnel from which they would make clothes. Sometimes they would make clothes for warders' wives and children. This brought the warders quite close to the detainees. For warders would come to our quarters and engage in conversation with the detainees. And detainees engaged in tailoring would receive invitations to the homes of warders, where they would be treated to tea by the wives of warders. Akamba wives who knew a little Gĩkũyũ would jokingly address people as "Mũthoniwa" or "Inlaw".

There were two motor-car mechanics—Mwololo Somba and Njũgũna. When the camp lorry broke down, they would be called to repair it.

25 November 1955

The detainees delegated Pinto to request the commandant to ensure the canteen was stocked with the kind of things we would need and at the same time afford.

Could he ensure an ample supply of loaves of bread, butter, soap, sewing thread and needles.

30 November 1955

Warders were heard to complain that the people in Block 4 did not show maturity in their affairs; the Block 4 detainees had quarrelled among themselves and had gone as far as invoking the commandant's intervention. It appeared these people could not act in unity, for those who had confessed the oath considered themselves better and more favoured by the authorities; others had chosen to act as spies on others in order to pass on information to curry favour. We "Jock Scott" detainees considered it an abomination for one detainee to report another one to the colonialist commandant; we had virtually taken an oath on this when we were in the camp at Kajiado, and it had become taboo.

December, 1955

5 December 1955

We received a big supply of Gĩkũyũ sweet potatoes from the people we had left at Manda. All blocks in Takwa camp, including the "Indian" block, obtained a share. People would comment that the farm work which we had first resisted had turned out to be really for our own good. Others countered that the authorities had seen it differently: what they were after was not persuading us to work for our own good but the achievement of our ideological capitulation; we should, therefore, maintain the stand that we had accepted certain actions without changing our basic way of thinking.

One could sense that many people had mellowed—they no longer seemed to relish a "strong-position" argument.

12 December 1955

The commandant announced the regulation that detainees should no longer pay visits to the homes of warders. A warder, he said, had complained that detainees were visiting the homes because of the women. Even the warders were not pleased with this allegation for they were convinced that the detainees had all along been treating the wives of warders with dignified respect. It turned out the warder who had made the allegation was not even married! The regulation was never seriously enforced because the chief warder never saw the need to enforce it.

16 December 1955

We closed the camp school. We held the closing ceremony outside block 2. Rev. Kĩgondu led us in prayers. Principal Cyrus Gakuũ gave a brief history of the growth and development of the school. He thanked the teachers for their contribution and the camp commandant and the Rehabilitation Officer for their assistance to the school. The secretary of the school committee read out the names of the top pupils, who would then stand and receive a round of clapping. We had invited the elderly detainees who were not enrolled in any classes to stand in as "parents" and to rejoice in their children's progress. Everybody was very happy.

Three people who had recently come from Manda—John Mbũgua, Kĩbuci Ndiang'ũi and Godfrey Mwaũra—opted to go and live in block no. 4. Francis Rũga voluntarily transferred to block 3.

18 December 1955

Joel Warũũĩ came from the office and informed us that the radio had announced the formation of a political party called Kenya African National Congress. This had been done after a meeting by African people resident in Nairobi. The chairman of the new party was the African lawyer Argwings Kodhek. We rejoiced that we had acquired a new voice.

25 December 1955

From a fund to which we had contributed using our wages, we bought two bulls which we slaughtered. We had a big feast for Christmas. People from Nyeri district organised a little tea party which they described as a party for taking a body count.

I had been requested to organise Gĩkũyũ cultural dances, such as we used to have in Manda, but the commandant refused to allow us to perform them. His reason was that he had been reliably informed such dances carried a Mau Mau message. It became known that some of our people had maligned our cultural activities while trying to curry favour.

All the same, after we had had our fill of meat, people danced inside the living quarters. Some danced the *mwomboko* to the improvised music of one piece of metal beaten against another. And Gĩcohi, Gacangi and Gacago led an enthusiastic group in dancing the *kamanũ* in joyous abandon.

26 December 1955

Prizes were awarded for the best football teams in the league and knock out games. Simba club won in the league games. The fifteen members of this club got a fountain pen each. Haraka club was in second position. Its members got a rubber-tipped pencil and a razor blade each. Sungura club won the knock-out games. Members got a writing pad and a pencil each. Members of Chui, which was placed second in the knock-outs, got 5 packets of Jet cigarettes each.

The prizes had been bought with the profits made by the camp canteen; discounts given on bulk purchases of books had also been saved and they went into the buying of the prizes.

People in the whole camp were in a mood for celebration.

31 December 1955

As was our custom, we exchanged the New Year greetings at midnight. People did not leave their respective living quarters. We held prayers of thanksgiving. Ordained church ministers led the prayers. In those blocks where there weren't any clergy, an elder would lead the prayers.

January, 1956

3 January 1956

We reopened the School. My new class had elderly men who did not know how to read and write; one of them was Ex-Chief Gũtũ of Ndia. I had taught other similarly elderly men, for example Ngatia Kangangi, Njiriri Mũkoma, Ng'ang'a Kĩboobo and others who hadn't known how to read. They could now read quite well.

15 January 1956

I received a letter from my sister, Mary Watare, informing me my mother and my wife had all along been under detention at Kamĩtĩ. I asked the commandant's permission to have letters and small parcels to my mother and my wife posted. I sent them two headscarfs; as well I sent the fountain pen I had received as a member of the winning Simba football club to my wife; she could use it to write letters inside her camp.

* * *

During the month of January there was a tour by the Assistant Commissioner of Prisons and newsmen from the British imperialist press. They talked to a good number of people. They saw for themselves the progress the school had made as well as the school in session. We asked them what kind of assistance they could render to the school. The journalists took down copious notes after listening to myself, James Karũga Koinange, Victor Wokabi and Kagĩĩka Kũhũtha.

A British soldier came to Takwa to assist the Commandant. He started to oversee the manufacture of fish traps. Mbūrū Njoroge and the team of fishermen he had worked with in Manda took over the work of fishing. The assistant commandant would also take Mbūrū Njoroge's team to hunt for tortoise's eggs. For a tortoise leaves the sea to lay its eggs far inland where it buries them in the sand.

In the month of January we also received newspapers which carried the news that D.C.'s and P.C.'s had been deprived of the Emergency powers which had enabled them to carry out arrests and detentions. We rejoiced at this and people expressed their conviction that victory was in sight and that we would be released soon. Those of us who had been detained under the Governor's Detention Order had already languished in exile for four years, and people's minds were focused on their homes.

The elderly men were examined by Dr. Shah. Some of them, for example W. Wambūgū Maina, Kamūmbū and Gīcūhī, were declared unfit for heavy work and they were assigned to compound cleaning duties. A number of elderly men who had been kept off heavy work by detainees themselves out of consideration for certain of their physical disabilities were now declared fit for this kind of work. Such were Mwangi Mathu, Mūtahi Gatheemia and others.

A new regulation was also introduced in January under which people who were involved in domestic work could no longer draw the Shs. 8.00 wages; to be eligible for payment a detainee must have worked outside the domestic area.

February, 1956

3 February 1956

A rehabilitation officer who was also a Catholic priest, Father Joseph, saw me and said these words: "You, Gakaara Wanjaū, you are the man who has set out to disrupt in 5 short months the good work the established church has done in 50 years! Whoever is going to follow you?" I did not say a word to him.

Later, however, we conversed. He informed me that the people who had killed my father had been arrested. One of them was a homeguard from Kaheti-Mīhūtī and another one came from my own location, Kīrīmūkūyū. There were others, but he couldn't recall them. Investigations were still continuing. My conviction grew that my father's murder had been planned right from my home and extended family and it was motivated by hatred bred by disagreement over my father's land ownership.

14 February 1956

Rumours were rife that Takwa Detention camp would be abolished—the detainees would be released to go home and the warders would go to Nairobi prisons on transfer. Warders themselves would conspiratorially drop hints about our imminent release and their imminent return home for their work "was now finished". Another version of the story was that we would be replaced in the camp by forest fighters who had surrendered in acceptance of the Surrender Terms.

Many people trusted our release was indeed imminent. They had even started to plan their post-detention lives back home. Some would picture the ecstatic welcome that awaited them from their wives and their children.

17 February 1956

A large group of very senior British officers came to Takwa: the Commissioner of Prisons, the Coast Provincial Commissioner, the Commissioner for Rehabilitation and their assistants as well as the D.C. of Lamu. There were also senior British army officers and African soldiers. They toured the camp but inspected only block 1 where most of the 20 October 1952 detainees were housed. They were shown the Takwa Camp School which was run by and catered for detainees. At the school they met the top student, one Gatabaki Mũũndatĩ who had qualified for Form 1 in secondary school. They also looked at a display of students' handwritings presented at a handwriting competition which had been conducted on 14th February 1956.

Because of this visit of the great rumours now grew wings about the imminence of our release to go home.

18 February 1956

We closed the school for the mid-term holidays. The Principal thanked the students for acquiring text books worth Sh. 670.00 and for buying syllabuses for use by the teachers. The textbooks were tailored to the syllabuses operative in Kenya schools.

After that people went to look at the display of handwritings presented in the competition; the winners' names from each class were also displayed. The handwriting was displayed on the walls of one room in block No. 2. People took about two hours watching the display—from 2.00 o'clock to 4.00. It was evident many students had achieved brilliance in their hand-writing.

After this I, who was the secretary to the school committee, explained how the handwriting competition had been organised and presented prizes to the winners; the prizes, comprising exercise books, pencils and envelopes, had been donated by the teachers. Romano spoke about the need for respectful cooperation among pupils and teachers; we should sometimes forget our detainee status or the age of people. When we were in school we should take on the humility of little children. That way we would acquire something very valuable during our detention.

19 February 1956

We read the English newspaper *East African Standard* and Kiswahili newspaper *Baraza* which carried stories about us—written, no doubt, by the journalists who had toured Takwa during the month of January. There was a positive mention of the fact that we were running our own school. We were quite a closed community, the report said: we were shut out of affairs outside the camp. We were a hard-hearted lot, the newspapers said negatively. We persisted in refusing to cooperate with the Government. Many of us were veteran politicians who had been rounded up under the "Jock Scott" operation.

Some of the things in the papers pleased us; others, we felt, were not meant to reflect well on us.

26 February 1956

Our people from home had started to make our longing for home intense. Mwangi Thabuni's wife wrote from their home in Mŭrang'a. She had been spending her days at the D.C.'s office waiting for him to arrive, for rumours were rife in the villages that detainees from Manda island were on their way home.

29 February 1956

Some people had already been released from camps in Manyani, Mackinnon Road and Mwea. They would write to us and encourage us to take heart—our release was a future certainty. Thus, even when we were threatened with further exile in the camps of the hardcore—Mageta, Lodwar or Yatta—we did not take the threat seriously.

March, 1956

2 March 1956

I finished writing my book, *Mĭhĭrĭga ya Agĭkŭyŭ* ("*The Gĭkŭyŭ Clans*"). I had been lucky in that all the nine Gĭkŭyŭ clans were represented in Manda island.

This book describes the characteristics of each Gĩkũyũ clan as well as the character-traits associated with people from each clan. Are people from the clan querulous? given to magic and inclined to medicine? close-fisted?, and so on.

17 March 1956

Kamũtoto, who was to have been released on 1st October 1955, was finally allowed to go. He was virtually smuggled out of Takwa camp. It was said the delay in his leaving was occasioned by active opposition by certain people to his release. He was awakened very early in the morning. He boarded a plane at Mukowe. There were rumours that two other people—Mũirũ Bedan and Gĩteru—were also to be released, the Chief Secretary in Nairobi having signed their release orders; Baker's Rehabilitation Committee, however, were acting as a stumbling block in the matter.

20 March 1956

Ten Gĩkũyũ collaborators came in the company of a senior Rehabilitation officer. There were eight elders drawn from the three Gĩkũyũ districts as follows: Kiambuu, 3; Nyeri, 3; and Mũrang'a, 2. As well there was Ndegwa Gĩkuhĩ who acted as an assistant to the British Rehabilitation officer; and a secretary to the committee. They told us they had come to take us home. Once a detainee had made a full confession he would be eligible for transfer to Athi River from where he would be taken to his home "Working Camp" before being finally allowed to go home.

When we put questions to them, they told us that the policy had just recently become operative to suspend the General Detention Order for the good elements among detainees. Detainees at Athi River Camp would be eligible first for suspension of the G.D.O. and release. People who confessed to having committed murder would have to undergo detention in Yatta Camp but even they would be eventually released.

The British Rehabilitation Officer told us that there were no more detainees at the moment at Manyani. However, the camp would begin serving as an isolation camp for Mau Mau elements who refused to offer a full confession of their doings.

The collaborator elders said they were happy to see that it was not true what was generally alleged that we would refuse to talk to people who were helping the Government. Many people back home had renounced us and had heaped the burden of all kinds of wrong doing on our names; it was as if we would never return home. It was our chance, the elders said, to put these people to shame by hastening our return and surprising them by our reabsorption into our local communities.

In the afternoon people gathered according to their district of origin and held discussions with the elders from their respective districts. These are some of the things we discussed: the reallocation of land, life in the new colonial villages, communal work for women left back home, children's education, accusations and calumny against people in detention camps and prisons or people who were dead; opening of shopping centres and village markets; etc. The elders told us the armed conflict was simmering down; many fighters had already left the forest in compliance with the Surrender Terms.

After they left, the elders said, interrogators would arrive soon. We should, they exhorted us, treat them well and tell them about ourselves so they could recommend our transfer to Athi River which was nearer home. Here our wives could even be allowed to come and see us.

We learned that the British rehabilitation officer who had come was none other than Major Breckenridge the commandant of Athi River Detention Camp. And Ndegwa Gĩkuhĩ was a very senior Interrogation Officer.

Breckenridge said how pleased he was to see the dedication the educated among us had shown to the educational advancement of other detainees. He had always operated under the faith that every human being, unlike a rock and being endowed with a mind, can bring about his own transformation; for a man can review tomorrow his thinking yesterday. He had seen to the release of many erstwhile detainees. He was happy because we had worked towards our release, for education, if conducted in a straightforward manner, was a means of changing people for the better.

Breckenridge's team left for Mwana Camp and Manda, after which they departed from the island.

23 March 1956

A British Special Branch Officer named Goodale arrived and started to carry out hurried interrogations as well as classification of individual detainees. He had a record for each detainee of all information obtained from previous interrogations. He would put three or four questions to you and then ask you to leave.

Information had it that he had earlier carried out a similar exercise in Manda, the outcome of which was that 30 people had already left that camp.

26 March 1956

Goodale completed the interrogation of 356 detainees. I myself appeared before him on 24th March 1956, and we couldn't see eye to eye. Kahara, however, assured me Goodale bore me no ill-will. He had already been briefed on my writing activities by the CID officers who had come to Takwa on 29th September 1955. Kahara recommended that I should appear before Goodale again. So early in the morning on 26th March I went to see Goodale. He asked me whether if he assigned me a job to do I would do it. I told him I was already regularly assigned to office duties. He glared at me and asked, "Do you want me to have you transferred to a hardcore camp?" And I answered, "To what purpose, and I have already agreed to work?" He put down some notes and told me to leave.

Three detainees, Nyamŭ, Gakuŭ and Romano were persuaded into serving as clerks in the interrogation court. Nyamŭ was shortly asked to leave—his work was not satisfactory. Gakuŭ and Romano, however, worked up to the evening, to the amazement of most of the detainees. After work, they were asked to retire to Block 4, where they were escorted by guards. They were told they would soon be going on transfer to another camp.

I saw Kahara who assured me I would not be transferred to a "bad" camp—as if the colonial system could manage "good" and "bad" camps!

30 March 1956

I and five other detainees were ordered to "Confession Camp", as Block 4 had come to be nicknamed. The five other people were Njenga Njoroge, Naaman Ikahŭ, James Mbŭgua, Ngure Mbugŭrŭ and Mŭragŭri Maruru. When we asked the camp commandant the reason for the transfer, he told us he was following the instructions of Goodale, the Special Branch Officer, who had by now had three days of interrogations. Would we require a guard escort to Block 4? asked the commandant. We said no.

When we went to our quarters to collect our belongings, the other detainees offered to help us transfer our things and congratulated us on what they said was our imminent release. I did a hurried handover of my books as secretary to the school committee to Wokabi.

All those who had been ordered to Block 4 had denied that they had ever taken the oath. It was being speculated that we were being transferred to another camp—we suspected it would be Athi River. In Block 4 we were informed we would stay here for three days before being transported out. We signed for the wages we had earned. There were rumours that they would bring detainees from Manda to Block 4.

31 March 1956

There was a meeting for all the School teachers. Gakuŭ, the Principal, announced that six teachers were just about to leave, including himself and myself, the secretary. Mũrage Wokabi was elected the Principal and Mwangi Mathu his secretary. I gave a little handing over speech during which I exhorted the teachers who would remain to work with all love and devotion to promote the education of our people. Wokabi and Wamũthenya gave a vote of thanks for all departing teachers. They would never forget the good work we had done. They would endeavour to carry our work forward in developing education in Takwa.

After the meeting some people who were familiar with life at Athi River Camp in recent times advised me to maintain an alertness there and to fortify myself against the hardships of the place.

April, 1956

1 April 1956

26 detainees arrived from Manda. However, these did not include the teachers we had expected to come like Kali, Cege and Waiyaki. These people informed us that the recent transfers from Manda had taken people to Kwale Detention camp in Kwale District.

2 April 1956

The camp commandant, imperialist Westrop, came to Block 4 and told people who were travelling out the next day to gather. He told us about the authorities' plans for us. We were being taken to Athi River Detention Camp, which however was no longer like the detention camp of old; it now had a Rehabilitation Centre where C.I.D. officers would recommend people for release. Elders from detainees' homes would be coming to collect those who had been recommended to take them home. There were 15 of us from Takwa Camp, 9 from Manda and one from Mukowe. We had been informed that some of us had been recommended for "upgrading" by Rehabilitation Officers while others had been recommended by C.I.D. officers.

Earlier, at around 5.00 p.m., teachers and students from the Camp School had bidden us farewell in Block 1 where everybody had gathered for this purpose. Two teachers and two student representatives made speeches; the students bade us farewell and thanked us on everybody's behalf. Then they went for classes and we went back to Block 4 to prepare ourselves for departure.

3 April 1956

We woke up at 5.00 o'clock in the morning. Everybody woke up early and took up positions at the barbed wire to see us go. We boarded the lorry at 6.00 o'clock and they handcuffed us two by two. Dawn had broken and we could see the detainees from the whole camp as they waved us goodbye.

The lorry dropped us at Mwana Camp at the boat landing. Two motor boats carried us across the sea to a landing on the shores of Mukowe. A British officer and 7 warders kept guard over us. A bus had been rented from its Kenyan owner to carry us from Mukowe, which we left at around 9.00 a.m. to Mombasa. We arrived in Mombasa at around 11.00 o'clock at night. They removed our handcuffs and put us into Fort Jesus Prison for the night.

4 April 1956

In the morning prisoners brought porridge to us. One prisoner, Nderi by name, was known to us. He told us a larger number of detainees from Manda were being held here at Fort Jesus. We remained locked up until 12.00 noon, when we were taken for lunch. We ate *ugali* and tasty cabbage relish after which we were manacled again and taken to the railway station in two lorries. A large crowd stared at us before we boarded a train which was carrying all kinds of passengers. During our short stay at Fort Jesus we hadn't met a single man from Manda.

We left Mombasa at 1.00 o'clock in the afternoon, travelled the whole day and the whole night and arrived at Maboko, Athi River, at 6.00 a.m. the following morning.

5 April 1956

At the Athi River Railway station we found the camp commandant and a group of camp warders waiting for us. We boarded two lorries which took us to Athi River Detention Camp where we arrived at around 7.00 o'clock in the morning. We disembarked on Compound no. 9. As they removed our handcuffs many detainees passed our place of disembarkation on their way to work and exchanged greetings with us. After they had carried out a body inspection on us we were allowed to go and bathe and take a rest throughout that day.

7

Brainwashing in Athi River

5 April 1956 to 15 February 1957

After getting to Athi River I was no longer able to record events on a day-to-day basis as I had generally been doing earlier. However, I remained quite conscious of events and what follows in these three final chapters concludes the story of my seven years' life in colonial detention camps in Emergency Kenya.

The effect of our removal from Manda island far from being beneficial proved to be traumatic. It was part of a colonial design—to break what had been a community of detainees and scatter the fragments to all the corners of Kenya Colony. Our people were scattered to far-flung detention camps in Kwale, Lodwar, Mageta, Seyusi, Mwea and Athi River, while a remnant remained on Manda island. The idea was to break the spirit of mutual support, the authorities being unhappy with the way we took actions in the strength of solidarity, not least of these actions being our constant petitions to higher authorities in the colonial administration. Thus the colonialists invoked the principle they had always applied in the administration of subject Kenya: "Divide in order to rule!"

Our people were thrown from the generally homogeneously-administered camps on Manda island to various categories of camps: "Special Camps", "Work Camps" (where hard labour was imposed) and "Closed Camps" for the hardest of the hardcore. They now came into contact with many different kinds of detainees who at times even struck them with their strangeness: there were camps with many detainees who were captured during the forest armed conflict, the so called "boys of war"; there were the *komerera*, the "sly ones", arrested in the villages after playing a questionable role in the armed conflict; and there were people whose spirits had been broken by long detention who would obey the will of the authorities like zombies.

We found Athi River camp caught in a feverish dispute over the work of the Moral Rearmament (MRA) movement. The authorities were carrying out a purge against the Moral Rearmament, which included the mass confiscation of all books and literature associated with the MRA. I became anxious for the diary I had kept in exercise books—for these materials could be confiscated during this upheaval. I pleaded with a man who hailed from my home area and who was working at the camp, one Paulo Gatuurŭ, to deliver the box containing the exercise books to my home. I did not disclose to him the box contained these writings. Gatuurŭ offered to have the box delivered to his

175

shop at Karatina market. When my wife was released from Kamĩtĩ Women's Detention camp in 1957 I wrote to her and instructed her to collect the box from Paulo Gatuurũ's shop.

Athi River detention camp was far bigger than all the other camps in which I had been detained. The camp was constructed during the Second World War (1939-1945) for incarcerating Italian prisoners-of-war. There were 10 buildings for housing Mau Mau detainees. These were surrounded by a high fence of densely arranged barbed wire. Each building block was a vast hall divided into 4 areas by barbed wire. Each area would accommodate about 80 people. The whole camp at any one time would hold about 2 000 detainees. Blocks 8 and 9 were built separately from the other blocks. As we learned from detainees who had been at Athi River during 1953 and 1954, such as Nahashon Ngarĩ, Kame Mũhoro, Maina Gĩthĩnji and others, Block 9 had been used to house women detainees since Kamĩtĩ Women's Prison was not in use at that time. Some of those women were the same women who had been arrested with us at the beginning of the Emergency: Rebeka Njeeri, Sera Sarai, Cecilia Wanjikũ, Wangũi Gakũrũ, Priscilla Wambakĩ, Nyagĩcirũ Mbote, Flora Wanjũgũ, Miriam Wanjirũ Ndegwa, Wanjukũ Gordon, Nyamacaki Kagondu, and others. There were 200 women in all.

Outside the camp there was a big cinema hall built by the Italian prisoners-of-war. People would also use this hall for concerts; and on Sundays it was used as a church.

In accordance with the plans of the colonial administration Athi River camp was intended to serve as the Main "Rehabilitation Centre". Athi River stood at a major junction near the end of what the authorities called the "pipeline": for detainees would leave the other camps like Manda, Manyani, Mageta, Lodwar and pass through Athi River for rehabilitation, or, more accurately, brainwashing, before being allowed to move nearer home.

On 6th April 1956, the Liaison Officer and the Chief Rehabilitation Officer, Major Breckenridge—J.M. Kariũki in his book *Mau Mau Detainee* refers to him by the fictitious name Rochester—came to see us where we were quartered. He said he would deal with our cases later; for he wanted us to experience at first hand people's confessions at a mass meeting, as had become the practice at Athi River. Breckenridge was no stranger to those from Takwa—he had come to Takwa on 20th March 1956 in the company of Ndegwa Gĩkuhĩ and other collaborator elders from Gĩkũyũland.

On the same day ten people arrived from Manyani camp. I saw Cange Waciira among them. He was a laboratory worker with the Government Chemist before his arrest. After searches had been carried out on their bodies and belongings they were taken to another block; we had earlier heard they would be brought to our block.

When we got to Athi River we found 26 people, allegedly fanatic members of the Moral Rearmament (MRA), had been isolated in Block 10. They would not be allowed to get into contact with us, for fear that they may infect us with MRA beliefs and ideas. One young man, a member of the MRA, came to grief for as much as saying hello to us: he received a ferocious slap from an imperialist British Special Branch officer. He was warned to keep his distance for we were not MRA people; it did not matter that we were bewildered, in our ignorance about what MRA was all about. But we did learn the names of some of the 26 people condemned to isolation for belonging to the MRA: Mwanīki Mūgwerū, Lucern Kīguta, Nahashon Ngarī, Kībūthū Mūturi, David Mathu, Jeremia Njīrainī, Paul Gītata, Kenneth Thugī, S. Njomo Njūgūna, Stanley Kīnga, Albert Thimba, Nahashon Wawerū, Benjamin Kahīīhia, Thuū Kīgera and Peter Kahūūra.

As I would later learn, these friends of ours were being maligned for being serious believers in the ideas of the MRA movement and for insisting on propagating these ideas. I was also to learn that the MRA was neither a religion, nor a political party; and it was not any particular individual's ideology. MRA was a movement which drew membership from the whole international community; it was an association of individuals who were committed to transforming their lives by making their hearts new. MRA accommodated people of all races, nationalities, and religions as well as all types of professions— doctors, teachers, the very wealthy, the very well educated and the not so well educated could all become members of the MRA.

Central tenets or ideas in the movement's teachings are: 1. Trustworthiness or Honesty; 2. Humility; 3. Cleanliness; and 4. Love for One Another. The movement believes in promotion of genuine and lasting peace; in the creation of wealth for one's country and in the rejection of oppression and exploitation between people. The movement rejects the kind of self-righteousness where people tend to accuse others and allocate guilt. It teaches that when you point your finger at another person, three of your fingers remain pointing at you!

This idea really used to please the detainees, but the interrogators were hardly amused, and the saying about the pointing fingers seemed designed to demand self-questioning for the interrogators whose actions and behaviour were hardly beyond reproach.

How did MRA ideas infiltrate the camp? The colonial authorities without first studying all the implications assigned MRA people to the work of rehabilitation. They were supposed to induce confessions of the Mau Mau oaths by the detainees. The MRA rehabilitation people, in the absence of clear working guidelines from the colonial authorities, used their own methods of obtaining confessions. Their method was simple: to make good MRA people out of the detainees by teaching the basic ideas of the movement to them: honesty, humility, cleanliness and love for one another. And the detainees embraced many of the MRA ideas as their own, interpreting them in their own way and in their favour. When the movement taught that people should not oppress and exploit others, they were clear in their minds that it was the authorities who should stop oppressing them, for what greater oppression could there be than confinement and exile in a detention camp? And they welcomed the idea of establishing a relationship of mutual love—and solidarity—among themselves.

The MRA's method of never using physical methods to extract confessions also appealed to the detainees. Their argument was that before a person can make any meaningful confession of the oath and other wrong doing he must first have a genuine change of heart; the mere fact of making a confession by one's mouth did not constitute genuine repentance. The MRA people, therefore, used reasonable persuasion to make people confess the Mau Mau vows they had made, and the bad things they had done.

The white leaders of the MRA in Athi River were Col. Alan Knight, G.B.W. Anderson and Guy Grant. But a large number of officers affiliated to the MRA used to come quite often to carry out work in rehabilitation. In addition they used to obtain assistance from Gĩkũyũ and non-Gĩkũyũ church people, among them Daudi Mĩtaarũ, Kĩhũũrani Gatundu, Johana Nyenjeri, or white priests like Rev. Church of the Anglican Church and Father Colleton of the Roman Catholic Church.

The ultimate objective of the MRA movement was to wage a subtle and cunning ideological struggle against the Mau Mau movement. A person who joined the MRA in effect ceased to be a member of Mau Mau—he had been won over. The MRA made a spectacular success—for many detainees were deceived into joining it. Almost all the detainees we found at Athi River had become members of the MRA and they had confessed to having taken the oath. Furthermore they became convinced that it was wrong to have taken up arms and to have used violence in demanding back land and national independence. They had accepted the MRA position that it was possible to continue the struggle for land and freedom without bloodshed.

And yet the colonial authorities were not completely happy with the work of the MRA. The reason for this was that many detainees did not see MRA as hostile to Mau Mau's objectives; indeed they seemed to equate the objectives of the MRA and those of Mau Mau. The authorities, seeing that detainees made confessions to the MRA while still holding to their fundamental nationalist positions and hardly making a clean break with their past, suspended the work of the MRA in rehabilitation. Further, the authorities ordered fresh interrogations of those people who had joined the MRA; these interrogations should be carried in accordance with a new procedure that had been introduced in Athi River. Rather than these people who had been in the hands of the MRA moving further down the pipeline, they remained in the camp while others were exiled to Mukowe in the Coast Province.

When we arrived at Athi River we found the new interrogation/rehabilitation procedure, only recently introduced, in force. This procedure was the brainchild of imperialist Breckenridge and his wife, whom the detainees had nicknamed Njeeri. The people who were assisting Breckenridge in carrying out this procedure included, Jeremiah Kĩereinĩ, who was a Rehabilitation officer, and Benjamin Wang'endo, who was Kĩereinĩ's assistant. Ndegwa Gĩkuhĩ was the leader of the interrogators. Finally they had brought a whole team of collaborators and loyalists from Gĩkũyũ, Embu and Merũ and employed them as "screening and classification elders". There were more than 10 screening and classification courts at Athi River to which these elders were assigned. These are some of the elders: Johana Nyenjeri and Junias Kĩmarũ (who were also church preachers); Bedan Mbangwa, Pharis Wahome, Nehemia Kigoro, Paul Gatuurũ, Girshon Waciira, Habili, Wilson Gĩtumbu, Robert Kang'ethe and Anthony Kĩronji.

Each screening and classification court had a clerk who would maintain a record in the English language of the questions put to the detainee and the answers given by the detainee during interrogation. When we got to Athi River the following people were serving as clerks: Kamau Mĩthiori, Andrew Kamau, Jethel Gatume, Matthew Kĩmani, Njenga Kĩmani, Mwathe Ndegwa, George Gĩthii, John Kĩmiti and Joshua Mwanĩki.

There were also Special Branch offices at Athi River. People who had been actively involved in politics before detention and people who had held positions of leadership in the actual Mau Mau war had to appear before the Special Branch committees. After making their confessions before these committees detainees would be taken to Yatta camp where further screening would be carried out; some would be released, others would be condemned to imprisonment for terms of many years while others would be condemned to life imprisonment.

After we had been two days at Athi River Goodale, the Special Branch officer who had come to Takwa in March to carry out a classification of detainees, came to our quarters and asked four of us —myself, Romano Njamumo, Cyrus Gakuũ and Samuel Mbũrũ—to follow him to his office. As we went past an interrogation court we heard a man crying out in pain as they assaulted him to obtain confessions. As we followed the imperialist officer we whispered among ourselves that perhaps we were going to meet the same fate—to have our intestines cleaned inside out. The Special Branch offices were at the far end— beyond the interrogation and screening courts. Goodale entered one of the offices and left us sitting on a form outside the office, under the guard of a warder.

After about five minutes the imperialist officer came out and asked me to follow him in. Inside I found another imperialist officer sitting in front of a large pile of books, many of them in Gĩkũyũ, heaped on the table. He ordered me to pick out the books I had personally authored. There were books written by Henry Mworia, Mwanĩki Mũgwerũ, and Kĩnuthia Mũgĩĩa; I also saw Kenyatta's book *Kenya Bũruri wa Ngũĩ* ("Kenya, Land of Disputes") and Peter Mbiyũ's *Ithaka Ciarĩ Ciitũ* ("All the Land Belonged to Us").

I picked out my books as follows:

1. *Ngwenda Ũnjũrage* ("Go Ahead! Kill Me"); 2. *Roho ya Kiume na Bidii kwa Mwafrika* ("The Spirit of Manhood and Perseverence for Africans"); 3. *Wanawake Siku Hizi* ("Women Today"); 4. *O Kirima Ngagũa* ("To Whatever Destination"); 5. *Ihu Nĩ Rĩau?* ("Who Caused the Pregnancy?"); 6. *Mageria Nomo Mahota* ("Make the Attempt to Succeed"); 7. *Mũrata wa Mwene* ("The Owner's Friend"); 8. *Kĩenyũ kĩa Ngai Kĩrĩma-inĩ gĩa Tũmũtũmũ* ("God's Own Fragment (Warrior) on the Hills of Tũmũtũmũ"); 9. *Kĩguni gĩa Twana* ("What Benefits Little Children?"). As well there was a printed copy of the pamphlet *Wĩtĩkio wa Gĩkũyũ na Mũmbi*, "The Creed of Gĩkũyũ and Mũmbi", and copies of *Waigua Atĩa*, my monthly newsmagazine. Other books had been written by different authors and published by myself; they were now on display: 1. *Kenya nĩ Yakwa* ("Kenya Is My Land"); 2. *Mĩikarĩre ya Thikwota* ("The Conditions Under which Squatters Live"); 3. *Mwarĩ Mwerũ nĩ Magambo* ("A Beautiful Woman is a Woman of Woe"); 4. *Riua Rĩtanathũa* ("Before the Sun Sets"); 5. *Nyĩmbo cia Gĩkũyũ na Mũmbi* ("Hymns to Gĩkũyũ and Mũmbi"); and 6. *Kamũingĩ Koyaga Ndĩrĩ* ("Unity Is Strength").

The imperialist officer picked the little book in Kiswahili, *Roho ya Kiume na Bidii kwa Mwafrika*, which I had written in 1948, and asked: "What was your objective in writing this pamphlet?"

I answered vaguely that I was simply putting to paper ideas gathered from different people.

He asked, "What are the readers supposed to do? 'It is better to die,' you say. Why?"

I answered I used the licence of hyperbole to underline my ideas. He said I was lying. I said I did not know of an alternative way of putting it—but the book had said everything and had given reasons for every statement.

He closed one eye, regarded me and declared: "Didn't you take the Mau Mau oath and then become terribly embittered, with your conviction that your land had been taken? Don't you demand in another part of the book: 'For how long will we endure this deprivation?' "

I didn't say a word, and the man went on, "All your doings have demonstrated beyond any doubt that you are a sower of the seeds of conflict and insurrection. You are a dangerous man for you fan the flames of bitterness and anger in people's hearts so that people may revolt against the Government.

My well considered opinion is that you are incapable of changing, you can only resort to deception; you should be held in detention until peace is restored to the country."

He read briefly from the file of my case, then looked into my eyes and said, "Even interrogation officers who saw you in Manda and Takwa have put it on record that you have been instrumental in preventing Christianity from taking firm roots in Gĩkũyũ country where you have been implanting creeds of darkness."

He asked sarcastically, "Can Gĩkũyũ and Mũmbi ever be the object of people's belief?" and then broke into a diatribe, "The Devil's own creed! Darkness, darkness and more darkness! And you shamelessly teach adults and children to express belief in Satanic ideas! Can you find your way to repentance for misleading your own people, thousands upon thousands of them?"

This time I did say "Yes, I will repent if there are people I have misled."

He sprang to his feet, glared at me and shouted, "What did you say? Do you want a demonstration that all detainees at this camp regard you as an enemy? You don't know they have all denounced all your books as Satanic. I am warning you! This is Athi River and not Manda where you were given to all kinds of boasting. Here you must confess all the Mau Mau oaths you have taken, for they are known; here you must yourself renounce in a mass meeting your past actions, such as these writings written out of misdirected pride and the songs you have been teaching people!"

He took the copy of a book of songs whose cover bore the portrait of Mathenge wa Mĩrũgĩ and said, "In the opinion of the interrogators this man, Mathenge Mĩrũgĩ, who calls himself a Mau Mau general, is your friend. Is this correct?"

I answered he was known to me before I was detained.

He asked, "Is he not from your home, Nyeri?"

I answered that my home was Mathĩra whereas Mathenge was from Ũthaya.

He asked, "But both of you were staying in Nairobi when you composed these songs?"

I said yes.

He commented, "So you were aware how he made preparations to launch a war from the forests ! "

"There was no war," I said, "when I was arrested."

He snarled at me, "What can you teach me I don't know? We know when you started planning the Mau Mau insurrection. We have records of your history in these very offices. We know you were a major propagandist for Mau Mau; you taught terrorism and ideas steeped in dark ignorance. You should have been charged in a court of law so that you could be imprisoned for a long term. All the necessary evidence was available—in these books of yours!"

I took courage in my hands and said that I had committed no offence beyond writing those books.

After the officer had taken some notes on a piece of paper, he called the warder and instructed him to take me to my block. Before I walked out of the door, he called out that he would be seeing me later after I had confessed all my oaths; then he paused and said with final emphasis: "for confess you must and will!"

Outside the office my colleagues had disappeared. I asked the warder, a Kipsigis man, where they had got to. They had been taken to Mbagathi, he said. I was surprised: "To do what there?" I asked. The warder explained that this was a work camp nicknamed "Luvai's place". This camp was the venue of punishing labour where people worked under the lash like draft cattle. People would stab their feet with their digging fork (mattock) so that they could earn a respite in hospital from the back breaking work.

I did not allow myself to worry unduly about my friends. I reasoned that they hadn't had their personal belongings so they would only be away from Athi River temporarily. But when I got back to our block I learnt to my chagrin that they had been brought to collect their things. They did not return to Athi River.

At 3.00 p.m. on the same day Ndegwa Gĩkuhĩ and another interrogator came to our Block. With them were four detainees who had been displayed to us as the exemplary people who had been cleansed. Ndegwa explained that a person must first confess all the oaths he had taken and all the crimes he had committed, and then demonstrate his repentance by offering full cooperation to the Government. Pharis Wahome, the other interrogator, said it was futile for a detainee to continue withholding information from the interrogators. Most people back home had already made their confessions and they had disclosed the names and acts of people in detention camps. Then one of the exemplary detainees spoke. He had confessed the oath because it had become evident that the initial objectives had been betrayed by some people. We had not taken the oath to indulge in murder among ourselves. The world had seen the actions of Mau Mau—and it had already passed its judgment. We should confess our oath so that we could be allowed to go home, there to work towards the restoration of peace.

Ndegwa Gĩkuhĩ announced that we would soon transfer to Block no. 5, where we would be able to mix with our friends who had come from other camps. Tomorrow was Sunday, he reminded us, and all detainees were required to go and pray to God. In the morning of Monday we would attend a confession session at a mass meeting, so that we could see and hear how such confessions were made.

We had been in Block 9 before shifting to 5. Block 9 would later become the home of the cleansed and the accepted—those who had freely talked about their past doings. They were rewarded by being made assistant interrogators in classification courts; others became clerks, others interpreters while yet others were assigned work in the Camp hospital.

There were many detainees in Block 5 who had, like us, just recently come to Athi River. They had come from Manyani and Mackinnon Road. I met people who were known to me such as Josto Kĩnyoori, Kamau Wang'ombe, Thũmbĩ Weerũ, Hiram Gatimũ and Kĩmani Ruo, who had acquired a B.A. degree just before he was arrested. Quite a number of people from Manyani had made fake confessions to save themselves from beatings. People would incriminate fictitious people in giving information about their oathing: A person may say he was oathed by one Mũtharitĩ wa Riigĩ ("Door Handle son of Door") and that he had been taken to the oathing venue by one Rũrĩĩo wa Mũitĩrĩro ("Potato Vine son of Roofing Beam").

These people told us they had been rounded up on 24 April 1954 under Operation Anvil. This operation was greater than any other that had taken place before. According to these people, the operation had put all Agĩkũyũ, Embu and Merũ people under siege in Nairobi, and especially in Bahati and Makadara locations where most of these people used to live. The men had been rounded up and transported to a camp at Langata where they had been beaten up by homeguards and soldiers and robbed of all their money. All their clothes and shoes had been taken from them—except their underwear. Then they had been screened: hooded spies-cum-Government-informers (wearing large gowns which covered them from head to toe and only left two slits through which they could study people) had picked out the people who were "guilty" and were to be detained. Some people were released, but the majority, about 10,000 people, had been transported to detention camps in Manyani and Mackinnon Road. The wives and children of people who were rounded up had been taken to their villages.

I spoke with Kĩmani wa Ruuo. Why this unceasing song in Athi River about confessing the oath? I asked him. Nobody was talking about anything else. Kĩmani explained that things started going wrong when those drifters called komerera, the sly ones, started to move to the civilian villages. These people had gone to the forests to fight but had no clear understanding of the cause they were fighting for. They were expelled by the honest freedom fighters from the forests for deviant behaviour and actions that damaged the whole ideology and manner of execution of the Mau Mau armed struggle. When they came back to the civilian villages nobody knew exactly where they stood, they used a strategem of deception and in their directionlessness they alienated, and incurred the hatred of, both antagonists in the struggle—the colonial Government and the Mau Mau freedom movement. When they were rounded up and detained they showed themselves up for what they were—spineless drifters who revealed all the secrets of the people's movement without any compunction. They became the greatest danger to genuine freedom fighters both in the camps and prisons and in the forest. The *komerera*, according to Kĩmani wa Ruuo, infected the detention camps with the epidemic of confessions.

But Nahashon Ngarĩ had the story quite different. Large-scale confessions of the oath dated back to the beginning of 1954. At a detention camp in Rũkenya which had come to be called "Luvai's Place" after the name of the brutal imperialist commandant, who used to speak Kikamba, detainees were forced to make confessions after terrible torture and beatings. There had been no way out: detainees had seen many people die under torture.

Many of the detainees who had come from Manyani had been at the fore-front of the armed struggle. Some of them had held positions of command; others had participated in particular battles in the countryside. Others had operated from Nairobi to back the war effort—collecting money for buying weapons, stealing guns, buying metal piping and other material for home-manufacture of firearms, organising the delivery of drugs, medicine and food to the forest fighters, as well as other necessary activities.

In their resistance to confessions, they developed an uncanny cunning and sought to escape from having to confess by deceiving the authorities. In their cunning they readily adopted the colonial authorities' theory that there was not a single Mũgĩkũyũ, Mũembu or Mũmĩĩrũ who had not taken the oath. But they would give a fictitious version of events—talking about things like enforced oathing at night by strangers and oathing venues holding faceless multitudes who took the oath under threat and intimidation. They would also claim to have gone through mass cleansing ceremonies. They did not manage to fool the authorities for long, and a policy of deporting such people to hard labour camps—to Mwea, Gathigiriri, Karaba, Kandongu and Tebere, where vast areas of marshland were being prepared for rice-growing—was adopted. People would be required to do designated amounts of work and they would get no evening meal if they failed to complete the day's measure of work.

On Monday morning we went to work. The Manda group of detainees was formed into a dam-digging work gang. We had to go out of the camp area to a rocky patch of earth. We would dig using mattocks into the hard rock and murram. We were shown how to carry *karai's* (iron basins) of murram on our heads by older Athi River detainees. People would form a round crown of dry grass and place it on their heads to cushion the heavy *karais*.

Other people went outside the camp area to work on a large farm, which was more than 30 acres. It was planted with a big variety of crops—cabbages, onions, sweet potato vines, bananas, cassava, maize and beans. This farm used to feed the whole camp, supplying cabbage as relish for the detainees' *ugali* and food for the white and black camp personnel. The Rehabilitation home-guards owned individual plots within the boundaries of this farm.

Compound cleaning was allocated on an alternating basis—people from one block doing the work for a week before another block took over. Cleaning also included disposal of the night soil. Other domestic work included cooking, clothes repair, car repair and carpentry.

Those people who went to work outside the camp went under the escort of armed guards. We were told about an incident that had happened in 1954. Ten people had been taken out of camp to dispose of night soil by guards armed with guns. They had surprised the guards, and seized their guns and left them with their hands and legs tied. The ten people had then fled to the forest.

At Athi River people would work in the morning hours, up to 1.00 o'clock in the afternoon. After work arrangements would be made for people to be involved in other activities. Sometimes people would go and listen to lectures on the history of Kenya. Such lectures would invariably demonstrate the bene-ficence of the British imperialists; for Kenya and Africa in general had been areas of great darkness; the British had brought a reign of light and profit. On other occasions detainees would go to the field to perform cultural songs, dances and concerts, or they would go to play football in club competitions which were expertly organised by one Dickson Kabui. Or they may be taken to watch films at the cinema hall or concerts presented by other detainees. The films and concerts were meant to provide a soothing escape from our troubled and heavy condition.

But the central concern of Athi River Detention Camp remained the extraction of confessions and carrying out of brainwashing. Each day about thirty people would be candidates for interrogation. The names of candidates for interrogation the following day would be called out through the loud-speaker public address system during the night. Every house had a loud speaker connected to this system. When they read out the names of people who would be interrogated, they would also indicate which screening court each detainee should attend.

The public address system was used for other purposes, for example to deliver sermons, and to make announcements about things that had happened. But the system was essentially a colonial propaganda tool: loyalist collaborators like colonial chiefs who had visited Athi River would use it to address us, and sermon upon sermon would be given on the system about the virtues of con-fession, the evil of Mau Mau, and the benefits of being allowed to go home.

The system was a constant source of irritation and nagging torture for those people who had withheld confession, whom it would persistently revile. Some people would bury themselves in their blankets immediately the system started broadcasting, in an impotent protest against the propaganda of the colonialists and their lackeys.

And yet it was not an easy thing to repudiate the nationalist vows in order to escape the constant nagging. Many detainees held tightly to the vows of the nationalist Mau Mau movement, living under the conviction that once a person gave away the secrets under which these vows were made, he would have made the ultimate betrayal of the cause, and as it were he would be divested of his nationalist courage and love for his land. Defeat was *not* in arrest and detention; it was in giving all the secrets to the enemy. And some people had been initiated into deep secrets and made grave vows—especially the commanders of the nationalist war. People had made vows and sworn secrecy by invoking the name of Ngai, the Almighty God, and invoking the eternal Earth. This was not a light thing. Some detainees would go for interrogation carrying a symbolic lump of earth on their bodies for strength and courage.

Monday 9th April 1956: this was the first day for us "Manda people" to attend the ceremony of confession in a mass meeting. Every detainee attended this ceremony and all interrogation and rehabilitation officers and screening court workers were present. The venue was a field in the quadrangle between the camp buildings. Detainees sat on the grass in the wide field, and the Rehabilitation officer, the screening and classification court elders and clerks sat on chairs facing the multitude of detainees.

As was the custom, the ceremony opened with the Chief Screening Officer making an announcement. He announced that a group of detainees, who had been rounded up under the Governor's Detention Order, had recently arrived from Manda island where they had been held since the declaration of the Emergency. One of these detainees, the Rehabilitation officer declared, was Gakaara wa Wanjaũ, "who is no doubt very well known to most of you. He is the writer of those songs you used to sing to demand land and freedom. He is also the author of Mau Mau creeds and prayers. We went and collected these people from Manda to come and witness for themselves a confession of the Mau Mau oaths; up to now they are not aware the oaths were confessed a long time ago!'

He then made remarks about detainees from Manyani. They had not done a proper disclosure yet and they should stop lying, he said. He then explained that once a good number of people had done satisfactory confession they would be collected by the chiefs from their home areas and assigned to their District or Division Work Camps. After that they would be eligible for release if they satisfied local Government workers and local community leaders. The chiefs were just about to visit Athi River and arrangements were in hand to give an opportunity to the G.D.O. detainees to confess their doings so that they could go home as soon as possible.

After that the Rehabilitation Officer said all people who were prepared to make their confessions should stand up. A young man called Toto Karība, who had been in the forest fighting and who had made a detailed disclosure of his doings, was asked to stand and demonstrate to the Manda visitors how proper confessions were given.

Toto Karība, "Little Karība": the name meant the young man was General Karība's assistant. He moved in front of the crowd of detainees and spoke facing us all.

His first evil act, he told us, was to take the Mau Mau oath, for all his wrong doing flowed from the vows of that oath. He had taken his first oath in January 1953 when he was still in school. He gave the names of the people who took him to the oathing venue and the person who administered the oath to him; and he disclosed that he had been confirmed as one of Kenyatta's soldiers. He disclosed how he took the "Platoon" oath, his second oath, how he left school and went to the forest to join the army under General Karība's command. He disclosed how he took his third oath, the oath of the fighters, in the forest. How he had joined a band of fighters which had raided a white settler's farm in Naro Moru and made away with firearms, how he and others had beaten up and maimed homeguards who had spied on them as they collected food from the villages and how they had raided a settler's ranch in Nanyuki, seized cattle and killed the herdsmen. He said where they used to hide in the forest. He explained how they organised the famous Battle of Rūirū River in Kaaruthi village and how they were treated after their victory to a feast where two bulls were slaughtered by the community of Kaaruthi. He explained how his exploits at the battle of a place called Kabaru earned him promotion to become General Karība's assistant or Little Karība, and he went on to talk about how he had been captured.

After Toto Karība's confession, five other detainees made their confessions. Some of them confessed to having killed collaborators, putting their bodies in sackcloth bags before disposal in rivers. Others disclosed that they used to keep money for the Mau Mau movement and they indicated how much money remained in the hiding places. Others talked about carrying out weird ceremonies including killing dogs and cats and impaling their carcases to the ground.

After a detainee had completed his testimony questions would be put to him or he would be reminded of certain other things for his personal confirmation. Finally, the detainee would declare that he had offered himself wholly to the Government to assist in any work towards the restoration of peace.

In later confession ses ions we were to notice that many detainees mentioned only a few of their past actions and waited for prompting by the interrogators. And it became clear that the interrogators' satisfaction rose in proportion to the number of people implicated in oath taking and acts of violence during the confession. If those people whose names were mentioned had not made their confessions, a record of their names and their alleged actions was opened.

This mass meeting confession was a spectacle of amazement to those of us who had come from Manda. Yes, we were to see people competing to disclose secrets, to open up about the vows of the oath. Why this drastic step? There were many theories. We were told a number of detainees had already arrived home from Athi River and they were writing from the villages to detainees left at Athi River urging them to get it over with, to make their confessions and earn a passage home. And the colonial propaganda machine never ceased working—telling the detainees about the imminent visitation by the chiefs from their home areas.

And another theory rested on the nature of the initial oath taking. As far as the ideologically clear Mau Mau leadership was concerned the oath was necessary to foster a deeply-felt unity and solidarity and to instil devotion for the land and its people as well as single-minded courage and determination in waging struggle for land and freedom in order to create, on the ruins of the old colonial order, a new equitable and just order. The leadership's policy was, therefore, to have oaths administered on a mass-basis in all the land of Agĩkũyũ, Aembu and Amĩĩru. The result was that different people took the oath for different reasons and understood the oath differently. A good number took the oath out of a clear-sighted conviction. Others took it out of the fear of reprisals from the movement, and yet others took it because it was part of a mass political action and they were carried by the mass wave. When the epidemic of confessions broke out these latter people were again carried off on the wave—and they confessed.

Again, many people had become weary of their stay in detention camps. Others felt the urgent need to go home when they heard stories about the suffering of their people back home; some were bereaved, after home-guards killed members of their families; the children of some had virtually been left without a guardian or helper; others had lost property and land to loyalists and homeguards, and the houses of some had been razed to the ground by vengeful homeguards. There was no end of problems back home for detained people.

The colonial authorities had tried to understand the situation in order to effectively exploit it. They needed to know what kind of people they were dealing with then asking for a confession: how deep was a person's Mau Mau convictions and how hardboiled in nationalist politics was a person? This was why "classification" courts had been set up. People who were thought to be hardboiled were handled by "special courts".

But it was not all smooth sailing for the interrogators. The hardhearted among the freedom fighters had made it an extra and secret vow—never to accept voluntary confessions. They would only confess after physical torture, this offering some consolation. And it remained a puzzle to the colonialist authorities the great hold the Mau Mau oath had on the thinking of the Mũgĩkũyũ, Mũembu or Mũmĩĩrũ. For they had in the past gone as far as carrying out mass cleansing ceremonies, to eradicate once and for all the taboo effects of the oath, only later to hear that the very people who had been cleansed had again taken vows under a new oath.

What colonialists never knew was that confession or no confession, cleaning or no cleansing, no Mūgīkūyū, Mūembu or Mūmīīrū could take this enforced undertaking seriously, that he would stop agitating for land. For he longed to go back home to the solace of his own land or his clan's land. And for those three peoples land is a man's and man's family's mainstay and a man without land is a person of little substance.

My interrogation started in a "special court" on 9 May 1956. For two days I was interrogated under the supervision of "Rehabilitation" officers, and on the third day I was taken back to the Special Branch department. The fact that I had taken the oath would have been obvious to the initiated from a reading of my books, and especially from the things I had written in the news-magazine *Waigua Atīa?* and the introductory comments I had published on the card carrying "The Creed of Gīkūyū and Mūmbi". For on the card of the Creed I had written that it should be bought or read or kept by any person who was 'unclean". The Rehabilitation elders readily and correctly interpreted "unclean" to mean unoathed.

The imperialist Special Branch officer and his African lackeys found it difficult to believe that I had taken only one oath, the first, called "the oath of unity", of 1952. The imperialist British officer was under the impression that a person who spoke or wrote out of a deep conviction, or did acts of real courage must have taken a multiplicity of oaths. Furthermore, there was my book *Roho ya Bidii* which had been written in 1948 and which seemed to exhibit a spirit of determined defiance. Therefore, the interrogators suspected I had taken the Platoon Oath before writing this book.

I would like to state here that it is not only the interrogators who doubted the verocity of my story that I had taken only one oath. From the books I had written and the newspapers I had published before my 1952 oathing many people had taken it for granted that I was an initiated nationalist. But they fact that was I had started my major nationalist activities before taking the oath.

How had I come to take the oath? I and one Gītuīku Njogu, who was a relatively senior officer with the Nairobi City Council, joined the Nairobi branch of a new home-based organisation called Kīrīmūkūyū Parents Educational Association. (This organisation collected funds for Karani Mūriūki's education abroad; he read for a degree in engineering in India from 1952 and later went to England.) Gītuīku was elected chairman of the branch council and I was elected secretary. The other members of the council were: Mwangi Mbeū, Kaigīrīra Gaithi, Nyagīcirū Mbote, and Mathūthi Mūikia. These are the people who took us to Njirū in Nairobi to be initiated through the Mau Mau oath into the heroic service of our people.

Around this period imperialist Breckenridge granted "parole" to a small number of detainees: under this arrangement the detainee would become an employee of the Government administration for six months before his case would be finally reviewed for release. A detainee on "parole", would be given a khaki uniform, would be supplied with food and receive a token salary of Shs. 20.00 a month, and would stop living in Block 9 and get housing away from the other detainees. He would also receive a pass card bearing both Commandant Breckenridge's signature and the signature of the Camp Chief of Security allowing him to go outside the camp confines up to 8.00 o'clock in the evening. If a paroled detainee so chose he could obtain a "pass" to enable him to go to Nairobi and back. People from Kĩambuu whose homes were close to Nairobi even made it to their homes and come back to Athi River.

Before I could be placed on parole the chief Rehabilitation Officer decided to put me on test—to see whether or not I had repudiated the Mau Mau ideology. I became eligible to live in Block 9 on 18th May 1956 and I was assigned my old work—writing. Only this time I must write anti-Mau Mau propaganda such as anti-Mau Mau songs, plays and concerts. There I was, I was told: I would be tested in work of my experience!

I was put into an office all alone. Those books which had been confiscated from the MRA disciples were all there. I was curious to know what this MRA was all about, and I stole time to delve into some of the books, including *Remaking the World* by Frank Buchman, *The World Re-built* by Peter Howard and Peter Howard's play *Forgotten Factor*.

Titus Mbathi had just recently arrived at Athi River to take the post of Assistant Community Development Officer (A.C.D.O.). Now and then he would come to my office to make suggestions about the kind of things I should write. But most of the time he was busy teaching the camp teachers what to teach about the history of Kenya, good agricultural practices, forest conservation, or about the requirements of community life, and so forth.

I was able to look at the anti-Mau Mau songs which the MRA had written for the Government's propaganda effort. Most of the time the writer had simply substituted anti-Mau Mau words for the words the Mau Mau movement had used in *its* songs. I would write my own materials, songs and plays and take them to Rehabilitation Officer, J. Kĩereinĩ for vetting. Kĩereinĩ would verify whether or not I had reviled Mau Mau satisfactorily. He would also discuss the materials with the senior British officers, after translating them from the Gĩkũyũ to English. If the materials were passed by the imperialist authorities, the plays would be eligible for performance by the detainees; normally, I would direct the plays and concerts I had written.

It was during this period when I wrote a fairly long play entitled *Reke*

Aciirithio nĩ Mehia Maake ("Let the Guilt of His Crimes Weigh Heavy on His Conscience"), which left a lot of doubt about the state of my rehabilitation in the minds of the interrogations and rehabilitation officers. The main character in the play was Zakayo, a detainee who had organised a secret council in the camp whose aim was to prevent people from confessing the oath. But one day a pastor from home came to preach the word of God at the camp, after which he had a conversation with Zakayo. The pastor informed Zakayo that his older wife had been arrested and detained at Kamĩtĩ after she had been denounced to the authorities by Labani, Zakayo's business partner. The preacher informed Zakayo that Labani had become a homeguard. He had removed Zakayo's son from their joint shop and was cohabiting with Zakayo's younger wife. His home was in shambles. He should give up his resistance, make a confession in order to go back home to restore the integrity of his home.

Zakayo had immediately gone to the Rehabilitation officer and made a clean breast of all the things he had done in the past. He was released and prepared to go home to restore his broken home. When he got home he found that his older wife had returned from Kamĩtĩ. His younger wife welcomed him home and revealed that she had all along been secretly setting money aside from the shop, which had been under her management since Zakayo's son was sent away by Labani; all along she was deceiving Labani and waiting for Zakayo's return. She took out bundles of the money she had set aside. It was when the money was being handed to Zakayo that Labani came in, intending to offer an insincere welcome to his old business partner. At the sight before him he collapsed and fainted. As he lay there unconsious, Zakayo, his wives and son would comment, "Let the guilt of his crimes weigh heavy on his conscience."

The play with a cast of 20 actors was rehearsed under me and performed under my direction on 20 July 1956 for the first time. All the detainees, warders and workers in rehabilitation courts watched the play. The first performance was not attended by Major Breckenridge. But after "Njeeri", Breckenridge's wife, as we used to call her, Kĩereinĩ and Mbathi had seen it, they said the Commandant must see it. So the play was performed for Breckenridge's benefit on 21 July 1956. And then the Major recommended that the British Special Branch officers should see it. So a large group of Special Branch officers, some of them invited from Nairobi, came to see the play on 9 August 1956.

I was under the impression, from the demands for extra performances, that everybody was deriving a lot of pleasure from my play. How mistaken I was! The rehabilitation authorities saw the play in a very different light. In their view, the play was not designed to urge a change of heart in detainees, but rather to foster hatred between detained people and loyalist homeguards. So on 12 August 1956 I was summoned to the Special Branch offices and subjected to rigorous interrogation. What were my objectives, they demanded,

in writing a play in which the homeguard was portrayed as the guilty party.
I assured them I never intended to foster a negative response in the detainees.
They warned me sternly against ever again writing a play which antagonised
one side. My play, they declared, should have come to an end at the stage
where Zakayo made his confession and earned his release.

It was determined that I should be placed a whole step back from parole
for my heart still harboured some resistance to reform.

Some of the cast for the play were: Bedan Kabirũ, Mwangi Wambũgũ,
Paul Gĩtata, Nahashon Wawerũ, James Njenga, Kĩbũĩ Gacuũrĩ, Kenneth
Ng'ang'a, Mũgambi Ndatho, Josia Kamau, Maina Karanja, Gakuũ, Kababwe
Ndũng'u, Kamakia Kariũki, and Jeremia Wanjaũ.

Another assignment was added to my playwriting in August 1956. This was
editing a weekly Camp newspaper called, *Atĩrĩrĩ! Gĩtugĩ kĩa Mũciĩ* "The
Pillar of the Home". It was published in Gĩkũyũ but there was a limited circulation English-language edition entitled simply *The Pillar*. J. M. Kariũki,
assisted by people like Ben Mwega and Linus Maina Gĩthĩnji, would do the
translation from Gĩkũyũ to English.

J. M. Kariũki in his book *Mau Mau Detainee* refers to the workers on
Atĩrĩrĩ. He has used a fictitious name for me—"Benjamin". He describes me as
a good and prolific writer of books in Gĩkũyũ. He says I valued solidarity
among the detainees and always used my cunning to avoid putting fellow
detainees into trouble. He has also said I went on with my work as an author
and a publisher when I left detention.

Other workers on the Camp newspaper were: Kĩnja Kĩbacia, M. Mũũgĩ,
Nahashon Ngarĩ, James Njenga and Cyrus Gakuũ.

In the month of June 1956 colonial chiefs flooded into Athi River Camp from
the Gĩkũyũ, Embu and Mĩĩrũ countrysides. They were housed in a large building
for approximately a week. Each of them brought his own folding bed. The
"good" detainees prepared their food. Some of these people had become chiefs
during the Emergency and they were consequently designated "loyalist" chiefs.
Many of the loyalist chiefs had earned themselves a bad reputation, for they
had sought to excel in waging a ruthless struggle against Mau Mau people,
many of whom they had murdered while having many others sent to detention
camps and criminal prisons. Such were most of the people who would now come
to gloat over information that such and such erstwhile Mau Mau hardcore
had undergone a transformation. I obviously didn't know all the chiefs who
came in January, but I did pick out the following: Charles Koinange, Mũhoya
Kagũmba, Kĩmani Warũhiũ, Daudi Wangũhũ, Karangi Mũrigũ, Perminus
Kĩritũ, Samuel "Speaker", Stanley Kĩama, Mũgane, Nahashon Ngigĩ,
"Chorio" and Benedito Wamũtitũ.

Benedito Wamũtitũ hailed from Mũhĩto ridge where my Father had been killed. He confirmed to me that the people who had been in the murder conspiracy had been unearthed and arrested and they were now detained at the camp at Kangũbiri, Nyeri. I harboured no vengeful feelings against these people. I had come round to accepting that my Father's murder was but one of the manifestations of the fury of a state of war; God had fated my Father to die in this fury. But the question of compensation by the Church of Scotland Mission, which had sent my Father to Mũhĩto, was yet to be settled.

I wrote a letter to my mother who was still being held at Kamĩtĩ, apprising her of the information I had received from Chief Benedito Wamũtitũ. I advised her to give all this information to the interrogation officers at Kamĩtĩ Women's Detention Camp so that the false charge against her and my wife to the effect that they had played a part in the conspiracy to murder my father would be dropped.

The interrogators at Kamĩtĩ refused to believe my mother and in March 1957 I was taken to Kamĩtĩ to give personal testimony. I found my mother waiting for me at the interrogation court. I testified that the chief from Mũhĩto had himself passed on information to me which exonerated my mother. The interrogators said they would carry out their own investigations and if they found the information truthful they would see to the early release of my mother. I enquired about the fate of my wife and the interrogators claimed she had not been implicated in the murder conspiracy, that she had been held on the charge of giving assistance to the terrorist bandits from the forests and keeping funds for Mau Mau. I was not able to see my wife because she had been assigned work, digging up murram, at a site distant from the camp.

My mother was finally released on 14th April 1957.

At Kamĩtĩ there were many women, among them the wives of prominent Mau Mau leaders who had been held under various charges. These were some of the women at Kamĩtĩ: Ngĩna Kenyatta, Mũkami Kĩmaathi, Ng'endo Koinange, Mũthoni wa Mathenge Mĩrũgĩ, Wambũi wa Mbiyũ, Ngunju Karĩba, Rebeka Njeeri, Pricilla Wambakĩ, Sella Kanuthu Kang'ethe, Nyagũthiĩ, Kariũki, Karugi Mũtahi, Njeeri Karanja, Miriam Wanjirũ Ndegwa, Njirikũ Kabũthĩ, Serah Sarai, E. Wairimũ Wagaca, Wangũ Mathia Mũthanjĩ and Miriam Cabangui.

There were six Blocks at Kamĩtĩ Women's Detention Camp. The Block for the extreme hardcore of the women detainees was referred to as the *Magaidi* Block (or Robbers'den); the inmates of this Block were made to wear three armulets on their arms. Then there was the "Hyenas" Block for the lower category of hardcores; they bore two armulets on their arms. Then in descending order there were the "Goats'", "Calves'", and Mĩtaama Blocks—inmates of which bore only one armulet. The "Cows'" Block housed the "good" elements who had already confessed all their doings. Many of them had come from

Athi River.

Sometimes men detainees would travel from Athi River to Kamītī to see and talk to their wives who were still holding out against making a confession. Some of the women exhibited a single-minded determination which put many men to shame. Some women would refuse to talk to their husbands for the reason that these men had sold out by making a confession. Others would insist that their husbands, who had already confessed, should only talk about domestic affairs and should by no means discuss matters relating to detention. One woman told her husband point blank that she would have no dealings with the sellouts and traitors from Athi River. The response of the women taught me that when women really set their mind to a cause they are capable of a remarkably single-minded commitment.

Just adjacent to the Women's Detention Camp was the great Women's Prison, where women who had been tried in courts of law and convicted were imprisoned. Some of the prisoners had been women soldiers in the nationalist Mau Mau army. Those who were captured bearing weapons of war were tried, convicted and sentenced to life imprisonment. Some of these "*Maisha*," 'life', people were Wanjira wa Kīmiti, Wambūi Gacanja, Wanjirū Kīmiti and Mū-thoni, wife of W. Gakūrū. Some of the work they had to do in prison was to bury the bodies of Mau Mau people who had been condemned to death by hanging. They would bury the bodies with the heads facing Mount Kenya on whose magnificent top God dwelled. Guards would try to thwart the carrying out of these burials of honour and would subject these women to brutal beatings; but the women were adamant and no amount of beatings would thwart them. Eventually the guards left them alone—to bury the corpses of their own people as they chose.

These young women were housed in little houses that had been constructed with the materials from the demolished buildings of the Gīthūngūri Kenya Teachers College. The imperialists had constructed gallows for hanging Mau Mau nationalists on the ruins of that erstwhile great nationalist school.

My wife Shifira Wairire was released in July 1957. Released with her were others including the following: Miriam Wanjira, Susan Waraū wife of Tiras, Daina Nyambura, Joyce Wanjirū, Njeeri wa Kībirū, Nduta Njenga, Mūcirū Kīrīīka and one Grace from Meru.

I wish at this point to say that I was not altogether happy with my stay in Block 9. I was very upset with the kind of treatment "reformed" detainees were meting out to those detainees who still resisted confession. With the licence of the leaders of the interrogation exercise, the "reformed" detainees would torment the unreformed ones by doing things like pouring cold water on their exposed bodies or rubbing irritant soapy water on their eyes. Such actions were meant to goad people into making confessions.

It used to work like this. Detainees who had resisted rehabilitation would be collected during the night by guards. Those who would agree to make a confession were readily accepted into Block 9. Those who persisted in resisting were subjected to torment by the reformed throughout the night. At the break of day they would be returned to their Blocks.

The aim of this torment of the "unreformed" by the "reformed", which included verbal abuse against the stupidity of those who refused to confess, was to demonstrate in an extreme form a reformed detainee's complete readiness to accept cooperation with the Government. It was a vile way of seeking an early release.

But the authorities put a stop to this programme of detainees abusing one another when one detainee who spent a whole night under torture died. The reformed had kept pouring icy cold water on him throughout the night during the cold weather of the month of July. He froze to death. In the subsequent enquiry everybody who had been instrumental to this shameful murder— the "reformed" detainees, the interrogators, even the Camp Commandant— wanted to insist on his distance from this affair. The people who had carried out the torture tried to conceal themselves. Nobody was tried for it since the Government pathologist who carried an autopsy on the dead man conveniently attributed the cause of death to long term lung disease. But the death left these people who had acquiesced in low acts smeared in ignominy.

My personal interpretation of the affair is that the people who stooped to such meanness were never true freedom fighters; they never had a real grasp of the people's cause, its objectives and its methods. Such people, easily turned "reformists", are a great danger to a people; they are sometimes referred to as the drifting scum of the nation.

Prior to the detainee's death, J. M. Kariũki had been subjected to brutal assault by imperialist British officers and two senior African officers. J. M. subsequently wrote a complaint to the authorities which included the assault on himself, the happenings in Block 9 and the death by torture of the detainee. After about two months the Government carried out a reorganisation of Athi River Camp—many camp officers, interrogators and rehabilitation officers and workers were transferred from Athi River and some of them lost their jobs.

During the months of July and August 1957 200 people arrived from Mageta detention camp. They had been captured while waging war in the Gĩkũyũ, Embu and Mĩĩrũ countryside. These were militant people who had maintained their resistance and great sense of solidarity in the detention camps. When they got to Athi River they were housed in Block 5. They immediately gave a demonstration of their militancy and solidarity when they violently resisted separation which was being imposed to make the work of interrogation easier. The leaders of that battle of resistance right in the Camp were: Mtu-Manyara, Paulo Mahehu,

Kang'ethe Waiganjo, Maina Mathenge, Kĩbuĩ Kĩmunyi, Nyaga Njirũ and Kagambe Kaguamba.

It had happened like this: The leaders of the Rehabilitation exercise had ordered that the new detainees from Mageta should be scattered to the other Blocks at Athi River. To this purpose a band of guards and interrogation workers tried to make an appearance in Block 5 where the Mageta detainees were already quartered. To their surprise they were forced to retreat when missiles of camp utensils and stones were hurled at them. A special platoon had to be brought from Nairobi to subdue these people. But even this platoon received determined resistance from people who fought with great courage but were defeated because they didn't have proper weapons. A fight like this had never been seen in Athi River. The Mageta detainees were forcibly separated. Some of them were taken from Athi River altogether and exiled at Sayusi, Lodwar and Mwea 1. And Athi River from that day acquired the reputation of violent resistance.

I finally achieved "parole" on 11 October 1957. I left Block 9 for a room which I shared with another paroled detainee, one Kame Mũhoro. I obtained my permit to go beyond the confines of the camp; and I started visiting Athi River town. One day I obtained a pass to visit my sister, Priscilla Wangarĩ, in Nairobi.

At this time, I, like most other detainees, was preoccupied with the idea of going home. All my family was aware of this burning desire for return and reunion. But I did not know there was an enemy back home who would work against my return.

During these days of my parole it was intimated to me that matters didn't stand well for me for there were people who had indicated that it would not be good to allow me to go home. At that time my mother was pursuing the issue of compensation for my father with the C.S.M. Tũmũtũmũ. Up to now she had received only token money. Back home it was known that I was the person advising my mother on the issue of compensation. It appears the minister in charge of this Church did not want to have me home and thus physically near to the affair.

Again a young clansman of mine, one Paul Gacanga who was working with the Athi River Meat Commission, told me that some elders from our clan did not want me to obtain a share of the clan land. I wrote to the Nyeri D.C. and requested him to intervene on my behalf. And I wrote to my mother and my brother Hunja and asked them to intervene with the clan on my behalf.

Because people had opposed my return home and because I had been guilty earlier of writing a questionable play, it was decided I would lose my parole and go back to the Camp. But before the end of one month after this action was taken, I and another detainee, one John Gĩathĩ, were informed that we were marked for transfer to a special camp at Marigat. We would be eligible for allocation of land there and we would be free to invite our families to live with us. We were told to get our belongings ready; we received our "token money" for work done, and then waited for transport. It never came and we were told to go back to the camp, the journey had been postponed. We went back to the camp—and the whole Marigat idea died.

During the month of December 1957 commandant Breckenridge and his wife "Njeeri" left Athi River for good, and Dennis Lakin became commandant. He immediately took measures to have all those detainees who had already made their confessions transferred to district and divisional camps nearest to their homes. He endeared himself to detainees by insisting on the principle that it was not reasonable to continue holding a detainee at Athi River if he had already completed his confession.

And so it happened that on 15 February 1958 I and other people from Mathīra Division were transferred to Karatina Detention Camp which was under Shadrack Gathekia's administration. Some of the other people who went with me were: Colonelious Kanyīrī, Mbuthia Gacuīrī, Mūcooki Mbūitū, Maciira Mūkenya, Joseph Kīrīra, Gītonga Kībirū and James Mwani Wanarua.

8

My Exile in Hola

2 May 1958 to 19 August 1959

From my home near Tūmūtūmū, it is only 4 miles to Karatina. My entire family therefore came to see me at the Karatina detention camp and we had a warm and joyful reunion.

I learned from them that I had not been allocated a share of the clan land. I made a complaint to the D.O. at Karatina who allowed me to go home, under the escort of warder Kahiga Kaboi, to put my case before the clan elders. I never managed to speak to all the elders.

After two days Kahiga Kaboi intimated to me that three clan elders had come to see the D.O. to make representations that I should not be released, for my presence in the village would be inimical to the good and just allocation of land during the ongoing land adjudication exercise.

And the offshoot of it was that I became one of the people who were rejected by their own local community, and had to be taken a step back in the "pipeline". The British D.C. explained to us that it was not the Government itself that had blocked our path to final freedom but our own people. This of course was not completely correct, for I was aware that in their sinister cunning the colonial authorities encouraged and welcomed this division among people from the same community while at the same time self-righteously exonerating themselves from all blame; for the authorities had been working all along to create animosities between the people who were left behind and the ones who were exiled in detention camps. But I felt terribly hurt and very bitter. However, whoever was instrumental to my continued banishment from home, I was determined to fight for my just interests. My mother pleaded with me to renounce my right to a share of the clan land, but I told her it was not just to accept robbery of one's birthright. Therefore, before my banishment and exile to Hola, I delegated my brother to look after my interests; I gave him all the necessary letters and papers. I also asked the sympathetic clan elders, led by Timothy Mwīhu, to demand another hearing of my case in the clan "court".

The officer in charge of the land consolidation exercise in my area at that time was Eliud M. Mahīhu. Elders from other clans listened to the case and ordered that I should get a share of eleven acres. At the end of the day I only got seven acres, for dishonest surveying was introduced when they took my contribution of land to communal amenities. I received information about the allocation through a letter from my wife which reached me in my exile at Hola, in the Kenya coast, where those of us who had been rejected had been banished.

All Nyeri people who had been rejected by their communities were brought together at the main Nyeri Kĩng'ong'o Prison. On 2nd May 1958 at 5.00 o'clock in the morning we boarded several buses and were driven towards Hola through Thĩka, Mwingi and Garissa. We arrived at Hola around 1.00 o'clock in the afternoon. We found other detainees there, some of whom had been known to us in other detention camps. Some of them had been rejected by their communities before they had left the main camps for the home district or divisional camps. They were therefore never taken to the home camps but were directly transported to Hola. These are some of my old friends whom I met at Hola: Wanjohi Solomon, J. D. Kali, Job Mũcucu, Mũrĩithi Goci, Wamũthenya Kang'eri, Richard Aloo, Maranga Mbaria, Joseph Gĩkonyo, Moses Kĩng'aarũ Maciira Mũkenye, David Mathu, Japhat Njagĩ, Romano Njamumo, Hezekiah Kaguĩrĩ, Charles Wanyoike, John O'Washika, Paul Mahehu, James Njogu and Karĩambũri.

Hola had become the dumping ground of the unreformable Mau Mau hardcore, the eternal enemies of the loyalist homeguards Many of these people had been in detention camps for more than 6 years and they had gone the rounds of all the harsh-regime detention camps scattered all over Kenya. And yet they had been found wanting. Another group of the Hola exiles comprised military detainees—the generals, majors, captains and sergeants of the Mau Mau liberation war. They had never relaxed their attitude of resistance to the colonial authorities and they had been a constant thorn in the flesh of the camp administration.

Our exile coincided with the launching of the giant Irrigation Scheme at Hola by an agricultural Company called ALDEV. This company was constructing a huge canal to deliver irrigation waters from the Tana River for irrigating the Hola plains. This would eventually lead to the creation of a settlement subsisting on irrigation agriculture—the Hola Irrigation Settlement Scheme. The plan was to integrate detainees into this scheme. To this end detainees were eligible for allocation of 4 acres on which they could build a home and if they wished invite their families (wives and children) to settle with them.

That is how I became a farmer at Hola. And in October 1958 I invited my wife and my younger daughter, Waarigia, to come and live with me. My young sons, Wanjaũ and Mũturi, were, however, left in school in Gĩkũyũ country.

The detainees built the first settlement village at Hola in June 1958. We christened this village Kĩarũkũngũ, or the Place of Great Dust, because of the terribly dusty nature of the place. We elected a representative council called Hola Detainees Advisory Committee which would make any necessary representations on our behalf to the District Officer and other Government workers. We also put up a school building roofed with *makuti*. We named our school Hola Settlement Scheme Primary School. Our children started attending classes at Standard One. Nursery school children would receive their lessons—and their milk—under a tree. My wife and Grace, wife of Japhat Njagĩ, were the nursery school teachers. In addition we launched, with the assistance of the C.D.O., an adult education school to which detainees could volunteer for classes. The following were the teachers for the adult education school: myself, Japhat Njagĩ Ndabarũa and Mbũrũ wa Nene. Some of the adult pupils who immediately come to mind are: Gĩtukũ Kamaitha, Gĩtangũ Marima, Mbũgũa Ng'ang'a, Ex-chief Wamũgane, Kĩmani Gĩcũhĩ, Mwangi Kamunyũ and Mwanĩki Nderi.

We introduced ourselves to Hola agriculture by planting cotton and soya beans. Some people ventured into growing maize and sweet potatoes, which did quite well. We would receive our seeds from the Government. We would sell our produce to the Government, who would recover the cost of the seeds before they paid us. We would, still in our detainee status, teach farming to the Apokomo and Agala people and hire them to help in cultivating the land, to mud and plaster the walls of our houses and to thatch houses which we used to build for ourselves.

The second settlement village came up later and we called it Nyakĩambi—the Village of the Beginners.

There were detainees who opted not to become involved in farming. These people lived in a camp which kept its doors open—Hola Open Camp or Kĩamũnyaka (The Place of Good Luck), as detainees used to call it. They used to carry out other kinds of work; they had permission to go four miles beyond the precincts of the camp without any escort. They used to pay us visits and we would sometimes invite them for communal work in the Gĩkũyũ custom. Large numbers of them would come and help to clear a whole farm in a matter of a few hours.

At the end of 1958 a detention camp which kept its doors locked—Hola Closed Camp—was built. This was for exiled detainees who persisted in rejecting all other kinds of work—except cooking their meals—while still in colonial detention. Colonial officers—Prison Commissioner Lewis and his assistants—feeling terribly affronted by this behaviour, took the law into their hands and decided to force these people to work. Their decision was received sympathetically by the Hola Camp Commandant, one Sullivan. He had known many of these defiant people since their detention at Mageta near Kisumu. The animosity he had felt towards these people was more than reciprocated by the detainees: on one occasion, the detainees had conspired to carry out an attack on Sullivan when he entered their quarters; luckily, Sullivan had kept off but this had not saved Sullivan's white colleague from being severely attacked. Sullivan saw his chance. He requisitioned a special platoon to come and intimidate these people to work in digging a huge water canal; should they resist they should be beaten without pity.

On 3 March 1959 more than 100 soldiers of the special platoon invaded Hola Closed Camp. They were armed with guns, hoe handles, clubs and they carried iron shields and wore iron helmets. They confronted about 85 detainees who were sworn to rejection of work. They set on them and subjected them to brutal assault, hitting at the detainees' bodies and heads indiscriminately, until they had driven the detainees out of their quarters.

The toll of the vicious attack was taken later. 11 detainees were battered to death; many others were maimed. The bodies of the dead were collected and locked in a little shed. The injured people were taken to the hospital in Hola.

Those of us who were working on our farms, about three miles away from Hola Closed Camp, learned about one hour later about the massacre. So we trooped to the hospital with heavy hearts and the women wept and wailed when they saw the battered bodies of our people. The injured men lay in a mass with bandages covering their broken limbs, skulls and ribs. Well might they weep with springs of bitterness bursting in flow at the realisation that the act of hateful carnage had been perpetrated not by white colonialists but by our Black brothers. For the white imperialist is uncannily adept at using ignorant Black stooges to oppress and destroy their own people. And our heroic people who had been battered into a mass of broken limbs and ribs also carried injured psyches, for these stooges had beaten them and subjected them to verbal abuse and insults. "What kind of freedom do people like you demand, you ignoramuses!" they had shouted. "Stupid people like you: how can you ever hope to put a case for a return of land?"

The next day some imperialist members of the Legislative Council flew to Hola to carry out an enquiry into the massacre. They were fed with lies by the killer imperialist authorities of Hola who put out a story—which the Legco members accepted—that people had died out of drinking poisoned water when it was being delivered on the water-carrying vehicle. The Legco people were not ashamed to have this unlikely version of events published in the newspapers. But the detainees sent a secret memorandum to the British Colonial Secretary, with many copies to African political leaders, and detailed the correct version of events over which the Hola imperialists were determined to impose a cover up.

The bodies of the dead people were flown to Nairobi and were then taken to Kamīti' Prison where they were buried after autopsies had been carried out on them. The autopsies confirmed the cause of death as beatings. A pathologist who examined samples of the water which had allegedly caused the deaths declared the water wholesome.

The Governor of Kenya, the Commissioner of Prisons and other senior officers of the colonial government in Kenya received a battery of questions about the Hola deaths from Britain. The British Government eventually ordered the Governor to institute a commission of enquiry under the chairmanship of the Solicitor-General. At the same time African trade unionists from Mombasa under the leadership of Dennis Akumu, M. Maigacho and Tom Mboya hired a lawyer to hold brief for the detainees during the deliberations of the commission of enquiry.

And thus did it happen that a colonial judge sat in judgement over colonial officialdom that had sought to preserve the colonial status quo by resorting to the murder of the enemies of colonialism. And the outcome was that Sullivan had his services terminated—in all honour and with full service benefits. And the Commissioner of Prisons offered his resignation in view of protests by people in Britain.

These are the names of the people who were murdered in the infamous Hola massacre: Ndũng'ũ Kĩbakĩ, Karũma Mbũrũ, Kahũthia Kamau, Mwema Kĩnũthia, Kĩnyanjui Njoroge, Mĩguĩ Ndegwa, Mũngai Gĩthu, Ngũgĩ Karite, Karanja Mũrũthi, Kamau Karanja and Ekinu Ekira.

The aftermath of the massacre was that the Closed Camp was abolished and some of the detainees from the former Closed Camp were integrated into the Open Camp, "The Place of Good Luck", while others were now housed in a new Camp christened *Matanya* or "Expectations", where General China and other detainees from the forests were living. But before long these people were separated and scattered to other camps like Lodwar, Mwea and district camps—like Kangũbiri, Nyangwethũ, Kĩgumo, Gĩthũngũri and Waithaka— which had already earned themselves a nasty reputation for gross maltreatment of detainees. Here the homeguards maintained a reign of terror and they would beat people to maim or even to kill. Detainees referred to these district camps as "Komesha Camps", that is Extermination Camps. At this time, during the middle months of 1959, many exile detention camps had been closed down as the bulk of the detainees had been released.

As a memorial to those Mau Mau heroes who were murdered at Hola during the struggle for freedom, the first President of Independent Kenya Mzee Jomo Kenyatta ordered that Hola Secondary School be renamed Mau Mau Secondary School. This secondary school had grown out of the Hola Settlement Scheme Primary School which we started in 1958. President Kenyatta's act of remembrance was hailed by the veterans of the Mau Mau Liberation struggle, for only in Hola does a memorial to Mau Mau stand. These people still long for the day when the Government of Independent Kenya will erect Mau Mau Memorial Halls in all the major cities and towns of our nation, in eternal commemoration of the nationalist struggle for independence.

The Hola exiles became used to living there, they learned how to practise irrigated farming, they sold the cotton they had grown, they opened up retail kiosks near their living houses and opened up butcheries that sold meat of goats bought from the Agala people, and some of them became carpenters and craftsmen who set up shop in their houses. The exiles started to create wealth and to acquire property and to achieve a certain settled feeling of peace of mind.

No doubt those of our people back home who had instigated our rejection and our banishment heard reports of our hard-earned success In June 1959 some elders from Gĩkũyũ, Embu and Mĩĩrũ, people of devious cunning, came to see us in our place of an exile they had engineered. With them was a Gĩkũyũ colonial D.O. whose name was Kĩhoori and his clerk, Mathew Kĩmani. And Ndegwa Gĩkuhĩ, the erstwhile interrogation man, arrived to take the post of chief at Hola Settlement Scheme.

These people had been sent by the colonial Government. They were amazed to see the progress we had made in our exile. They probably did get the impression that we had achieved greater prosperity and happiness than our own people who had been living in freedom back home. And they started to urge people—those who had become farmers and those who hadn't—to go back home. The fear of us our communities had felt had died down, they now said. We were free to return home.

A good number of detainees decided against returning home and went on with their farming in Hola. Later they acquired title deeds for the plots they were working. They became permanent Hola dwellers. I can remember some names of such people: Mũngai Ikumi, Justo Kĩng'ori, Gĩthũng'a Njoora, Njenga Mũruria, Duncan Kĩmenyi and Ndĩritũ Gĩkomo. Some of these people have become quite prosperous; they own shops and workshops. They have come to regard Hola—currently known as Tana River Irrigation Scheme—as their first home; they would visit their original homes in Gĩkũyũ, Embu. or Mĩĩrũ once in a while, only to return to Hola.

Other people were not immediately recommended by the team of elders for a return home and so for a period they remained in Hola without choosing to do so. Eventually these people started going home depending on when they became acceptable to their communities. But there was a large group of hardcores who persisted in their total rejection of cooperation in their Hola exile and these people remained in their banishment until 12 January 1960 when the state of Emergency was formally ended.

I was one of the people who decided to go home after the elders lifted my prohibition. Before we left, I organised the performance of some plays on 4 July 1959; in the evening we had a farewell dance. Paul Mahehu, Aram Ndirangũ and Stephen Oloo had come from the Open Camp to our village, Kĩarũkũngũ—the Place of Great Dust—and they played the music instruments for the dance. They and other Open Camp detainees were allowed to stay at our village up to 10.00 o'clock at night.

One week after the farewell dance, the women and children were put on transport in advance of the men who would be going home. The Hola doctor had objected to my wife's leaving since she was pregnant and he considered long journey risky. My wife had insisted on leaving. I had been asked to sign a declaration to the effect that I was aware of the risks and I shouldn't blame anybody in case anything went wrong. All the same the doctor kindly offered to travel with my wife up to Thika; he did not leave her until she had boarded the Nyeri-bound vehicle. She had not experienced any complications.

I and a number of Nyeri colleagues left Hola on 19 August 1959. We arrived at Mbaaini Camp at Rũrĩng'ũ, Nyeri, during the night. We spent the night there. On 20 July 1959 we were taken to the office of the Nyeri D.C., one A. J. Foster. He read out the regulations to us: after a detainee had arrived at his home, he should never go outside the boundaries of his administrative location; he should regularly report to the D.O. and the Chief of his area until the Governor's Detention Order or the District Commissioners Detention Order (D.D.O.) had been suspended in three months' time; a detainee should not join any political party or be associated in any way with a secret society.

I arrived at the Karatina office of the D.O. of Mathĩra Division at around 5.30 o'clock in the afternoon. To my surprise I found the D.O. was the same British officer Dennis Lakin who had approved my release from Athi River. He was amazed to see me, after this long intervening period, still carrying with me the status of a detained person. He gave me a letter to take to the Chief of my Location in accordance with the regulations, and formally released me to go home.

I walked from Karatina to the Chief's office on Kĩrĩmũkũyũ ridge, a distance of three miles, arriving there around 6.00 p.m. The Chief's name was Robenson Wangome. He had become chief during the state of Emergency, and had been brought from his home area in Ũthaya Division to Kĩrĩmũkũyũ in Mathĩra Division. He, therefore, did not know me. When in 1958 he had rejected my release and re-integration into my home community with the consequence that I had been banished to Hola, he had simply gone by reports about me made by the traitorous collaborators of my ridge. He had learnt to be suspicious of me.

When he had studied the D.O.'s note, he regarded me for a long time, then cast his eyes behind me as if to ascertain whether or not I had come under the escort of an *askari*, before asking, "Are you Gakaara?"

I answered, "Yes, I am."

"Who brought you here?"

I answered, "I came all alone, as you see me."

He engaged me in conversation about how I had managed to get out of Hola. I told him. He seemed inclined to disbelieve my story, were it not for the D.O.'s note that he had already read. He said it was already rather late and I should go home and come to see him first thing tomorrow morning, at 8.00 o'clock.

It is only about one mile from the Chief's camp to my home in a village called Thaithi. Nobody was expecting me at home. It is not possible to convey the ecstatic joy with which my homecoming was received. Some people were so overwhelmed by the joy of our reunion they wept.

A woman called Wamũcii wa Gacara from our neighbourhood said these words in her amazement: "Is this Gakaara we are seeing with our own eyes? And we were told repeatedly through aeroplane-borne loudspeakers that we would never set out eyes on him again! Oh, the terrible terrible lies of the white man!"

One Mwaniki Mbariti who had been released shortly before me commented, "Haven't you realised yet that we have achieved victory?"

These words put new life in me as well as a sense of great relief. People here still talked about the deception of the colonialists and about victory over the colonialists! Yes, indeed, they nurtured the hope of our eventual liberation.

In 1957 when my wife had been released from Kamĩtĩ Women's camp, she had been allocated a building plot in Thaithi village by the village headman, one Arthur Tutu. She built a little house similar to the little houses people used to build in colonial villages. It was round, had walls of mud and had a roof of grass thatch. It had three little rooms—a kitchen, a dining and sitting room and a bedroom. It was to this house that I returned, to start a knew life in a colonial village with my wife and our three children.

9

My Life As a Restricted Person

20 August 1959 to 19 May 1960

The matter of top priority for a released Mau Mau detainee, or prisoner or even a forest fighter who had returned home, was to rehabilitate and restore his affairs to a state of normality. Such affairs lay in wreckage and ruin after many years of the disruptive work of the colonialists and their lackeys. But besides looking after personal interests, a genuine freedom fighter continued to give any possible assistance to the process of liberation to ensure that the fruits of our protracted struggle would eventually be reaped.

I think it has been evident from the story told in this book that certain genuine nationalist leaders consistently championed the cause of liberation throughout their careers in detention in spite of many odds and obstacles. They left detention with their nationalist vision undimmed. The imperialists had studied the different types of nationalist leaders in the historical arena of struggle and they had realised that there were those who would carry on with the struggle for land and freedom, quite undaunted by the terrible repression and horrible torture the imperialists had resorted to—including the castration of men and the insertion of bottles in women's birth canals and outright murders. He (the imperialist) discerned them all—those leaders of great courage who would raise an unstoppable roar against their oppressors, those thinkers who conceived and executed strategies of struggle, those people who embodied the popular will and aspirations.

Armed with such understanding the imperialist authorities used a strategy of cunning in releasing such leaders. It was part of a general plan that if they came from the same area, such leaders should not be released at the same time. If such people were allowed to come together they could incite the "pacified" villages to defiance of imperialist authority. Therefore, to keep these people away and thereby buy time, the imperialists incited local collaborators and colonial chiefs to reject the return of these people, arrogating to themselves the role of spokesmen for local communities. When banishment and exile had become no longer tenable and Mau Mau detainees had to return home, the policy of whysically restricting the returnee to his home ridge was adopted. This, coupled pith the prohibition against joining political parties, was deemed an effective method of curbing the influence of nationalist leaders on a supposedly pacified community.

When I went to see the Chief on the morning of 21 August 1959, he gave me the same regulations we had received from the D.C. of Nyeri. He, however, did add that I would be required to participate in communal work which would be assigned from time to time by our community leader. This requirement would apply until such time as the Governor of Kenya suspended my Detention Order.

On 24th August 1959 I participated in communal work, under the supervision of homeguards, for the first time. A night crier using a loudspeaker had announced the night before that people should congregate at the little ridge of Kiawambigo which would be the work venue. Communal work was twice a week during this period. At the bridge I met about 20 people, both men and women, who had come to attend the work session. Many people fell on me and embraced me in welcome. I knew the following people in the workgang: Joeli wa Micūkī, Kīama Njũũrī; Ndegwa Mũturi, Ndīritũ Thīũri, Kīgaga Gatoogo, Ndīritũ Ngarami, Kahwaī Kīmarũ, Zelipha Wangũi Kībīra, Mũmbi Sethi, Hiũko Wambũgũ, Mwerũ Gītahi, Gathoni Ndīritũ, Wanjirũ Njũũkia and Nyagũthiī Wanjigua.

I was curious to study the behaviour and attitude of homeguards towards freedom fighters, and expected to see an overbearing man imposing an oppressive discipline. But this man did not exhibit much confidence and in fact self-effacingly allowed the detainees to carry on in their own way. Why this attitude? I asked myself. I reached the opinion that this man probably retained the sense and the imagination to realise that some of the people he was supervising had been his social betters before they were detained or imprisoned.

And yet this could not be the whole explanation. The truth of the matter was that our return, for long demonstrated as not possible by the white imperialists, had dampened the aggressive enthusiasm of the loyalists. Many of them had lost heart in pursuing their reactionary cause, the turn of events seeming to herald a new era where the loyalists' influence was on the wane and where our political star was on the rise, for now it did seem that the Mau Mau insurrectionists might eventually seize political power. The loyalists were on the retreat—even in a literal physical sense. Some of them permanently left the homes of their birth to live in areas where people had not known them or the crimes they had perpetrated.

I went to the work venue carrying no tools—neither a hoe nor a *panga*. My Mau Mau colleagues said I shouldn't worry, could I work with the people who were laying the grass which was being dug up on the frame of the bridge. In spite of our awareness that this work assignment was designed for our punishment, we carried on diligently, our major concern being to build a solid dependable and serviceable bridge for our two ridges and travellers from other parts. At 11.00 o'clock in the morning when our work was meant to end, we had finished making a little footbridge to be proud of.

We did the work assigned to us to the best of our ability. But our spirit was pained by the humiliation it was designed to inflict on us. For here we were back home, after years of wandering and oppressive punishment, being expected to work under the critical gaze of the public and the children like a pack of malefactors. We had been denied what should surely be our right—rest and solace at home as well as social and companionable contact with our communities at large.

After two days in the village Wambũgũ wa Gĩcũhĩ, who worked as the Chief's clerk, hinted to me that if I managed to obtain any kind of employment within the Division of Mathĩra, the D.O. would raise no objections. I therefore requested my brother Isaac Hunja and his business partners—Musa Matũ, David Mwangi and Mĩthamo wa Waciira—to employ me in their photography business in Karatina. Their studio was situated quite close to the office of the D.O. of Mathĩra, on Konyũ ridge in Karatina town.

My status was that of a restricted person which means I was required to live on my ridge of Kĩrĩmũkũyũ. I therefore gave a letter to my wife to deliver to the D.O. requesting him to look at my case in view of my need to work at Karatina. He granted me permission to work in Karatina during the day. However, I should spend my nights at home. Another condition was that I should always walk along the main road on my way to and from work; under no circumstances should I use little side paths. The Chief was informed about these conditions.

After walking to and from work for a whole week I complained to the D.O. that I was finding it very tiring to walk eight miles daily; I requested him to allow me to spend the nights at Karatina. He granted my request on condition that I reported to his office once every week. He informed the Chief that I was no longer under his (the Chief's) jurisdiction. And so I had the opportunity to reside at Karatina and would visit my home as I chose.

At the end of August 1959 the D.O. summoned me to his office. He informed me my Governor's Detention Order had been suspended. However, I was still subject to the Special Restriction Order as a Mau Mau adherent; under this Order I should not travel outside my administrative location. When I put a number of questions to the D.O. he told me his only instructions were to give me the information he had. But if I was interested in knowing the reasons for my restriction I should write to the Appeal Tribunal on Detained and Restricted Persons in Nairobi.

So I wrote a letter to the Tribunal. After two full weeks I had received no reply. I wrote a reminder on 25 September 1959—and even this one received no response.

Also on 25th September and on 30th September I wrote to the Nyeri D.C. and the Attorney General, Nairobi, respectively, petitioning for a suspension of a restriction imposed on the distribution of my books. I argued that these books did not disseminate Mau Mau ideas and I needed to make reprints and to sell them to earn my daily bread.

Not long after these things D.O. Lakin left Karatina and he was replaced by a Mũgĩkũyũ D.O., one H. Mũragũri. I went to see him and requested him to give me a permit to go to Nairobi to see if I could recover any piece of property I had owned there before my detention. My real purpose was to see a lawyer who could fight for a suspension of my restriction order, as well as to attend an interview with East African Breweries who had replied to my application for a job. D.O. Mũragũri gave me a pass authorizing me to stay in Nairobi from November 1st to 7th November 1959.

In Nairobi I contacted advocate Henry C. Warĩithi who wrote to the Appeal Tribunal asking them to order a suspension of my restriction order. Warĩithi's letter provided a pretext for laying false charges against me. Little sneaking spies from the Tribunal carried out an investigation about my visit to Nairobi and filed the following charges: 1. I had visited Nairobi without a KEM (Kikuyu-Embu-Meru) Passbook; 2. I had written a provocative letter to Government authorities demanding a lifting of restrictions on my publications which I knew to be pro-Mau Mau. I was to receive a copy of these charges back home and the warning that I could be liable for re-detention.

I immediately wrote to Advocate Warĩithi, apprising him of the Appeal Tribunal's charges. He took the trouble to come and see me in Karatina where I showed him the D.O.'s Pass and copies of the letters I had written concerning my books. On 26 February 1960 Advocate Warĩithi wrote to this imperialist court whose officers seemed to be mainly motivated by a fathomless hatred and malice. He tore to shreds their false accusations and destroyed their malicious case against me. But Warĩithi's legal rebuttal did not get the matter closed. He received communication that my case would be heard at the Nyeri D.C.'s office on 19th May 1960 before a court instituted under the instructions of the Special Commissioner of Detainees and Restricted Persons.

So on 19 May 1960 I and my advocate reported at the D.C.'s office in Nyeri. At the court room we found the D.C. himself, who was to chair the court, an imperialist spy from the intelligence service, and three African traitors turned out in neck-ties. My advocate was invited to sit down and I was left standing.

There was hardly any trial since my advocate had successfully put a case for my innocence. The fact was that we had been made to make our appearance simply for the "court" to announce its findings. The chairman announced these findings: 1. The pass issued to me by the D.O. of Karatina to enable me to travel to Nairobi was valid. 2. The Government had asked a commission to review my writings and publications—books, newspapers, etc.—which had been restricted in accordance with State of Emergency Regulations. It would rule whether or not the restrictions should be suspended. 3. The court had considered Advocate Warĩithi's submissions and prayer for the suspension of my restriction order and was satisfied about the desirability of this suspension.

From today I should consider the restriction order suspended.

In spite of this outcome Warĩithi was terribly annoyed by the time wasting scenes set up by the colonial authorities. Here they were instituting a useless court to deal with a case which had no substance, a court simply designed to cause annoyance and vexation to African people while wasting public funds. And then Warĩithi told me there would be no legal charges for handling my case! How could he charge me when he knew I had lived in detention camps all these years? How could he when he knew I had been fighting for the advancement of our country? He mentioned that his own father, Mũtahi, had been detained with me. His father used to be assaulted by homeguards who would taunt him that he had sent Warĩithi for studies in England using Mau Mau funds.

By the time my restriction order was revoked, it had been in force for ten months. During this period I collected Mau Mau freedom songs which people used to sing in detention camps, prisons and forests. In June 1961 I went to Nairobi. For a brief period I joined Pio Gama Pinto, George Gĩthii and Joe Kadhi on the staff of the Kenya African National Union party newspaper *Sauti ya KANU*. This nationalist paper was at that time championing the release of Mzee Jomo Kenyatta to come and assume leadership of the nationalist forces in the drive to Independence.

I left this paper to resurrect my publishing and printing venture. I published books I had written in detention, notably *Mĩhĩrĩga ya Agĩkũyũ* ("The Gĩkũyũ Clans") and *Nyĩmbo cia Wĩyathi* ("Freedom Songs"). I also collected Kiswahili songs which were at that time very popular with the Nairobi youth wing of the KANU party and published them under the title *Nyimbo za Uhuru*. Many of these songs sang praise to the heroes of the freedom struggle and the victory of Mau Mau. We used to sing them with great enthusiasm and verve, our hearts aflame with hope and great expectations as we looked forward to creating a new nation and serving in the new independent nationalist order.

The new nationalist order did arrive and Mzee Jomo Kenyatta presided over an independent Kenya. One of the cornerstones of Kenyatta's policy was the creation of a broad spirit of national reconciliation; the animosities and hatreds and bitterness of the Mau Mau war must be dissolved and absorbed in a new spirit of magnanimity and forgiveness.

That Mau Mau people embraced Kenyatta's philosophy wholeheartedly has never been challenged. They saw forgiveness and national reconciliation as necessary for a restoration of peace to the ravaged land. But it is only fair to state that the Mau Mau fighters seem to have given more than they got and history may record that they made great sacrifices for a land and its people—

and then they were ultimately made into a sacrifice.

In the implementation of the new national policy, the imperialist settlers who had robbed us of our land never had the same land seized from them for restoration into the hands of the rightful owners. Those of them who felt they could not live under an African government were asked to sell the land and other property. Never had the Mau Mau ideology made allocation for such a scenario. It would have been unimaginable to think of people paying money to imperialist settlers in order to acquire rights to our own land, unjustily seized from us in the past. But Kenyatta's plan was to have the lands peaceably restored to indigenous African hands—without fanning new conflict with the settler clique.

But the interests of unmonied Mau Mau people were thereby compromised and sacrificed. When the vast and fertile settler farms started to change hands, the Mau Mau fighters could only sit as spectators while wealthy Africans, the new "Smiths", took over thousand-acre farms from the while Smiths. They had only recently come from detention camps and were struggling to gather together the broken pieces of their lives, to rebuild from the destruction and disruption of the liberation war.

The Mau Mau watched as wealth changed hands, but also as power and office changed hands. For homeguards and loyalists were forgiven for the terroristic and inhuman acts they had committed against the freedom fighters as well as the abuses they had subjected them to. But this was not the end; for those very good servants in the colonial administration were readily absorbed into the Government administration of nationalist Kenya. It was no longer correct, in spite of the facts written large across the face of history, to refer to these people, now entrenched in the African Government, as homeguards and traitorous collaborators. Some of these people had cruelly taunted the Mau Mau fighters: "We will fight against you now under the British; and when self government arrives we will rule over you."

The Mau Mau fighters were pained to witness the fulfilment of this taunt. But they subdued their agonised spirits and learnt how to work and live with these Government administrators and workers who had been faithful servants of British imperialism and colonialism but were now conveniently serving an African nationalist Government. Finally they did manage to expel the cloud of bitterness from their souls and settled into their activities and careers enjoying the real freedom that Independence had ushered in.

But they had to accept the sacrifice of their political and material aspirations. Their aspiration for active participation in the nationalist Government, which they had been instrumental in making a reality, fell into the river of history. And national gratitude in the form of magnanimous gestures to individual Mau Mau fighters or in the form of memorials to the movement was quite absent, for such gestures had few champions and many detractors.

What is more, the land for which they had fought and for which they had expected an equitable redistribution plan was divided out to people with money. Some Mau Mau people could not even afford a decimal point of an acre. Many Mau Mau people and their cripples from the war were left living in deprivation and squalor in colonial-created villages, until some of them later managed to make contributions to land buying-companies which planned to settle people on former settler farms.

And so in this great historical sacrifice and sacrificing, the Mau Mau became that proverbial farmer who is denied a meal. The Gĩkũyũ have this saying: "It is not the farmer who eats the food he has grown."

Appendices

Appendix 1: Kenya's Nationalist Leaders

Below, you will find the names of Mau Mau leaders who were arrested on 20th October 1952. Included are the names of the Leaders of the Kikuyu Central Association (KCA), the Kikuyu Karing'a Schools Association (KKSA), the Kikuyu Independent Schools Association (KISA), the Kenya African Union (KAU), the Youth Wing of KAU and Workers' Unions. There are also names of traders and businessmen and well known taxi drivers. As well, I have included the names of cultural workers like publishers of books and newspapers. Most of the people listed below were leaders of more than one organisation, although it has not always been possible to give a full indication. And all of them were members of KAU. Each person's district is indicated.

A. The Kikuyu Central Association and the Kikuyu Independent School Associations

1. **Jomo Kenyatta.** Kīambuu. National Secretary, KCA. Chairman, KAU. KISA. Editor, *Mũiguithania*.
2. **George K. Ndegwa.** Kīambuu. National Secretary, KCA in Kenyatta's absence. Editor, *Mũiguithania* when Kenyatta was in England.
3. **Job Mũcucu.** Mũrang'a. National Treasurer, KCA.
4. **Willie Jimmie Wambũgũ Maina.** Nanyuki. KCA. Chairman, KISA. Treasurer to Kenya Teachers College, Gīthũngũri.
5. **James Beauttah.** Mũrang'a. KCA. KISA. Chairman, KAU, Mũrang'a Branch. Brought the Bishop who ordained KISA church ministers.
6. **Samuel Koina Gītībi.** Rift Valley. KCA. Head of a clan land committee.* Ex-Chief, Olenguruone.
7. **Joseph Kang'ethe.** Mũrang'a. National chairman, KCA.
8. **Amos Wagaca.** Kīambuu. Chairman, KAU, Limuru Branch. KCA.
9. **Giitwa Ndimũ.** Nanyuki. KCA. Ex-Chief, Mũkogondo, Nanyuki.
10. **Mussa Mũturi.** Mũrang'a. KCA. Manager, Gīkũyũ Club, Pumwani, Nairobi. Conductor of *mũthīrīgũ* song and dance.
11. **John Mbũgua Kamotho.** Kiambuu. KCA. Head of a clan land committee.
12. **Kũng'ũ Karũmba.** Kīambuu. Chairman, KAU, Cura Division. KCA. KISA.
13. **Johana Kīraatū.** Nyeri. KCA. Ex-Chief, Pumwani, Nairobi.
14. **James Njoroge.** Mũrang'a. KCA. Trader in Nairobi. First African driver in Kenya.

*Such people had been elected by their own clans to look after the land interests of the clan.

15. **Paulo Thiong'o.** Rift Valley. KCA. Chairman, KISA, Rift Valley.

16. **Henry Wambūgū Gathūngū.** Nyeri. KCA. Assistant Chairman, KAU, Nyeri.

17. **Johana Karanja.** Kĩambuu. KCA. National Chairman, KKSA.

18. **Paulo Gicaana.** Kĩambuu. KCA. Chairman, clan land committee, Gĩthũngũri.

19. **Mariko Kaambuĩ.** Kĩambuu. KCA. Chairman, clan land committee, Ndĩiya.

20. **Bongwe Icaũ.** Kĩambuu. KCA. Chairman, clan land committee, Cura.

21. **Solomon Meemia.** Kĩambuu. KCA. KISA. Leader of clan land committee.

22. **Cege Kiraka.** Kĩambuu. KCA. KISA. Chairman, Kenya Teachers' College, Gĩthũngũri.

23. **George Waiyaki Wambaa.** Kĩambuu. KISA. Engineer and architect during construction of Kenya Teachers' College. One time principal, KTC.

24. **Mĩnyaru Kahĩa.** Kĩambuu. KCA. Ex-Headman, Ndĩiya.

25. **Tandeo Mwaura.** Mũrang'a. Chairman, KISA, Mùrang'a Branch.

26. **Peter Gatabaki Mũndatĩ.** Kĩambuu. National chairman, KISA.

27. **Stephen Ngure Gicũgũ.** Kĩambuu. Chairman, clan land committee. Cura.

28. **Samuel Kĩhara.** Kĩambuu. Chairman, KISA, Kĩambuu.

29. **Rev. Arthur Gathũng'ũ.** Kĩambuu. KCA. KISA. A church minister in Kĩambuu.

30. **Rev. Petro Kigondu.** Mũrang'a. KCA. KISA. A church minister in Mũrang'a. He swore Kenyatta to loyalty to the nation before Kenyatta was sponsored by KCA to study in England.

31. **Rev. Ephantus Waithaka.** Kĩambuu. KISA. A church minister in Kĩambuu.

32. **Rev. Stefano Waciira.** Nyeri. KISA. A church minister, Nyeri.

33. **Peter Karanũ Kahoro.** Mũrang'a. KISA. KCA. A church leader. Gatanga, Mũrang'a.

34. **Daniel K. Mũgekenyi.** Kĩambuu. KISA. A church leader, Gatũndù, Kĩambuu.

35. **Nehemia K. Kĩbũũthũ.** Nyeri. KISA. A church leader. Agũthi location, Nyeri.

36. **Arthur Mahiga Kĩmani.** Mũrang'a. KISA. A church leader. Marĩira, Mũrang'a.

37. **Joram Wawerũ.** Kĩambuu. KISA. A school parents' association leader, Gatũndũ.

38. **Solomon mtu'Mwiricia.** Merũ. KISA. A school parents' association leader, Merũ.

39. **Benson Gatonye.** Nyeri. KISA. A church leader. Kĩricũ, Nyeri.

40. **Henry Kahoya.** Mũrang'a. KISA. A church leader. Kĩgumo, Mũrang'a.

41. **Danstan Kiboi Wariũa.** Nyeri. KISA. A school parents' association leader, Ũthaya, Nyeri.

42. **Crispus Mwaniki.** Kiambuu. A school headmaster and teacher, Githunguri, Kiambuu.
43. **Rebeka Njeeri.** Kiambuu. KISA. Women's leader at Kenya Teachers' College, Githunguri.
44. **Harrison Waciira.** Nyeri. KISA. A school headmaster, Uthaya.
45. **Ngarama Wagakura.** Kiambuu. KKSA. A school parents' association leader, Muguga.
46. **Girshon N. Tharau.** Kiambuu. KISA. A school parents' association leader, Kirenga.
47. **Johnson Rugio.** Murang'a. KISA. A church leader, Weithaga.
48. **Philip Ngugi Muibu.** Kiambuu. KISA. A school parents' association leader, Mang'u.
49. **C. Mwaura Marite.** Kiambuu. KISA. A school parents' association leader, Kanyariri.

B. The Kenya African National Union

50. **Fred Kubai Kibuuthu.** Nairobi. Chairman, KAU, Nairobi Branch; leader of trade union groups, e.g. East Africa Trade Union Congress.
51. **Anderson Wamuthenya.** Nyeri. Chairman, KAU, Nyeri branch.
52. **Joel K. Weerehire.** Eldoret. Chairman, KAU, Eldoret.
53. **Waira Kamau.** Kiambuu. Chairman, KAU, Kiambuu.
54. **Josaphat Mburati.** Embu. Chairman, KAU, Embu.
55. **Philip Gicoohi.** Nanyuki. Chairman, KAU, Nanyuki.
56. **Onesmus Gacoka.** Thomsons Falls. Chairman, KAU, Thomsons Falls. Chairman, Tribunal Court, Thomsons Falls.
57. **Achieng' Oneko.** Nairobi. National Secretary, KAU.
58. **John Adala.** Kakamega. Chairman, KAU, Kakamega.
59. **Paul Ngei.** Machakos. Assistant National Secretary, KAU. Editor, *Wasya wa Mukamba.*
60. **Bildad Kaggia.** Murang'a. Secretary, KAU, Nairobi. A leader in the East Africa Trade Union Congress. Editor, *Inooro.*
61. **Isaac Kitabi.** Machakos. Treasurer, KAU, Nairobi.
62. **John D. Kali.** Machakos. Member of National Central Committee of KAU. Editor, *Sauti ya Mwafrika.*
63. **Mwinga Chokwe.** Mombasa. Member of National central committee of KAU.
64. **John Mbiyu Koinange.** Kiambuu. Member of central committee of KAU, Nairobi.
65. **Charles M. Wambaa.** Kiambuu. Secretary, KAU, Kiambuu.
66. **Gitahi Waciira.** Nanyuki. Secretary, KAU, Nanyuki.
67. **Samuel Kiragu.** Nyeri. Secretary, KAU, Nyeri.

68. **Romano Njamumo Gĩkunju.** Embu. Secretary, KAU, Embu.
69. **Jackson mtu'Angaine.** Meru. Secretary, KAU, Meru.
70. **Ndeng'era Mũriithi.** Nyeri. Secretary, KAU, Mathĩra.
71. **Kahũgi Gituro.** Kĩambuu. Treasurer, KAU, Kĩambuu.
72. **Daniel Wawerũ.** Elgon. Chairman, KAU, Elgon, Nyanza.
73. **Gacuuru Ngorano.** Nyeri. Treasurer, KAU, Nyeri.
74. **Mbũrũ Mũgwĩra.** Mũrang'a. Member of central committee, KAU, Nairobi.
75. **Wahome Kĩĩhia.** Nyeri. Assistant chairman, KAU, Mathĩra.
76. **Ngũnjiri Kimondo.** Nyeri. Central committee, KAU, Kĩricũ, Nyeri.
77. **B. M. Kamau.** Kĩambuu. Central committee, KAU, Gĩthũngũri.
78. **David Nyamu.** Nyeri. Chairman, KAU, South Tetũ.
79. **Josaphat Wandimbe.** Nyeri. Treasurer, KAU, North Tetũ.
80. **Mũngai Gacũgũ.** Kĩambuu. Central committee, KAU, Limuru.
81. **Paulo Ndũrũ Ndekere.** Nanyuki. Central committee, KAU, Nanyuki.
82. **Mwangi Thabuuni.** Mũrang'a. Central committee, KAU, Mũrang'a.
83. **Njoroge Mbũgua.** Rift Valley. Central committee, KAU, Njooro.

C. Editors and Publishers of Books and Newspapers

84. **Victor Mũrage Wokabi.** Nyeri. Editor of the 2 weeklies, *Mũthamaki* ("The Good Leader") and *Gĩkũyũ na Mũmbi*.
85. **Nyamurua, wife of Henry Mworia.** Kĩambuu. Editor of the weekly *Mũmenyereri*. ("The Care Taker"). Publisher of books.
86. **Gakaara wa Wanjaũ.** Nyeri. Editor and publisher of the monthly news-magazine *Waigua atĩa?* ("What Is the News?"). Author, editor, publisher and printer of books.
87. **John Cege Kabogoro.** Mũrang'a. Editor of weekly, *Wĩyathi* ("Freedom").
88. **Griggory Mbiti.** Embu. Editor of weekly *Mũgambo wa Embu* ("The Voice of Embu").
89. **Isaac Gathanju.** Mũrang'a. Editor of two weeklies, *Wĩhũũge* ("Stay Alert") and *Mũramati* ("Care Taker").
90. **Morris Mwai Koigi.** Nyeri. Editor of the weekly *Mwaranĩria* ("Conversation Maker").
91. **Mwanĩki Mũgwerũ.** Nyeri. Author of the book *Wĩyathi wa Andũ Airũ na Kamũingĩ Koyaga Ndĩrĩ*. ("Freedom for Africans through United Action").

D. Trade Unions and District Councils

92. **Cege Kĩbũrũ.** Nyeri. Domestic and Hotel Workers Union.
93. **John Mũngai.** Mũrang'a. Transport and Allied Workers Union.
94. **George N. Kamũmbũ.** Embu. Night Watchmen Union.

95. **Peter Mũtabi.** Machakos. Domestic and Hotel Workers Union.
96. **Nyamũ Marea.** Embu. Transport and Allied Workers Union.
97. **James Wainaina.** Mũrang'a. Transport and Allied Workers Union.
98. **R. M. Kinũthia.** Mũrang'a. Secretary-General, Domestic and Hotel Workers Union.
99. **Wamũti Mũhũngi.** Kĩambuu. Transport and Allied Workers Union.
100. **Dishon Kahiato.** Nyeri. Commercial, Food and Allied Workers Union.
101. **Isaiah Mũricũ.** Nyeri. A locational councillor, Ũthaya, Nyeri.
102. **Elsaban Mũrigũ.** Nyeri. A locational councillor, South Tetũ, Nyeri.
103. **Joel Warũũĩ Njũgũna.** Mũrang'a. Ex-Welfare Officer, Nakuru Town.
104. **Timothy Maina.** Mũrang'a. A locational councillor, Mũrang'a and a teacher, Kangĩma.
105. **Sera Serai.** A community worker in women's affairs, Nairobi City Council.

E. Traders, Businessmen and Farmers

106. **Simon Mbacia.** Rift Valley. Hotel business; a landlord with houses for rental in Nakuru.
107. **Harrison Karũme.** Nyeri. A trader in skins and leather.
108. **Kĩhara Wandaka.** Nairobi. Owner of a taxi business in Nairobi.
109. **Fred Mbiyũ Koinange.** Kĩambuu. Owner of a goods transport business in Nairobi.
110. **Kagiika Kũhũtha.** Mũrang'a. A hospital assistant in Nairobi.
111. **Gerald Gacaũ.** Nyeri. Trader and farmer in Nyeri.
112. **Mwangi Macaria.** Kĩambuu. Trader and farmer in Kĩambuu.
113. **Jackson Waigera.** Nyeri. Hotel business in Nairobi.
114. **Wallace Waciira.** Nyeri. Hotel business in Nairobi.
115. **Kamau Mwerũ.** Mũrang'a. Owner of a goods transport business in Mũrang'a.
116. **Maina Mũnene.** Kĩambuu. A commissioned salesman.
117. **Ng'ang'a Kanja.** Kĩambuu. A trader and farmer.

F. Taxi Business

118. **Nahashon Itati.** Kĩambuu. A taxi-driver in Gĩthũngũri, Kĩambuu.
119. **Mwangi Baarũ.** Nyeri. A taxi-driver in Nairobi.
120. **Karũũru Mũreebu.** Mũrang'a. A taxi-driver in Nairobi.
121. **Gacangi Gĩkaru.** Nyeri. A taxi-driver in Nairobi.
122. **Ndibũi Wawerũ.** Nyeri. A taxi driver in Nairobi.
123. **Mbũrũ Njoroge.** Kĩambuu. A taxi-driver in Nairobi.
124. **Mũtahi Kĩbiri.** Nyeri. A taxi-driver in Nairobi.
125. **Mũirũ Kinogu.** Nyeri. A taxi-driver in Nairobi.

126. **Ngarĩ Kĩgeca.** Nyeri. A taxi-driver in Nairobi.
127. **Maina Kahuumbĩ.** Mũrang'a. A taxi-driver in Nairobi.

G. The KAU Youth Wing

128. **Daudi Wanyee.** Kĩambuu. Party activist, Dagoretti Corner, Kĩambuu.
129. **Mwangi Wamweya.** Mũrang'a. Activist, Kĩharũ, Mũrang'a.
130. **Njenga Thagicũ.** Kĩambuu. Activist, Dagoretti Corner, Kiambuu.
131. **Ndua Thiong'o.** Kĩambuu. Activist, Dagoretti Corner, Kĩambuu.
132. **Ndegwa Njoroge.** Nyeri. Activist. Gĩkondi, Nyeri.
133. **Wang'ombe Gacerũ.** Nanyuki. Activist, Nanyuki Township.
134. **Mũtonga Karũri.** Kiambuu. Activist, Rirũta, Kĩambuu.
135. **Thuũ Thagicũ.** Kĩambuu. Activist, Dagoretti Corner, Kĩambuu.
136. **Ng'ang'a Kĩbobo.** Kĩambuu. Activist, Gĩthũngũri, Kĩambuu.
137. **Kibeera Gathũkũ.** Kĩambuu. Activist, Rirũta, Kĩambuu.
138. **Kĩhoro Mũriithi.** Nyeri. Activist, Agũthi, Nyeri.
139. **Maara Gatũndũ.** Kĩambuu. Activist, Ndĩiya, Kĩambuu.

Appendix 2: A List of Detention Camps During the Mau Mau Emergency

1. Kajiado (Senya) Detention Camp — Kajiado
2. Marsabit Detention Camp — Marsabit
3. Manda Island Detention Camp — Lamu
4. Manyani Detention Camp — Voi
5. Athi River Detention and Rehabilitation Camp — Nairobi
6. Mackinnon Road Detention Camp — Taita
7. Mageta Island Detention Camp — Kisumu
8. Sayusi Island Detention Camp — Kisumu
9. Takwa Detention Camp — Manda, Lamu
10. Lodwar Detention Camp — Northern Frontier District (NFD)
11. Malingat Detention (Exile) Camp — Rift Valley
12. Hola Detention (Exile) Camp — Tana River
13. Kwale Detention Camp — Tana River
14. Kamiti Women's Detention Camp — Kiambu
15. Mkogondo Detention Camp — Laikipia
16. Mwea Detention Camp — Embu

And in the Gĩkũyũ, Embu and Mĩĩrũ countrysides there were the following "District Work Camps".

17. Karaba Work Camp — Embu
18. Kandongu Work Camp — Embu
19. Gathigiriri Work Camp — Embu/Meru
20. Kangũbiri Work Camp — Nyeri
21. Mjini Work Camp — Mũrang'a
22. Kĩrigiti Work Camp — Kiambu
23. Nyangwethu Work Camp — Rift Valley

Again each Division had its own divisional work camp to which detainees were released at the end of the ("pipe line")

Appendix 3: How to deal with a Mau Mau hard core

This is the copy of the official memorandum normally sent to recommend the demotion of a Mau Mau hardcore detainee.

ATHI RIVER DETENTION AND REHABILITATION CAMP.

Re: _____

      Subject is a proved agitator who has been inciting others against confession or any other kind of co-operation. He has been spreading mau mau propaganda in the Camp. His behaviour has been highly unsatisfactory and is considered to be a thorn and a regular nasty type on the side of the Rehabilitation set-up.

      If he remain here he will severely prejudice the future progress and it will be a blow to our prestige. I recommend that he be moved down the pipe-line.

      Forwarded to the Special Branch Officer i/c., for concurrence.

LIAISON OFFICER,
COMMUNITY DEVELOPMENT AND REHABILITATION,
ATHI RIVER CAMP.

DATE:

==============================

SPECIAL BRANCH REMARKS:-

SIGNATURE:

SPECIAL BRANCH.

DATE:

Appendix 4:

The following six pages reproduce in reduction a camera copy of Gakaara wa Wanjaũ's book, *Mageria Nomo Mahota* which had been translated from the Kiswahili booklet *Roho ya Kiume na Bidii kwa Mwafrika*, and whose publication featured prominently in Gakaara's detention order (see also Appendix 9).

1

TUGUTURA TUTANGIKAGA NGINYA - RI ?

Athungu ni moi wega ati twi na uhoti, ugi ona umenyo wa gwika maundu manene ta nduriri iria ingi ciothe cia thi, ni undu ona ithui turi na meciria ota o, no tundu Athungu ni mendaga gutura bururi-ini uyu witu magiikaraga magithahagia maundu maitu ona gutumenereria ni getha ati na ithui twimene. Maŋakiugaga ati tutigaine a kwiatha ona angi magaturuma tondu wa kuga ati meciria maitu ni ta ma twana na ati atongoria aitu ti ogi matingihota gututongoria wega. Ici ciothe ikoragwo iri o njira cia ŋutucambia na kuhenia irimu na makiria gutunyururia ati niguo twimene o riria megukorwo makimenya ati gutiri kindu ona kimwe Ngai atatuhete na twahota kwiikira undu o wothe wikagwo ni mundu.

Gutiri mundu utoi ati thina nduri miri na ati uhunii etaga uria uhutii mukoroku. Nitui ati mundu o wothe angitonga ndangicoka gwithinia na ŋawira ma hinya mangikorwo matikumuhe umithio, na nikio Athungu aria marutagirwo mawira ta maya ni andu airu matikiendaga andu airu magie na njira cia gutonga narua, niguo mature mamarutagira wira.

Tungihura mbica ya mundu muiru umuthi uyu tukuona ati aturaga atarii ta ndungata ya nduriri iria ng'eni harī kumarutagira mawira mao marie mamarehagire umithio na utonga o hingo iria we mundu muiru ataiganagwo ona kairia ka ii. Ni kieha kinene tondu mundu muiru aturaga atakindiirie tondu wa kwagagio na njira nyingi cia kumuthinia na waara, tondu wa kuguciririo ona kuonererio maundu manene na mega ma kwiririria, o marie maingi we atahetwo kamweke kega ga kumanyita uhuthu. Tondu ucio mundu muiru agigakinyita ikinya riu onereirio akoragwo atangikite na akanoga muno. Ino ni hitho nene ya Comba na ni uhoro wa kieha makiria riria tukumenya ati o hingo iyo we mundu muiru egukorwo agiitanga ta uguo, we Muthungu ni akoragwo akimenya o wega ati minoga ya mundu ucio muiru niyo ariaga akanora na agatonga akeyona na akahota kuruma mundu muiru na kumwita kirimu tondu ndekwenda amenye hitho iyo. Riu-i, tungikirora wega na twicirie ni tukuona ati uthini witu urehagwo no njira imwe ta ici.

2

Athungu aria marutagirwo mawira ta maya na makiria Athungu a Migunda na Onjoria ni makoragwo na wihoko ona umenyo mũnene ati mangitabarira njira cia kugiriririra mundu Muiru agie na mieremano yakugia indo cia kumuigana hatiri na nganja ati ni egutura amatungatagira nginya mindi na mindi, na ni getha Athungu acio monage umithio kuma hari hinya ugi ona uruti wa wira wake. One mawira mothe ma hinya ona ma bata na umithio munene maratungatwo no andu airu. Wahota kuona ati mundu Muiru thii-ni wa mweri umwe ni arutaga wira wa kurehe umithio wa Ciringi magana maingi muno nowe-ri arihagwo kindu kinini muno kuringana na minoga, ona hinya wake uria atumiire hari guthondeka kindu kiu kana kuruta wira ucio. Undu ungi muuru makiria ni ati wira ucio na minoga yake yothe ndikoragwo iri na ngatho kana kuheo gitio wira-ini tondu hingo ciothe we arutaga wira agiathaguo na ciugo cia hinya, na gwitwo boi (ta kahii kanini) na kugatangagwo kamucara gake kanini, na gwikangagwo tuundu tuingi tungi twa kumurakaragia o hingo hingo, no getha ndak enda kahinda kega ga gucokaniriria meciria make, na niguo ndagekindire na ndakamenye ati ni areka undu wi na bata muno hari Muthungu. Ni hinya muno ona ungiruta wira mwega atia ndungiirua ugicokerio ngatho ati ni weka wega, tiga no muthungu amenyire na ngoro na ekirire. Ririkana hitho ino na wirute makiria, ati maundu maya mekikaga no getha mundu muiru akoragwo atari na kamweke ga gutonga ga menene, eyagire kiene, na ature ari ndungata ya ageni nginya tene. Tondu ucio ni handu haku kumenya haria urungii na niguo riu uguthii githoma haha kabere.

ATI TUGAYANITIO NIGUO TWATHIKE

Athungu nio moigite kaundu gaka ati gayania na ni ukuhota gwathana uhuthu. Ta wicirie kana andu airu umuthi uyu ni maiguaine na kana ni agayanie ? Uguo ugutuonia ati athungu ni moi ati tungicokaniriria ngoro ciitu bamwe tutuike kindu kimwe gutiri undu ungiturema. Tondu ucio ni turore kana ni tugayanitio ni getha tutige kuiguithanagiria

3

ona tukamenanaga ithui ene, tondu wa kuhurithanio ciongo na waara o riria o ageni acio mari na uiguano munene wa gutuma tumaheage umithio na minoga ona ugi witu tondu wa waara wao.

Tondu wa gutururio ta uu andu amwe ni morite o kuura, magatuika ta atumumu na agathurana, magakiugaga atiri : "Nii ndi wa ndini ya Mohamed" Uria ungi nake akoiga ni Mukristiano ona ungi nake-ri ni Mukaring'a. Hau noho hacokaga hakoima "Wee ni uretia tondu wa kwaria githungu ta uri muthungu" ungi : "Wee nduri na nguo theru tutingitkarania" ungi nake akemena akoiga: "Mundu muiru no mundu muiru" na mangi ta maya. Maundu ta maya monekaga gatagati-ini o ka andu airu tondu wa kuhurithanio ciongo magatururio niguo matikagie na uiguano na mature mahitanitie na niguo mahotage gutumirwo uhuthu tondu ni ta irimu.

Ta rorai ithaka ciitu, icio nigutunywo twagitunyirwo ni comba tondu tutiakimahere. Tondu wa gutunywo ithaka-ri ni twagite migunda ya gutuigana hari urimi mwega ona ya gutuigana hari uikaro. Riu Agikuyu matindaga magiitanga mbia ciao magicirithania o ene tondu wa migunda ithaka ona mibaka, o hingo iria matangihota guthitanga athungu aria marikitie guthi na ithaka ciao. Mahiu ma Agikuyu riu niguthiririkira marathiririkira tondu wa kwaga gwa kuriithia tondu mititu yothe minene na minoru ona weru uria munoru ni wathire na comba, na nikio Mugikuyu no agitindaga akiururia ng'ombe ciake agicicariria nyeki o riria itekunoneka ya kuigana. Riria Mugikuyu akiagite migunda na akaga mahiu-ri, kai akiri na utonga ona kana mwikinyiro ungi uriku ?

1. Kuma hau mundu angiaga mieremeno ya urimi mwega kana mahiu-ri ni kurutanitwo ati mundu ahota gwicariria wira kuri Ageni Kuu mundu muiru nikuo akiandikagwo kamucara kanini gatangiigana mabataro make ni getha ature arutaga wira. Ririkana ati hingo iyo yothe ya kuruta wira gwa Comba ucio mundu muiru ni akoragwo agikombonrithio nyumba, ni ariaga irio cia goro, todu wa kuguciririo na waara niguo tubeca twake tuthiririkagire. Marihi ma nyumba ni manene uu ati ni ta kugayana mundu agayanaga kamucara kau na mwene nyumba. Kaingi no nyumba uririkane ati nyumba icio ikoragwo iri cia comba o ucio ukwandikite na nikio mbia ciothe icokaga o kuri-o. Tuthendi turia tugugicoka gutigara-ri ni turiku ?

4

2. Ta no kirore ningi. Andu aria angi nao maturaga migunda-ini minene ya Athungu nio Thikwota. Gutiri andu maturaga thina-ini ta aya. Hingo iria mari kuu matiri na rutha rwa kuriithia ng'ombe nyingi kana mburi ati ni ikurehere ng'ombe cia muthungu murimu. Migunda nayo-ri gutiri mundu uri na rutha kurima gukira ika imwe ona ni gukorwo muthungu ucio ari na migunda minene atia. Mucara naguo ni ta gwathirwo mighayirwo kiria mekuheo, amu tumicara twa matikwota ona tutingithngerera nuthu yamabataro mao. Ni getha mundu one tubeca tuiganu, mutumia marutagira muthungu wira hamwe na mutumia wake na ciana ciake ciothe na matiendagwo mamenye maundu maria moimaga na mucii-ini kana town ni getha matikohige. Magiikaraga o ndumaini makarutaga wira wa hinya na mutumia munene o uria uthiaga na muthungu nao makoima ona minoga. Magithukumaga ona thina ati ona matigiaga na meciria ma kuma kuu tondu wa gutururio na kuhenio ati ni maiganagwo, ni undu wa kwaga kumenya maria marathii na mbere miena ingi. Githi nao acio matiguigitura minyamaro-ini ?

3. Gikundi kiria kingi nakio ni kiria gituraga Majengo. Tene athungu matanoka-ri ni kwari majengo ? Acio mendaga gutura micii-ini iria minene-ri mui ni kwao matari ? Indi nimahenereirio na hinya muno makonio ati ni wega gutura micii-ini ta ino ni getha monagire muthungu umithio na njira mithemba

222

ningi. Ta wicirie miturire yao kuo. Ona haria amwe
ne na nyumba nikuonekaga ati aingi ao maturaga
nyumba cia gukomborithio no athungu acio, amwe ni
nonaga thina muno wa nguo na irio, ririkana no
muhaka marutage igoti na no muhaka makoragwo
nandikitwo mawira, ni getha matigetwo mikora.
Nyumba icio makite no muhaka mathirwo uria
negukomborithia kana gutura kuo na makagucagio
na maundu ma gicomba muno o riria mataheagwo
micara kana maundu maiganaine na comba. Nituonaga
ati Muthungu atonga ni kuinuka ainuikaga kwao
Ruraya no acio matihotaga kuinuka tondu wa
kwagagio ni thina nginya mundu agakuira o kuo.

4. Andu angi nao ni Arimi aria meturagira
Gikuyu-ini na thina wao. Maturaga marutaga wira-
wa kurima tumigunda twao na gukuria irio
ciao o wega ta cie. Athungu, no hingo ya kwendia
makerwo ciao ti ngurie wega na kwoguo mathogora

5

makagia na ngurani. Hingo iria irio icio ciathio na
ithii ona kana ciarugwo tuticokaga kuigua mathogora
magitigithanio na guticokaga kugia mathogora ma
mutu wa mbembe cia Muthungu kana wa mbembe cia
Mugikuyu na ciothe icamaga o undu umwe. Ni kugiaga
na tumawatho twa kugiria maciaro matigatwarwo
kuma bururi guthii bururi ungi o riria we murimi wa
Muthungu atari na watho ta ucio. Ngwiciria murimi
Mugikuyu akuragia irio ciake niguo endie o kuria
guothe angiona thogora wa kumukenia, na tondu ucio
gutikiagiriire kugie na tumihinga twa kumugiria
eyonere umithio niguo ndagokire narua, o riria
arageria gwithondekera miikarire yake Gikuyu-ini
gwake.

5. Gicunji kiria kingi ni kia onjoria. Ni kuoneke
ati wonjoria niguo urarehe utonga Gikuyu-ini, ona uria
gutarii mabururi mangi. Agikuyu amwe ni mahotete
gutwara wonjoria wao mbere wega no atiri, kuringana
na uria o mundu wothe ekwiyonera ni ati mundu muiru
kaingi ni aremagwo ni kwagiria wonjoria wake tondu
wa mathogora manene ma indo. Marithenthi na magoti
ma nduka nene ni ma goro muno, ona ningi marithenthi
ma gutwara indo kana kurehithie indo kuma mabururi
ma kuraya monekaga na hinya. Ni kuri na
marithenthi mamwe mataheagwo andu airu ta ma
njohi iria nduru na ingi ta icio. Maundu ta maya ni
makirehage mihinga wonjoria-ini na andu airu na nikio
tutuka twao tutihotaga gukura wega tiga o hingo iria
mundu angikorwo erutaniirie muno nginya akona
kamweke na munyaka mwega. Nikio o nao onjoria
matuikaga ati ona Hingo iria marageria guthondeka
njira cia gwitongia mathikoragwo magika uguo uhuthu.

6. Ta nituone uhoro wa athukumi aria marutaga
mawira gwa thirikari mingara ya thirikari o nayo ni
itabariirwo iri o minini tondu ni tukuona ati kuri na
andu angi airu mari na ugi munene ona magakira
athungu amwe na ahindi indi mucara wao no munyinyi.
Uguo ugutuonia atia ? Amwe ao nimatonyaga magerio-
ini ma kuhakwo muno na makiria aria makonainie na
wathani ta anene na thigari ona angi ta acio. Tondu
wa micara kunyiha amwe ni matonyaga mageriori ma
kuiya indo cia thirikari kuu wira-ini niguo mahote
gwiteithia na thutha wa maundu ta maya mundu
agathuika ngumo yake ona iri njega. Kuma hau
gugatuika ati andu airu matingihokeka o riria egukorwo atonyete ihitiani ta riu ni undu wa thina. Amwe ao
nimakoragwo meriirwo ati ni makaheo iheo thutha

6

wa kuruta wira ta miaka 20, no atiriri ona angikorwo
mundu ni akaheo Shs. 3000/- kana 4000/- ageka nacio
atia o hingo iria arikitie gukura ? Ihinda riu riothe
ria gweterera kiheo giki akoragwo akiriirie mathina
o getha akona tubeca tuu turi tuingi hingo imwe.
Agituraga na thina wa nguo, toro ona irio ndahotaga
kuria igakinya na ii undu hingo ino yothe no
arateithia mutumia na guthomithia ciana ciake o
agitanyaga no akona mbia nyingi. Ndangitiga wira o
na atia tondu angitiga onakio kiheo no kiage ona
angikorwo atigairie mweri umwe. Mundu uria uui wega
ta ni anjire kana Shs. 3000/- ona kana 6000/- ciahota
kuigania mabataro ma mundu wa matuku maya na
ukwenda kurumirira gicomba ?

7. Aria angi nao ni athigari aitu aria me mbara-
ini. Aya nao hingo yao njega no hinya iria mararua
kana hingo yothe me ita-ini. Hingo iyo nimageragia
kuheo ikeno nene ona kuheo ngumo njega ona gukenio
na ikeno nene ona kugathiririo ta uria andu airu moi
mbara na matari guoya. Indi kuri o kaundu kamwe
gatangirekwo kaiganane nao nako ni mucara. No

atiriri angikorwo mbara-ini tuguthii muthitari o umwe
tugiikia mburuburu-ri tukwaga guthii muthitari o
umwe niki riria tukuheo mucara ? Ningiri muthigari
mweru-ri githi arathwo ni thu ndegukua o undu umwe
na wa mundu muiru ? Megukiaga kuigananio niki ?
Athigari hingo ya kwandikwo kana hingo ya guthii
mbara-ini nimakunguyagirio muno ona ningi riria
mekuo makerirwo maundu mega ati makaheo moima,
no hingo iria moima mbara-ini tuticokaga kuigua
ngumo ciao uria ithiraga. Aingi ao maturaga
manegenaga ati ni meragwo ni makaroragirwo maundu mao wega na hingo iria makinya kuuria maundu
ta maya no makerwo ati uhoro wa uthigari ni
wathirirre o riria oimire mbara-ini.

8. Ciana ciitu na Githomo. Ota uria mundu wothe
ekwiyonera ni ati hingo ino mundu muiru ni agite na
ng'aragu nene makiria ya Githomo tondu wa kumenya
ati maundu mothe mega marehagwo no ugi na nikio o
mundu ni arakorwo akienda mwana wake athome o
uria angihota. Tondu wa uria andu aingi matakoragwo
na miguu maikaraga makihurithanaiga na
thina wao ati no geka mwega nikio mbia cia guthomithia
ciana ciao. Cukuru cia githomo kia iguru ni ciagaga
tondu tutiri na macukuru ma kuiganu na tutiri na mbia
nyingi cia kuhota kwiyakira macukuru maingi manene

7

ta makoleji na Univasiti na tondu ucio kaana
gatihotaga kugia na ugi muiganu. Tondu ucio
gutingioneka handu ha guthomera kaana ka muthini
tondu wa marihi manene na mathogora manene
ma indo cia guthoma macio nguo ona irio. Angikorwo
kaana ni gatiga githomo tondu wa kwaga mbia-ri uria
kangigika ni atia ? No gagathii gwicariria wira
hihi ta wa Karani, Deresa, Dereva, Makanika,
Murutani na mangi ta macio. Ririkana ati kuria
gegucaria wira no kwa Athungu nao makoragwo
makimera ati matiri na ugi wa kuigana na tondu ucio
ekuheo kamucara kanini. Ungiciria thina wa mundu
ta ucio ihinda-ini riu no uigue tondu wa mathina
maria akoragwo akiona.

Ni Twagiriirwo ni Kwimena ?

Riu ni hindi hingo ikinyite ya mundu o wothe
muiru kuhingura maitho, one mawara maya na nikio
aigue ruo ngoro-ini yake tondu wa mathina maya.
Eiguire kieha tondu wa guikara ari kirimu na eyone
uria ari mundu wa bata bururi-ini wake ona ecirie haria
we arungii. Uguo ni ta kuga atiri, o uguo ageni acio
mekuhota kugia na uiguano wa gutunyamaria na thina-
ri ithui na ithui nitubataire tuiguane, tucokanie ndundu
niguo na ithui tuhote guthengia mihinga, iyo ya waara
ya gutugiririria tutonge ati getha tutikaigaane nao.

Gutiri kwoneka kihoto ona kinini gia kugiria
mundu muiru aheo mucara wa kumuigana kuringana
na umenyo ona uhoti wa uruti wake wira ota uria
Athungu, Ahindi na Arabu maheagwo. Gutiri hingo
mundu, muiru akaiganwo ndekuheo njira cia
kuigananio na ndururi iria ingi hari mucara ona maundu
na mawabo maria mothe mataringaine hari ndururi
ciothe iria ituraga bururi uyu witu. Ni undu-ri mundu
muiru ni akionetio ati kuria irio njega ni wega,
kwihumba nguo theru, guthii na mitoka ona, ndege,
gwaka nyumba njega guthoma muno na mangi ta
maya mothe no mega na monekaga ona mbia. Indi
kimako nakio ni ati o riria maundu macio monanitio ta
uguo ni hacokete hakagia na mihinga ona giririria cia
gutuma mundu muiru aremagwo ni gukinyira maundu
maya uhuthu.

Thiini wa nduka cia Athungu tutiri tuona kindu
kiandikitwo ati kiu ni kia muthungu na kiu ni kia
mundu muiru tiga no mundu wothe uria ungikorwo ena

8

mbia egurire. Igoti-ini kuria guciragirwo tuonaga
andu othe eru, atune ona airu magituirwo ona ituiro
rimwe kuringana na ihitia ria muthemba umwe. Tondu
ucio onayo micara ndikiagiriirwo ni kwamuranagio ni
undu uguo ni kuonia mundu muiru ati hingo iria
ekuruta mbia ni hakoragwo na uiguano no hingo iria
ekwamukira hakagia na utiganu. Kihoto kiri ha ?

Gutiri hingo mundu muiru agakira atonete ati
maundu ni marekwo kuringana hari nduriri ciothe na
makiria hatiri gitumi ona kiriku gia kuga ati ti ithui
twagiriirwo ni gukorwo tugiathana bururi-ini witu
tondu ni ithui ene guo-Gutiri hingo tukaiganwo
tutonete ati ni ithui turoiga na tugeka uria tukwenda
na uguo ni ta kuga ni tugie na wiathi.

Tondu wa gukimenya o uguo wiki ni hingo ya mundu wothe muiru gwitonyia hari wendi wa bururi uyu na makiria gwiciria uria tungicokerio Ithaka ciitu amu hau noho uthini witu woimanire naho. Kai tukiri iguoya cia naku ithui ? Hatari na uiguano gutiri na undu tungihota kwiikira, na nikio undu wa mbere nitwagiriirwo ni tuiguane, muthini na gitonga, kirimu na mugi, kionje ona mundu mugima andu anja ona arume, ithuothe tugie na ngoro o imwe ya kwenda bururi witu kuutetera na kwiatha. Tukiagiriirwo ni tuone ati turi na andu aingi ogi o gutuaririria na mari urume ni getha mahotage gukararukagia na Athungu hatari kuuna maitho hari njira cia kweherera mathina maya. Angikoruo turikoragwo na aririria anini Ciama-ini iria ikonainie na wathani wa bururi uyu gutiri hindi tutarihotagwo tondu maundu mahitukagio na kura.

Hamwe na uguo ti wega kurekereria andu amwe matuikage ta ari o matuitwo ateteri a bururi. Ona haria andu othe matangihota gutuika a kwaria Ciamaini hamwe na Athungu ona Ahindi ni wira wa mundu o wothe muiru kuona ati ari na undu arateithiriria hari gutetera bururi witu. Gutetera bururi to kwaria kana kwandika, no makiria ni kugia na wendi wa bururi na ruriri rwaku uguo ni ta kuga ukariranagia nao hingo iria mekurira na ugakenanagira nao hingo iria megukena. Tondu ucio ni urikoragwo hingo ciothe ukigia na mihang'o ya kwenda kumenya maundu maria marekika kana uria ubataire ni gwika hari gucaria wiathi.

9

NI KABA GUKUA

Mundu wothe muiru utendete bururi uyu ndabataire ni gutura guku Gikuyu-ini ni kaba angikua atige guturehere hathara ya gutuingihia o riria atari na uguni hari ruriri. Ucio-ri atari ota tumiti turia tuicuhagio ni Ikamba, na tutikwenda mihianano ya andu guku Gikuyu-ini.

Andu aingi maturaga mahana ta mareru kana cieha iria ciigwatagirira miti-ini ni undu icio ituraga iriaga hinya wa miti iria iri na miri na ikuraga. Ucio nguo thina uria wiragwo nduri miri, na nguo wee nawe utari angikorwo ndwendete gwitanga tondu wa bururi waku, amu o rimwe kihuhukanio gioka-ri no ukahubaniroi onarua ni undu uikaraga utehariirie. Ni thoni nyingi kugia na andu ta acio guku Gikuyu-ini, acio metagirira guthinikiruo ni andu aria angi o hingo iria o mekirire mategwitanga hari kuuna ukomboini. Ririkana o ringi ati andu ta aya nio aria aturuire maitho na tondu ucio maikaraga nduma-ini.

Ti wega kwiyamura ati wee uri wa ndini kana wee nawe wi Mwonjoria kana wi Murutani kana Karani na ati wee nduri muteti. Hingo iria ugwitia wongererwo Mucara ririkana ni urateta tondu ni urona nduiganitwo na nikio ni wega ukoragwo hamwe na aria angi hingo iria megwiciria uhoro wa kuiganano kwa mucara. Ona wakorwo wi munene wa bururi ririkana ati andu a bururi waku mangituika ni meguthamio bururi ucio gutiri hingo wee ungitigwo. Wee nawe gitonga ririkana githaka kiu giaku nikio gitindaga gigiteterwo ona aria magutetera no gukorwo matiri kagombe na ni maiguaga ruo na moiagaga ni kaba makue magithinika ta uria tungicokerio ithaka ciitu. Ona wakorwo wi muthini atia ririkana ati uriaga tiri, niguo nyina waku na noguo thoguo. Ugugikira niki riria andu megukorwo makiuga macokerio tiri wao ? Kai wee uriaga ki, na uturaga ku ? Wendaga gukenera minoga ya Ariu na Aari a nyukwa niki ?

Nima ati korwo mundu o mundu ahota kugia na wendi wa guteithiriria Ciama ciitu no tuone wiathi onarua. Tubataire ni kuona ati ni turikoragwo micemanio-ini yothe iitu ya uhoro wa bururi na kuhotha na wendi munene kiondo o giothe kiria kingikorwo gikiendekana ni atongoria aitu turi na ngoro o imwe.

10

Wee, tiga kuga ati ndukuhinga nduka yaku kana no muhaka wambe uthii kiumia kana ni kaba uthii ukanyue njohi kana ugekenie na ikeno ta cia mubira, thenema, na ingi ta icio, oriria ugukorwo ukimenya wega ati kwina mucemanio wa gwiciria uria tungiuma ukombo-ini. Micemanio ta ino igiaga mahinda mamwe na mamwe na nima wi na mahinda manene ma gwika maundu maingi maku. Ririkana ati maundu maria makoragwo magiteterwo ni andu airu ni magukonii tondu ona we ndukiri Muthungu ugugieterera wariririo

niki ? Riria turahoya macukuru-ri githi ti kaana gaku gagathomere kuo ? Kai wee utendaga twehererio watho wa gukuaga bathi na kunyitagwo ni Haraka uninwo ? Kana ningi-ri wee githi ndugaga ni wega tucokerio ithaka ciitu na tuongererwo micara ? Tondu ucio-ri thiaga micemanio-ini ukaruta mihothi angikorwo ni ukwenda maundu maya no akorwo ti uguo-ri hakiri bata wa kii wa gutindaga ukiuga na kanua ? Ni kaba gukira ki.

Tiga gwitigira kwaria undu uria ukuona ni kihoto amu kiunaga uta mugete. Wakiuga ati wi wa thirikari kana ati Muthungu uria ukwandikite ndendaga uthii mucemanio wa K.A.U.-ri hingo iyo egukorwo agikuguna kana agigute ? Muthungu ta ucio menya ni muugi tondu ekwenda uikare uri kirimu na niguo ndukamenye hitho yake uture umutungatagira etongere wee nawe ndukohige uture uri muthini. Twagiriirwo ni kuonia Athungu ta acio ati twi na bata na ni twendete bururi witu ona ati makienda gututaba mawira macio ni kaba matubute, na ithui twiyathe.

GUTIRI MUNDU WAMETIRE.

Ni uhoro uri thoni kuona ati riu ithui ni kuhoya tuhoyaga handu ha gwaka o riria turi bururi-ini witu ati ona njira iria tuguthiira-ri no turihaga na mundu uria wageria kwaria kana kuria uhoro ucio-ri akaringwo mutwe nao aria angi mona uguo-ri magethuna. Githi uguo tigukionania ati matiendaga mundu uria ukuona kaundu na akaria ma o hingo iria mundu abataire ni kwaria o uria angiona ni kihoto. Ithui tutiendaga mbaara. Ithui turiaragia na kanua na tutiri hingo tutakoiga ni tukwenda wiathi niguo ona ithui tuiganane na nduriri iria ingi itathagwo na twikage o uria tungienda gwika. Tondu

11

ucio thirikari iitu ni ikibataire ni kuona ati andu a nduriri ciothe iria iri Kenya ni igwikirwo maundu ma kuiganana hatari uhoro wakurora uhoro wa nduriri kana wa rangi.

Tukwenda tugie na Aririria aingi muno Kiama-ini ka Gavana ona ciamaini ciothe iria ikonainie na wathani wa bururi uyu. Ithui ni ithui aingi na nikio ni ithui tabataire nigukorwo turi na aririria hari Ciama-ini ta icio, na makiria ma uguo tutikwenda guthurirwo andu ta acio, tukwenda gwithuragira ithui ene tondu ni ithui tuui aria ega na aria matangihota ni undu "Kanyiri kainagio ni mwene". Akorwo tukwenda andu mirongo inana ni iguru riitu gwithutira ithui ene tondu ni ithui tui aria moi na matoi mathina maitu mothe wega.

Riria Athungu matokite bururi-ini uyu makorire o tukiyatha na tutiaremetwo ni kwiyatha. Gutiri mundu wametire ati moke matuonie gwathana tiga nio metonyereirie na waara ati ni guturuta megutuuta thina-ini. Riu amwe moiagaga ati bururi uyu ndwari witu ati waari wa Ndurubu angi noo moigagaa ni bururt wa nduma. Tugakiuria atiri, kai makiremagwo ni guikara bururi-ini ucio wao wa utheri niki ? Ningi tondu nio maragiathana-ri nuu wamaheire bururi uyu ? Ningi-ri ti kaba magithii kwao na ithui tugicokerie Ndurubu bururi wao ? Moigaga ati ni thayu matureheire tondu wa kunina mbaara ciitu na Masai no tungiciiria wega uhoro wa mbaara ciitu na Masai-ri ciari o kaundu kanini tondu ni ciana cia nyina umwe ciathakanagla. Masai maakiri thu ciitu atia na nitwakiguranagira, ningi mokaga Gikuyu-ini magataba ng'ombe nao Agikuyu magathii Masai-ini mageka o taguo, hathara yakiri iriku? Masai-ri matiatutunyite ithaka ciitu ona kana ithui tugathii gutura bururi-ini wao, na hingo iria gutari Athungu-ri kwari gikeno kinene ona irio nyingi na mahiu maingi guku Gikuyu-ini na twari itonga cia bata na njamba cia hinya.

Mbaara iria athungu matureheire ni ya uthini amu ni ya gutuikaria riera-ini tutari haria turi ni undu wa kwagagio ni uthini, na nginya hingo iria tukamenya hitho ino ithuothe gutiri hingo tutegutura turiraga. Tondu-ri wahota atia gwakania haria wa warikia kuruta utheri ukauhumbira na gitambaya mwena umwe ni getha utheri ndukoneke wothe? Angigikorwo ni tuonetio githomo ni kiega na ningi tutiri na Macukuru makuigana na mbia tukaimwo-ri githi kuu titagucumikio tucumikagio ? Ni kaba utarai ucio uikare.

12

Matanya Mao Ni Mamenyeku.

Riu tondu ni tumenyete mawara mao tukahun-
urania hitho ciao kamwe kamwe na makiria
ngaturwo ngoro ona miiri-ri, tugugikira niki ? Aca !
utingicoka kumiriria minyamaro ati tondu wa
witikagia maundu o maria tukuona ni magutwrekeria
chini-ni. Amu riu turiikaraga twihugite hari miario
iyo yao ya waara wa gutumenereria ati niguo na
hui twimene na twiyagire kiene.

Nitui nama ati ithui andu airu turi arathime ni
gai. Ini agituhe bururi mwega uu, ati niuiguagirwo
ru Ni munoru na uri na mitheruba yothe.Matituonaga
akimahoya irio ciao ni gukorwo ni ithui twirimagira
igunda iitu. Tukiagiriirwo ni gwitiia ni undu wa thi
o iitu, tumikumagie amu tiri-ini o uyu-ri noguo uri
a utonga wothe wa mahiga maria ma goro ta
ahabu. Mititu minene minoru ona njui nene iria iri
gumo Ngai aciyuritie kundu guothe bururi-ini witu.
ondu ucio kindu giothe tungienda-ri kiri a tiri-ni,
yu witu. Tugukiaga gukinyukia thi-ini ino iitu na
nya niki ?

Riu tutingicoka guthikiriria ciugo icio ciao cia
utumenereria magitwitaga ciana na athini ona kana
utebebio ni twiko tuu twao ati niguo tugegio nituo na
witigire. Nayo mihinga iyo ya guturigiriria tugie na
ndo-ri ati niguo tutikaiganane nao-ri tukumiciririra na
iyo twicoketie ndundu tumithengie o kahora na
iguano amu riu tuticoka gukoma na kugutara.
ukuruta wira na hinya o nginya tukaiganana nao na
imakire ona tumathe kana tumaingate mathii kwao.
o niyo ngoro iria twinayo kuma umuthi.

Ini tondu nitukimenyete ati gutiri na gitumi gia
utuma twitigirage mundu uri na thakame on muoyo
ta ithui tondu wa gutuhenia na ciiko o iria
a ithui turi na uhoti wa gwika o take, kana tukonaga
a ari na umenyo muingi gutukira. Undu uria uragi-
ikenia makiria ni kumenya ati tuturaga turi na guoya
ondu wa gwitigirithio na guoya ucio niguo utumaga
umenwo. Hi, Aca ! Riu hingo ni nginyu ya kwaria na,
ondu-ri twagitura twaragiria ngungui-ini na guoya-ri
ithi to gukimemendwo tukumemendwo ni thina na
iinyamaro. Nituonete ati kwororoa kuu gwitu ona
witikagia hingo ciothe nikuo gutumaga matutonyerere

a matunyarire amu kamuoroto kao no tuture
umatungatagira niguo nao mature makenaga na
natongaga kuma hari hinya wa miiri iitu, ithui na
hui-ri tuhinyarage miiri ona ngoro tondu wa thina
i, twagicoka gweterera kuhenererio na rurimi ruu
wa waara na uhinga atia ? Ni undu-ri magitutuaga
imu o irimu amu-ri matarii ta andu aria metagwo
huhi-ouria ni undu rurimi rwao-ri rututhaithaga
uororoete niguo tutonyio mitego-ini na noruo
ucokaga rugatumenereria na gutucambia ona gut-
nyururia. Kai gukiri na kihoto kiriku gia kurekereria
ndu amwe metage aria angi nugu na matingiurio
o riria andu metia ithaka ciao makeruo ati ni
narahenania. Kai kuri hingo ithui tugakira ?
Makiuagaga ati kirimu gitiagiriire ni kuheo gitio na
thui tugakihoka ati turi o irimu na tukemena. Hi riu
aitho ni mahinguku tukona haraya na tukamenya
utiri na kaundu tutiganite nao.

Onao-ri kai mangikiriganirwo ati kahiu kaha-
garagia karia kangi gagakohigia na gagacoka gutema
nukanori ? Ithui tugutumira o kihoto tondu nituklo-
ete ati turi na uhoti wa mithemba yothe. Ni amuri
ugukirwo tutiri na ugi niki? Ni undu uriku mundu
uiru atangihota gwika wikagwo ni mundu uri muoyo.
undu muiru ni athomete nginya muico wa githomo,
iu twina andu airu Majaji, Arutani me ngumo
Mandagitari a mithemba yothe. Mundu muiru ni
jamba akorogwo mbere mbaara-ini ni oi gutwara
dege ona meri, ari mbere mathakoini ta ma thenema
a ngundi kana mahenya na gutiri kaundu ona kamwe
tangihota gwika. Tugucicoka kwirwo tutiri undu
utangiikira niki ? Ningi ucio ukiugaga niwe uui
rukira aria angi guku thi niwe-u ? Mundu wothe
higaga ni undu wa kwiruta tondu Ngai
mbite andu na akamahe meciria muthemba umwe
ani handu ha mundu o mundu atumire meciria make,
nundu muiru ni erutite gwika ota uguo andu aria angi
merutite. Tugukimakio niki ithui ?

Ona riu ni tukenete makiria tondu wa kuhithura
aitho iyo yao ya gutugiririria tutonge amu tungiri
tonga-ri tungiaka Macukuru ma ngoroba igana, ona

twiyakire mikawa iitu matangithengerera. Tugie na
nduka ciitu nene na ngaari ciitu nene ona ndege cia
kumbukaga nacio, tutwarage ci_na ciitu nacio
mabururi ma kuraya igathome na hingo iyo-ri no mone

ati gutiri na undu matukirite naguo. Tondu ucio-ri
twagiriirwo ni kwirutaniria na kiyo ona twenda
guthigina thakame ni kaba o nginya tuone ni tuiganaine
nao. Tukunyitana mbutu ya uiguano ota tunyamu
turia twitagwo thuraku ni getha twerana tutharikire
undu muna tugeka o rimwe tuiguaniire. Ini ota uria
tunyamu tuu turi urume-ri ona ithui twiheane gukua
na kuhona. Akorwo ni gwaka Cukuru tugeka guo na
ngoro theru. Akorwo ni gutwara kaana Amerika
tugeka guo na ngoro ciguaniire. Akoruo ni kuhotha
mbia cia gutuma Mutongoria kundu agatwariririe
tukahotha na kiyo.

Ota uria mbumbui iyakagira nyumba yayo na
rurenda rwayo o ikiguaga na muico ikahota kurikia
ona ithui andu airu noguo tukwirutaniria na kiyo
onginya tukona wiathi. Ni undu-ri kai kanyoni gakiri
na hinya wa kwiyakira nyumba na kamuthece na
gakarikia na ithui twina meciria, moko ona maguru
tutingihota kwiikira kiundu gia kugegia kirindi. Riu
ni twiharirie-i, amu-ri mbere no mbere na thutha ni
mugiano. Kamuingi koyaga ndiri namo mageria nomo
mahota. Wetereire ki ?

MUICO.

WEE O HANDU HAKU NA NII HA KWA

UHORO WA MWANDIKI

Gutiri na uhoro wa njuku, gucambania kana kinyararano kabuku-ini gaka, no riu ihinda ni ikinyu haria uhoro uregagira kihoto kana mitheko, na ndiri na tha na kirimu kia Mugikuyu kiria gitari kirahinguka maitho ona umuthi uyu. Ndingitindanirira na mutumumu wa kwihinga maitho, ucio utarahota kuona ati no guthina turathina ungikimutua ta nduu ?

Kabuku gaka kaaritie muno uhoro wa mathina maria tuonaga na uria athungu matutuaga ta irimu tondu wa kumatungatagira na njira ya uhuthu. Nii ndiri na nganja ati mundu uria utaretanga na gwi ciria uria tugatura ucio ni mutururie. Mugikuyu wothe riu araigua ta ararutwo muoyo ni undu wa gutunywo utonga wake na nikio kabuku gaka ni kageretie kuonania ta uria o mundu o mundu abataire ni gwitonyia hari gutetera ithaka ciitu na gucaria njira cia kunyita wiathi niguo tume ukombo-ini.

Kubuku-ini gaka ni ukuona haria wee uigitwo ni Muthungu. Wakorwo wi wa ndini, Mwonjoria, Karani, Munene wa bururi, Gitonga, Thikwota, Munyahoro, Mugikuyu karing'a, Muthigari ona ciana cia macukuru na arimi aria maturaga Gikuyu-ini, othe ni monanitio ta uria comba utugayanitie ni getha tutururio na.

tuthuranage ithui ene. Uyu ni uhoro uri kieha na kurakaria mundu o wothe riria ukuuthoma, tondu kuigua ati athungu amwe moigaga ati Bururi ndwari wiitu. Tugakiuria atiri aria maari ene bururi uyu matuire ku ?

Ni gacokete gagakuonia uria ona Athungu acio matucambagia ta uria Ngai aturathimite agatuhe bururi mwega na uria ithui tutagiriirwo kwimena kuringana na uguo tucambagio turi irimu. Nikomiriirie ngoro ya Mugikuyu wothe kirimu ona mugi gakamuonia ati abataire ni gwitiia tondu wa tiri uyu wa na kuwendaga makiria ma ndege icio ciao kana mito ona nguo cia goro. Warikia guthoma kabuku gaka ukuigua ngoro yaku yagaruruka na wiyone wi mumiriru na Mugikuyu kuna kuna. Ni kana cararuku ni getha Mugikuyu ucio utendete rua rwake emene na eyone haria arungii. Ndukanae utonete, kiugo kia muthia.

Nairobi.   J. J. Gakaara.
April 1952.

Gacabithitio ni:-

GAKAARA BOOK SERVICE

P. O. Box 2122

NAIROBI.

An English Translation of the Pamphlet (Booklet) entitled in Gikuyu *Mageria No Mo Mahota,* or "The Spirit of Manhood and Perseverance for Africans"

Appendix 4 reproduces a camera copy of Gakaara wa Wanjaũ's booklet *Mageria No Mo Mahota* (in Gĩkũyũ), which had appeared originally in Kiswahili as *Roho ya Kiume na Bidii kwa Mwafrika*—the equivalent, in English, of "The Spirit of Manhood and Perseverance for Africans". The authorship of the pamphlet was one of the particularised grounds for detaining Gakaara, as evidence of his being an active supporter of Mau Mau (see Appendix 10). An English translation is provided herebelow of the whole pamphlet, from the Gĩkũyũ original.

Author's Preface to the Gikuyu Edition

It is not the intention of the author of this little booklet to bear false witness against anybody or to malign any party. But I have no intention of mincing words in talking about the truth. For the time has arrived when we can no longer be complacent and people must be shocked into the truth. I have no patience with the African who insists to this day in wallowing in ignorance, refusing to have his eyes opened by current reality. I have no patience with the man blinded by blinkers of his own making. I have no patience with those who refuse to acknowledge our grave impoverishment.

This booklet talks about experiences which are familiar to the reader—about the suffering to which we are subjected by the white man who takes us for fools ready and willing to slave for him. Its concern is to incite reflection on our fate, which should be the concern of every African. Any African who has no thought about our collective future is obviously a man of distorted vision. For the truth is that the life is slowly being strangled out of the African. This book seeks to demonstrate the need for each and every one of us to become actively involved in the struggle for a restitution of our lands as well as the recovery of our national independence and delivery from our slavery.

This little booklet demonstrates to you in what low regard the white man holds you. It exposes the regime of division that the white man has established over us and the bitter and destructive conflicts between ourselves this regime creates. And the regime, with its divisive tactics, works to the detriment of all of us Africans irrespective of our social class or standing—people in religious ministries, or those who consider themselves religious, merchants and traders, clerical workers, leaders, men of means, squatters, so called loyalists, people belonging to the Gĩkũyũ Karĩng'a Independent movement, soldiers, peasant farmers in the countryside, even school children.

The book exposes the white man's strategy of lies. The white man has ever posited the preposterous deception that this land did not originally belong to us. We demand in anger: To whom, then, did the land belong? The white man uses calumny to soil our name and to sow seeds of self-doubt and self-hate in us. But we are aware of the great blessings God has bestowed upon us, the greatest of them being our beautiful land. We should be people of dignified pride in spite of the evil lies of the white man to the effect that we are fools. This book seeks to foster justified patriotic pride in all of us, the wise and the ignorant; we should be proud of this our land and value it beyond the white man's aeroplanes; motor cars and expensive clothes.

After you have read this little book your heart will glow with a new found pride and confidence and you will rediscover yourself as a genuinely brave member of the Agĩkũyũ people. This book does not mince words; that person devoid of patriotic love for his people will find himself exposed to himself in his bankruptcy; hopefully he will, from seeing his real stand, react in revulsion and seek his transformation.

So reader, go ahead and read this book carefully—and don't stop until you have read the last word.

J.J. Gakaara, April 1952, Nairobi.

This book is published by
Gakaara book Service
P.O. Box 2122
NAIROBI

CHAPTER 1

Until When Should We Endure Our Oppression and Our Hardships?

It is the strategy of our white rulers, in order to ensure their dominant stay in this land, to cast aspersions on our abilities and to even sow seeds in us of self-hate and self-doubt; and this in spite of the fact that the white rulers are well aware that we are endowed, like all the other nationalities of the world, with the mental abilities and skills and wisdom to manage our own affairs for our own benefit and well being; they are quite well aware that we have a mind as good as theirs. They, therefore, spread the falsehood that we have not reached the maturity which would enable us to run our own government; and they insult us by claiming that our minds are the minds of children and therefore our leaders do not qualify for wise mature leadership. All these postures are meant to misrepresent our image and to mislead the foolish among us and to lead us into self-doubt; for the white man is constantly aware that God in his wisdom has endowed us with all the human capacities and capabilities and there is nothing Man can do which we, as part of Man, cannot do.

Thus the white man's strategy is one of calumny against us, but it is a strategy founded on the white man's vulnerabilities. For the white man requires our labour to acquire wealth and therefore live in luxury. And he needs to keep us in low-paying labour so that we do not make a break from our poverty and thereby our dependence on him. We only need to realise that the logic operating in our relationship with the white man is the logic between a poor man and a rich man. A man who is full of meat calls the hungry man greedy. And a man who has acquired wealth and gone beyond the poverty line now no longer will accept to do back-breaking work for subsistence, but will insist on reaping a handsome profit from any venture he undertakes. The white man's strategy is to keep us below the poverty line, in subsistence back-breaking labour.

We need to understand the position of the Black Man today. A look at his situation reveals that the black man is relegated to the role of a slave to all the alien races that have established dominance over him in his own land. For it is the black man who provides the labour to these alien races from which they reap huge profits and amass much wealth while the Black Man hardly obtains enough to satisfy an iota of his needs. And the African finds himself in the sad situation where the carrot of modern attainments is cunningly dangled in front of him while he is insidiously denied the means and wherewithal of ever achieving the good things of modern living. He must needs engage in hard struggle to obtain even a small portion of the good things.

The white man holds this secret closely—the need to dangle the promise of things which are beyond achievement. Sadly the white man gloats over the spectacle of the black man breaking himself in labour in the vain attempt to achieve the good life, while also relishing the knowledge that he gets fat and wealthy on the labour of the black man and indeed builds his insulting and arrogant confidence on the wealth he has been able to amass through the labour of the black man. The white man therefore anchors himself in deceit and abuses the "ignorant" black man, thereby seeking to consolidate the black man's lack of awareness of the real nature of the problem.

This strategy of deceit is employed by the land owning settler class and white merchants and traders. They try to ensure that the arrangement is in place where African labour is never adequately compensated to enable Africans to develop themselves. For if this arrangement continues in place the African's strength, labour, intelligence and mental abilities may be exploited for the benefit of the white man until eternity. For all difficult, important and profitable work actually done by Africans.

Our claims here are borne out by a casual look. An African worker produces wealth worth hundreds of shillings per month; yet he gets just a few shillings as wages for his labour. And to add insult to injury the white master never shows appreciation or gratefulness for services rendered. Indeed the white man makes sure the black man works under conditions of great humiliation and spiritual vexation: he is subjected to hard orders, called "Boy" like a young male child, has all types of deductions made from his meagre wages and is subjected constantly to all types of petty harassments. These conditions are created for a reason: to deny the black man the opportunity for quiet reflection on his situation and to prevent the African from attaining the awareness that this work is in fact vital for the white man's well-being. So the white man will never give a hint of appreciation of your work—although in the deep recesses of his cunning mind the white man knows just how important the African's work is.

Therefore, I urge you to be privy to the white man's secret. This situation, I urge you to note, is part of a grand design to keep the black man eternally enslaved to alien races. The reasoning works like this: deny the black man the opportunity of ever breaking out of the necessity of hiring out his labour, nurture in him feelings of inadequacy, self-doubt and self-hate and he will remain a slave for ever.

Reader, it is your duty to have a personal awareness of this insidious grand design. This book will seek to create this awareness.

CHAPTER 2

We Have Been Divided So That We can be Manipulated

It is the white man himself who said that in order to rule and manipulate easily, you only need to divide. Ask yourself these two questions: Are Africans today united in brotherhood? Or are they in fact divided? The white man realises that if we united our hearts together so that we become one thing, no obstacle would stand in the path of our pursuit for achievement. So, let us understand how divisions are created between us so that we may not agree between ourselves and so that antagonisms and hatred may exist between us. Let us understand how the alien races in their cunning and their solidarity conspire to make us surrender all the fruits of our physical and mental labour.

(4)

One way of dividing us is the creation of allegiance to alien religions and faiths. Some of our people have lost a communal vision and they have become blind in their sectarian antagonisms. You will hear an African declare vehemently: "I am a Mohamedan," while another declares, "I am a Christian," and yet another, "I belong to the Independent African Church".

And there are also class divisions built on alien values. You will hear one African say to another, "You show your pride and arrogance because you speak English like an Englishman." And another will say, "You and your dirty clothing, I don't want to associate with you!" And in the same confusion you will hear voices of self-hate: "A Black Man will be a Black Man!" you will hear an African say in disgust. And the cause of all this confusion is the manipulation of the white man who believes in dividing people, knocking their heads one against another's and generally making people behave like fools so that he can exploit them.

Witness the pathetic internecine struggles between Africans on the question of land! All our prime lands were seized from us by the white man. Since then we do not have an adequate supply of farming land and there isn't enough land to even accommodate all our homes. And the result of this is that it is the African victims of the seizure of land who engage in constant and costly litigation against one another, in disputes about who owns which piece of land or where land boundaries are supposed to be. But they are not capable of bringing a legal case against the white man who has taken all their land. The Agĩkũyũ people are on the verge of losing all their herds of livestock, for all the fertile grazing forest areas and all the fertile grazing valleys were taken by the white man. The Agĩkũyũ herders are therefore caught in a futile wandering in search of grazing grounds. Thus the Mũgĩkũyũ is caught in a desperate situation: without land and without blood wealth, and therefore without any substantial wealth or any real anchorage.

Let us look in greater detail at the situation of the African upon which the exploitation of his labour is premised:

1. Unable to engage in good profitable farming or livestock keeping, the African is forced to seek employment with aliens who hire him at subsistence wages which ensure he will forever remain a wage labourer. Do not forget that the white man ensures that he controls other departments of the African's life. The white man hires the African and provides him with housing at a rent fixed by himself. The African has also to buy expensive food from the white man. The white man makes sure that almost half the African's wages go into the house rent. Thus the white man pays out money which finally goes back to him. The African is at the end of it all left empty-handed.

(5)

2. Consider the case of squatters on white settler farms. These are the mo
terribly exploited and deprived people. They may not keep any substanti:
herds of cattle and goats, for the settlers claim *their* herds will become infecte
with diseases from squatters' herds. And a squatter may not hold more tha
one acre of farming land, however vast the settler landlord's farm may be
On top of this the settler determines the wages which he pays to the squatter:
making sure the wage paid could never pay for half the basic needs of th
squatter. To make ends meet the squatter is forced to hire out all his family—
wife and children—to the settler landlord. The settler landlord makes sure th
African family single-mindedly serves his interests—he shuts off their communi
cation with people back home and with people in towns, thus enforcing :
perpetual ignorance on the squatters' part. And so the squatters live in darknes
carrying out difficult work which builds up the wealth of the alien settler farmer
at the end of the day the squatters reap only their physical weariness. And s
the African squatters get used to a routine of hard labour and full preoccupation
never getting time to reflect on their situation, believing the lies weaved cunningly
by the white man and consolidated by their enforced isolation. Aren't these
people therefore condemned to lifetimes of exploitation, poverty and ignorance '
3. Consider also Africans living permanently in Majengo-like slums in the
major towns. Did Africans know of slums before the advent of the white aliens '
These Africans who have gone to stay permanently in slums, is it that they have
no homes in the countryside? Of course not. But they have been lured in all
sorts of nefarious ways into towns with the sole aim of serving the white man's
profit motive. Many of these people live in shanties rented out to them by white
men. It is a life of hard struggle obtaining daily food and clothes to cover their
bodies, for although they must needs be wage-employed to avoid arrest as
vagrants, they must pay taxes from their low wages. A few of the Africans may
have shanties of their own but the white man controls the conditions under
which they may live or the rents they may demand from tenants. And these
Africans perpetually live under the relentless pressure of fostered desires and
wants, for things of modern living which cannot be obtained from their meagre
resources. The white man who has amassed enough wealth may decide to go
back home; but the African slum dwellers are condemned to a lifetime of
deprivation until their squalid death in the squalid slums.
4. Now let us consider the case of peasant farmers who stick it out, in spite
of their poverty, to the Gĩkũyũ countryside. They devote a lot of hard labour
to farming on their small holdings. When they have grown a good crop and wish
to offer it to the market, the white man blocks them, for he insists that the price
for African-produced crops shǒuld be lower than the price paid for European-
produced crops. Mysteriously the quality of crops produced by Europeans is

(6)

upposed to be higher than that of crops produced by Africans. But once crops have been bought at a discriminatory price, products processed from these crops are then offered to consumers, the bulk of them Africans, at a uniform price. Once maize, for example, has been milled, nobody talks about maize-meal from African maize or maize meal from European-grown maize. The price asked for all maize meal is uniform. Neither do hotels ask for lower prices for cooked food bought from African peasants!

And discrimination does not end there. There are all kinds of discriminatory regulations. An African may not export his crop to another country while the European may freely do so. Yet it should be the right of the African farmer to look for the best market for his crops so that he may have his labour rewarded and so that he may develop himself within his home area where he has chosen to work with devotion. But the white man finds it necessary to erect barriers, in the form of discriminatory regulations, in the path of the African's search for profit and progress.

5. Let us consider the situation of African businessmen and traders. It has been evident that business and trade have great potential for bringing in wealth to Gĩkũyũland—just as business and trade bring in wealth to other countries. The truth of the matter is that some Gĩkũyũ traders have had considerable success in building up their businesses. But just as barriers are erected against Africans in other areas of enterprise, e.g. farming, there are many hurdles for Africans in business. An African retailer is hampered by the exorbitant prices charged by wholesalers. A lot of money has to be paid to obtain licences, and rents for business premises are exorbitant for Africans. It is either very difficult or downright impossible for Africans to obtain export and import licences. Africans are also barred from certain areas of business and trade: for example, Africans may not deal in wines and spirits. African businessmen and traders are therefore forced to operate within serious restrictions and the majority of them have to make do with small shops and small operations; it is only the exceptionally lucky African trader who gets the satisfaction of seeing his operation grow expand and develop. And so this avenue—of business and trade—does not offer an easy way to the creation of wealth, upon which Africans must base their emancipation.

6. Now let us look at the situation of Africans employed in Government service. The salary structure in Government service is discriminatory against Africans. There are obviously well educated Africans in Government service—better educated than some of their European or Indian counterparts—who are getting subsistence wages. The offshoot of this discriminatory pay is that some African Government workers—especially those with some authority and people in the police—succumb to temptations and accept bribes. Others are tempted to

steal property, all in a bid to make ends meet, so meagre is their pay. But once they succumb to these temptations, they compromise their honour and the white man grabs at their example as an indicator of the general dishonesty and lack of honour of the African, quite oblivious of the fact that white-created structures of deprivation have laid these people open to temptation.

If the Government does try to offer incentives to Africans they are unrealistic. Consider the prospect of obtaining "long-service awards" for example. How is an elderly man who has served the Government for twenty years supposed to benefit from a cash prize of Shillings 3000 or 4000? For a Government servant is supposed to endure a lifetime of deprivation—for the long-service award of a few thousand shillings! He has to struggle hard to keep his body and the bodies of his family members clothed; he is so worn with worry from maintaining his wife and educating his children on his little pay that he hardly ever enjoys a meal. He must keep at his job for those full 20 years, for he may even miss his long-service award for serving one month short. Those who know better: please tell me how Shillings 3000 or even Shillings 6000 may satisfy the needs of a modern man who wants to live in a modern European style?

7. Let us now consider the situation of our people who serve in the British colonial armed forces. Ironically for these people, the only time these people enjoy a feeling of well being is during periods of actual war. For it is only when they are in action when they are allowed to enjoy certain material privileges and when they are accorded respect and dignity and when they are praised for their bravery. Even then their pay must be lower than that for white servicemen. The following weighty questions arise from this fact: If on the front line we take the same combat positions with whites in order to shoot on the enemy, why are we not placed in a situation of equality in respect of pay for military service? When a white soldier is hit by bullets from the enemy's guns, does he not die just like a black soldier? Then why should they not be put in a position of equality?

But the situation is always that Africans are attracted to the armed forces by false promises; on recruitment they are told they will receive their reward during service; and when they are already serving they are promised great things on demobilisation. When the armed conflict is over and when Africans have actually been demobilised, there is hardly any reward even in terms of genuine appreciation of their service. And African ex-servicemen are actually told not to expect any rewards, for they are now no longer armed forces servicemen!

8. Finally let us look at the situation of our children vis-a-vis educational opportunities. As everyone knows, there is among Africans a widespread and intense hunger for education. For Africans realise the key to all good things is the knowledge and skills imparted by modern education. Thus they desire

the best education for their children. But general poverty stands as a hurdle to a realisation of this desire. It is a hard and impossible struggle for most people to raise enough money to pay their children's way through school. And this is not the only hurdle. Facilities for post-primary education are terribly limited and the African community does not have the financial means to create such facilities. Africans are not in a position to build their own colleges and universities; their children may therefore only obtain an elementary education. The children of the poor are in the worst plight, unable to even acquire this elementary education, for the means of the poor are consumed by basic needs like food and clothing.

Thus, unable to acquire anything better than a limited elementary education, what career opportunities are left open for African children? If they are lucky the highest they can hope for is employment as clerks, dispensary dressers, drivers, mechanics, primary school teachers and so on. And, of course, all employment opportunities are controlled by the white man, who is only too ready to decry the low level of education of Africans. And so our children are condemned to a life of meagre pay, exploitation and deprivation—right from the start.

CHAPTER 3

Is It Right That We Should Despise Ourselves?

But the time has arrived when each and every African must open his eyes to our desperate plight, so that a new vision of understanding of the white man's strategy of deceit may fire our hearts with anger against our tormentors. The process of gaining this new vision will start with a kind of sadness and sorrow at the realisation that each one of us Africans has been living in the darkness of ignorance, that each one of us has for long been duped in the white man's grand design of deception, oppression and exploitation. This sadness is followed by a new sense of worth, a new awareness that each one of us is a master of our own collective destiny in a land which in fact belongs to us. And this awareness in the final analysis translates into an appreciation of the need for unity and solidarity among ourselves in order to confront the insidious unity of our alien oppressors and exploiters and thus surmount the hurdles so cunningly erected across our path in our pursuit of liberating wealth.

For a start, we can fight for the just equality of pay for equal work, for there is no possible reason why Europeans, Indians and Arabs should get higher pay than Africans for work requiring the same ability and skills. The

African should never be satisfied with anything less than absolute equality in matters of pay and treatment under the law, with all the other races which have made this country their home. For the African has accepted as his own the material and cultural aspirations of modern life: he wants to get wholesome food, dress decently, be able to build good houses to live in, and acquire a good academic education. These aspirations can only be pursued if wealth and money are in African hands. The situation where these aspirations are fanned and at the same time hurdles erected against their realisation must be totally rejected.

When we go to shops owned by European aliens, we do not find goods for Europeans set aside from goods for Africans. Rather goods are offered at uniform prices to anybody who can pay the price. When people of different races go to courts of law they are asked to pay similar fines for similar offences. Thus when Africans are made to receive salaries and wages which are lower than those paid to people of other races, the situation is created where the African must receive less than others but must pay out as much as everybody else. Where is justice in such an arrangement?

In the final analysis this unjust arrangement is premised on the ultimately and larger unjust arrangement where we Africans have no self-determination. Armed with his new awareness, therefore, the African must never accept anything less than self-determination in this land which indeed belongs to Africans. We must be the masters in our own country, to determine what we should do for our own ultimate good. That is to say we must seize political independence.

Once each and every African has embraced this awareness he must actively join the patriotic service of this land. For a start this will involve joining the struggle for a return of our seized lands, for our disabling poverty has resulted from this deprivation of our major means of existence. What cowards have we become that we have failed to make these necessary demands?

Unity is the foremost requirement if we are to achieve our ultimate goals; without unity we can do little. We must join hands, the wealthy and the poor, the intellectually well endowed and those not so well endowed, the able-bodied and the disabled among us, men and women—all of us should become one force imbued with the spirit of patriotic love for our country, our life's desire being to struggle for its total emancipation. Our aim should be to get as many wise and brave people as possible to represent us in the councils that participate in the governing of our country, people who can stare the Europeans in the eyes in putting our demands for total emancipation. We must reject the situation where our African representatives are always in the minority such that whites always outvote them, for this situation simply perpetuates our subjugation.

(10)

I am not advocating that we leave our affairs in the hands of a few African epresentatives. Far from it. While it is true that not everybody can participate n the deliberations of councils of government, where Europeans and Indians are lready represented, it is vital that every African plays his own role in the struggle or African freedom. To fight for freedom does not only mean making political peeches and writing political tracts. More than that, to struggle for freedom s to be imbued with a patriotic love for your country and its people, so that ou become part and parcel of its suffering and its triumphs, so that, in your piritual unity with your people, you weep with them when they weep, and ou share with them their moments of joy. It is a deep and all-consuming involvement with your people. It motivates you to seek to know what is happening ill the time to your people; it motivates you to always seek to further the cause of freedom and independence.

CHAPTER 4

It Is Better If They Were Dead!

Any person who is devoid of patriotic love for this country were better dead. For such persons are not only a great liability but give by their mere presence the false impression of swelling our ranks, while contributing nothing to the welfare of our nation. Such people are like wooden carvings made by the Akamba. Surely we don't need these graven images in our land!

Many people are like parasitic mistletoe growths that thrive by sapping the life-strength of proper trees which have their own roots. They are the proverbial poverty and sorrow, rootless and therefore needing to attach themselves to real people.* Yes, if you are devoid of patriotic love for your country you are essentially like these parasitic growths. And this will not save you on the day of reckoning—for you surely must be swallowed in the cataclysm, for you will be caught unawares.

It is the depth of ignominy to have to live with these parasitic elements among us. They shun sacrifice for the common good—and expect that others will work for everybody's liberation from present slavery. These people have accepted to be blinded and they live in the darkness of ignorance.

Abdication takes the form of "opting out of politics"—on the grounds that a person is a follower of a certain religion or that he is by trade a merchant

* In the Gikuyu language two parasitic plants, like the mistletoe, bear names *kieha* (sorrow) and *thiina* (poverty).

or a teacher by profession. But in our circumstances you cannot and may not opt out of politics. When you are dissatisfied with the pay you receive for your labour and agitate for fair pay you are involved in politics. It is, therefore, necessary to realise that you should link up forces with those who seek to be part of a movement to fight for equal pay. Even if you hold some position of leadership you should realise that if the land is subjected to mass arrests and detentions, you are very likely to end up in detention. You man of means: you may have access to good substantial land, but you should realise that people involved in political activity are fighting for a consolidation of genuine land rights. Don't just sit on the fence: learn from the great sacrifice and dedication of poor people, some of whom do not even own a cow, who are committed to the bitter struggle even if it may result in their deaths.

But even if you are very poor you have no right to opt out of the political struggle. Your food, remember, comes from our precious soil and the land is your mother and your father. How then can you stand aside in silence while other people demand that our lands be returned to us? What do you eat and where do you erect your dwelling? Why should you be content to enjoy the fruits of the labour of your brothers and sisters, a labour of which you have refused to be a part?

The truth remains that if each one of us were prepared to assist actively in the councils of the people's movement, our independence would not take very long to be won. We should support the people's cause by attending all meetings called by people's leaders and we should contribute generously and with one heart our money or other material things needed in the work of people's movements as these needs are indicated by our leaders.

Recognise at all times the great priority of the struggle for our liberation from slavery. Do not allow trivial things to stand in your way of attending a nationalist meeting. Don't offer the excuse that you cannot attend because you cannot afford to close down your shop, or that you have to attend a Sunday church-service, or that you must go and have a beer or get entertained watching a foot-ball game or watching a film in a cinema theatre. These meetings are, in any case, only called occasionally and you have ample time to attend to your everyday business. Remember that every matter being championed by African nationalists touches you: you are not a white man. Why should you then stand on the side-lines? When we demand schools for Africans, is not your own child supposed to benefit from the availability of these schools? Don't you have a personal interest in the abrogation of pass laws that require you to carry a pass on your person on pain of instant arrest? Don't you privately say that we should get back our lands, and that we should get better pay for our work?

(12)

Therefore it is your duty to get actively involved in the people's movement —to attend its meetings and make tangible contributions to its work. It is not enough that you should pay lip service to the people's movement.

Banish the kind of fear that prevents you from speaking the truth and seeking justice, for as the Gĩkũyũ proverb has it, "Truth breaks a readied bow". Don't seek to escape from your patriotic responsibility and the pursuit of truth by offering such excuses as that you are a servant of the British colonial government, or that your white employer has forbidden you to attend meetings organised by KAU (Kenya African Union). When a white employer alienates you from KAU, is he helping you or alienating you from what is good for you? Such a white man is using his cunning to keep you away from enlightenment and self-awareness. He intends to keep you in ignorance so that you may not be wise to his insidious design to keep you serving his interests and creating wealth for him, while he keeps you in perpetual poverty. We should have the courage to demonstrate to these Europeans that our patriotic love for our nation is greater than our self interest; should they insist on taking away our jobs, we should be ready to lose these jobs.

CHAPTER 5

No One Requested the British to Come and Rule Over Us!

It is the depth of ignominy that we the owners of this land have been reduced to the status of tenants at the will of aliens: we have to beg for a place on which to build our homes and we have to pay taxes on the roads we use. To add to this great shame those of us who dare to question the justification for this state of affairs end up getting their heads bashed; the others see this and cringe in fear. People are not supposed to speak their mind; they may not insist on justice being done. We are therefore denied our freedom of expression.

But we will insist on the right to free expression. We do not want to resort to violent struggle. We will say it again and again that we must have our own independent nationalist government, for we have a right to equal membership in the community of independent nations; we have, like other nations, a right to self-determination. It is therefore the duty of the government of this territory to serve the interests of all the communities of this country in equality without regard to ethnicity, race or colour.

We should have as many representatives as possible in the Governor's council as well as in all councils involved in the government of this country. We form the great majority in this country and we should therefore be proportionately represented in such councils. But we also make another demand: on no account should representatives be appointed for us; we should freely elect those in whom we have faith to represent us. As the Gĩkũyũ saying has it, "Each person knows his needs best."

If we are to have a team of eighty people to represent us, we should elect each and all of them, for it is we who are in a position to assess the level of their sympathetic understanding of our problems.

We should remember a few home truths. Before the white man came to this country, we lived as independent nationalities; we managed our own affairs and our government ably. No one invited the white man to come and teach us the art of good government; rather he sneaked in and cunningly elevated himself to a teacher and our "redeemer" from alleged past problems. The white man erected a scheme of lies, now claiming that this land never belonged to us but to the Dorobo people, at other times saying this had been a land of darkness. We cannot but ask: Why hasn't the white man stayed back home to enjoy the great light with which his land is endowed? And if they sincerely think the land belonged to the Dorobo people, why do they insist on staying on it, instead of standing on their righteousness and merely demanding that we return the land to the Dorobo? And can the white man answer this ultimate question: Who gave him this land not only to live on it but to rule over it?

The white usurper in his cunning explains it away: they came to pacify us, to terminate our wars with the Maasai people. Just think about that! It is true that we fought some battles with the Maasai but there was no basic conflict or enmity between us and the Maasai and our scuffles were like wrestling matches between brothers. How could the Maasai be regarded as our enemies when we married from their community and they married from us? They would today carry out a raid for our cattle; and we would carry out a raid tomorrow, recovering the same cattle; the raids caused no significant disruption. The Maasai were not interested in taking all our land and leaving us without means of livelihood, and we had no interest in taking over their territory.

This is the naked truth: before the coming of the white man, our land was a land of joy and plenty, we had plentiful food and large herds of goats and cows, and our people were people of wealth and dignity and great warriors. And the white man did not usher in an era of peace. On the contrary, he introduced an era of perpetual war, war with ourselves as we struggle with desperate and hopeless poverty and deprivation. We have to come to grips with a realisation of this bitter truth; for until we change the situation our plight will remain one of sorrow and tears.

Our situation is as follows: a lamp has been lit, but a curtain covers the light of the lamp and only a little light escapes for illumination. We have been taught that modern education is good—but we have been denied school facilities for imparting this education. It is an insidious scheme of dangling what is desirable in front of a victim who may never grasp what is dangled. In truth, it were better if they hadn't allowed us that lingering taste of modern education.

CHAPTER 6

We Are Privy to Their Evil Designs!

Now that we know the evil designs of our alien rulers—nay, now that we have felt the pain and agony, of their actions towards us, both in our hearts and our bodies—can we be expected to keep silent about things? A hundred times no! We shall refuse to suffer in silence the oppression of our lives, we shall refuse to bear in patience our incessant drift towards ultimate impoverishment. And for a beginning we shall combat their cunning efforts to devalue our human worth in a bid to sowing seeds of self-doubt and self-hate.

We have a deep conviction that God has bestowed us Black People with his bounteous blessings. See, God gave us this land of great beauty and plenty, a land which became the object of envy among alien races. It is a fertile land with a rich variety of plant and animal life. It more than adequately supplies our food needs: we never go to them to beg for food. We are, and should be, eminently proud about this land which within it carries the potential of great wealth, including minerals of great economic value and precious stones like gold. The land abounds with great fertile forests and mighty rivers of reknown. On this land we can build our own self-sufficient life. Why then should we not step out in dignity, with our heads held high?

We shall never again accept their reviling words; we shall treat with contempt their claims that we are a nation of children, that we are a people handicapped by poverty: we are no longer going to be awed by the white man's little doings. And we are going to adopt a strategy of unity and patient thought and planning to dismantle those hurdles erected against our development towards equality with the white man. The era of lazy indifference and complaceny is over!

We have made a resolution today: to spare ourselves no effort in our concerted bid to ensure our own development until we not only get to the white man's level but surpass him, accommodate him under our own government or send him out of our country so he can return home where he belongs.

We shall implement this resolution because we have discovered the hollowness of the white man's claims to superiority, for the white man like us is a being of flesh and blood, and any achievements he has made are not beyond us. We have discovered to our joy that all along we have been inculcated with a false fear and awe of the white man to ensure our subjugation; we are now casting this fear aside.

From now on we shall speak the truth out loud and clear. We shall no longer whisper discreetly about our problems, for this only compounds the sense of fear and helplessness and would only mean our crashing under the destructive weight of our impoverishment and oppression. We shall repudiate our "soft" approach and our seeming acquiescence in our oppression—for these attitudes have resulted in a ceaseless attack against our interests, and our continued oppression in body and soul, and a ceaseless pursuit for ultimate and eternal white dominance over us, accompanied by the unequal enrichment of the white man.

How can we allow ourselves to be misled again by the false sweet talk of cunning people? For they treat us as nothing better than fools when they sweet-talk us inorder to entrap us and ultimately revile us. What just relationship can exist between us and people who compare us to monkeys and in the same breath deny us the right to claim back our land? We shall relentlessly demand justice. For our eyes have been opened and we have obtained a far sighted view of our interests and our fate.

We have become the proverbial knife which has been sharpened by the grinding of another. We have become the proverbial knife that cuts its sharpener. But we will be guided by truth and justice in waging our struggle. We will repeat it again and again, that our white rulers have no abilities beyond ours. Why should anybody cast doubt on our intelligence? Which achievement, made by a living human being, is beyond the Black Man? Black Men have reached the apex of the academic ladder; we have produced great judges, teachers, and people with doctorates in all fields. Black men have made brave soldiers on frontlines of war. They make great ship and aeroplane pilots. They have made a creditable contribution to the world of theatre and the cinema, and they have produced great sportsmen in sports like boxing and athletics. Our detractors are therefore discredited by facts. We can seize opportunities for the improvement of our knowledge and skills and our own development. What then is there to daunt us?

It is a source of joy and pride that we have unearthed the secret of the white man's strategy—to keep us enslaved to poverty so that we cannot initiate our own genuine development. (We, therefore, realise that we need to break from their scheme in order to create a new order where we can build up our wealth*.) Then, there will be no limit to our aspirations, and we will be able to build schools with multi-storey classrooms for our children to study in. We will put up big hotels and entertainment facilities which will become objects of envy to the white man. We will build big commercial centres and shops and will enjoy sophisticated means of transport, cars and planes, the latter serving our need to fly out our children to great schools in foreign lands. It will then dawn on the white man that he is no better than ourselves.

But to make the necessary break from the present situation, we need to exert great effort and sacrifice, we need to shed the sweat of blood. We need to be united into an army of hard-workers like *safari* ants, so that we can attack our problems in fierce unison. Yes, we should even nurture in ourselves the dauntless fierceness of these little insects. We should be ready to face the challenges of winning for ourselves a full life at the risk of dying. If, for example, we need to build schools, we should give all our hearts to the task. If we need to send a child to America for further studies, we should all jointly contribute to the effort. If we want to send one of our leaders overseas to champion our cause, we should diligently raise the funds to do so.

Let us learn from the example of the spider which builds its web using its own substances from itself; let us build self-reliance in our struggle for self-determination, independence and freedom. Let us learn from the little bird that uses its tiny beak to build its house. For we are better than that bird—we have a mind, hands and legs, why shouldn't we perform wonders to awe the multitudes?

There is not time to lose! We must seize the opportunity this very moment! A group of people working together finds it easy to lift a heavy mortar! You must make the attempt inorder to succeed! My, brother, what are you waiting for?!

Yes, you play your little part, and I will play mine!

THE END

*The translation of this section is nothing near literal. We have brought out the underlying meaning.

Appendix 5:

This is a copy of a circular sent out by the Press Office of the Department of Information expressing the colonial Government's view on the nature of Mau Mau.

NOTES ON THE MAU MAU MOVEMENT IN KENYA.

1.   Since Mau Mau is essentially a Kikuyu movement, it is generally recognised that the Kikuyu people themselves must play a large part in bringing about its eventual defeat. The policy of the Government in Kenya in fighting terrorism recognises this aspect of the situation, and accordingly every encouragement is given to the African loyalist movement known as the Kikuyu Guard. The Kikuyu Guard has shown a phenomenal growth from a scattered band of persecuted loyalists to a 30,000 strong movement today. The Guards not only take an active part in military style operations against terrorist gangs, but are the mainstay of agricultural and educational progress in the reserves. They protect the churches, and it is not uncommon for a fortified Guard post to contain, besides the garrison, a school, church and in some cases, the local dispensary. They provide much needed information about terrorist activities and by their own example influence the mass of the Kikuyu against Mau Mau.

2.   The power of Mau Mau is concentrated to an overwhelming extent in the oath. This oath, according to a recent report by a mental expert, stems not only from Kikuyu custom, but also from a more sophisticated source and has a close analogy to European witchcraft. Its seven grades range from mere savage rites to advanced forms of sadism, sexual perversion and bestiality. It is comparatively easy for a Kikuyu to rid himself of the influence of the first two grades, but once he has taken the higher forms of the oath there is little that can be done with him. In the early part of the emergency cleaning ceremonies by Kikuyu witch doctors were held frequently, but these did not prove a great success as it often happened that people who had been "cleansed" of the Mau Mau oath took a further oath a few days later. Today the principle method used in breaking the power of an oath on its subject is to encourage him to make a full confession and give all the information he can about terrorist activities. This is what is being done in the large detention camp for Mau Mau adherents near Nairobi.

    The team in charge of this camp is not made up of regular Prison Department officials but consists mainly of African and European clergy and laymen with a sound knowledge of Kikuyu psychology. Under detention here are some 1,500 members of the Mau Mau hierarchy and after a year's work some 200 of the detainees have confessed their allegiance to Mau Mau and expressed a desire to work for the Government. Their next step is to prove their new loyalty by actions as well as words, and then it is hoped it will be possible to release them and to restore them to normal society. The small number of confessions illustrates the tremendous task confronting the Government.

3.   The Kikuyu now in detention camps (apart from those at the camp near Nairobi) are being devided into three categories as a result of information gained by screening teams. First are the hard-core irredeemable terrorists; secondly, people with a lighter allegiance to Mau Mau; and third, those who can be released very quickly. It is planned to place the second category of detainees in "work camps" within or outside the Kikuyu reserve. Here they will be engaged on projects useful to the Kikuyu tribe such as bush clearing, irrigation and soil conservation. If they show a willingness to work, their families. may, in time, be allowed to join them and, once they have proved themselves worthy of a return to citizenship, they may be sent back to their land in the reserves or, alternatively, land may be found for them in the newly cleared bush round the camps /

camps. A few works camps have already been established outside the Kikuyu reserve, notably one at Baringo in the Rift
Valley Province, where the detainees are working on a large
scale irrigation scheme, and another in the West Suk district
of northern Kenya. These have proved remarkably successful,
as has another rice-growing irrigation scheme worked by
Kikuyu detainees in the Embu district. This scheme, if
successful, will put 60,000 acres of virgin bush under cultivation, providing a good living for some 10,000 families.

4.   The process of rehabilitation of Mau Mau is of necessity
a very slow one, and will probably continue for some years
after the state of Emergency in Kenya is over. There is no
doubt, however, that owing to the number of Kikuyu involved,
the task has to be tackled somehow, despite the cost. The
Government is very much alive to the problem and is energetically pursuing its objects in this matter. As regards the
mass of Kikuyu, there are encouraging signs that the tribesmen
are gradually turning away from Mau Mau. This is due largely
to the new policy of "villagisation", which needs some
explanation. The Kikuyu in their 2,000 square miles of high-
land country have never lived in villages. Each family
occupies its own piece of land and lives in family or clan
units, in many cases widely separated from neighbours. This,
coupled with the lack of roads and communications in the
Reserve, enabled terrorists to intimidate the ordinary Kikuyu.
By concentrating these scattered tribesmen into villages,
protected by Kikuyu Guard posts, the Government is not only
dealing a severe blow to the gangs but is also making a great
step forward in matters such as education, health and local
government. Each new village will eventually have its own
school, health centre, women's welfare centre and village
council. Already there are hundreds of villages in the Fort
Hall, Nyeri and Embu districts, and each of them has resulted
in the creation of a much happier and a more co-operative
attitude among the villagers now free from the fear of murder
and terrorist brutality.

5.   Side by side with these Emergency measures come the
Government's long-term plans for African advancement. Notable
amongst these is the Swynnerton plan for African agriculture,
which will result in the proper development of the 52,000
square miles of African reserves, some of which contain the
most fertile land in the country. The Swynnerton plan places
emphasis on the development of cash crops such as coffee, tea,
sisal, and pyrethrum which will enormously increase the
African income and afford greater prosperity to the ordinary
tribesman. Education, both academic and technical, is also
making great strides, and the Government is spending much
money on the opening up of new land. The first requirement
facing the Colony is, of course, the end of the Emergency,
which is placing an intolerable financial burden on the
Colony. The large Emergency expenditure now amounting to
£1,000,000 per month has handicapped, but by no means halted,
measures for African progress. Once this expenditure is ended,
the way will be clear for even greater efforts than are being
made now and have been made in the past.

PRESS OFFICE,
DEPARTMENT OF INFORMATION,
NAIROBI.   11th August 1954.

Appendix 6:

Suspension of Detention Order

THE EMERGENCY POWERS ORDER IN COUNCIL
1939 and 1956

THE EMERGENCY REGULATIONS, 1952
(G.N. No. 1103 of 1952)

SUSPENSION OF DETENTION ORDER

DETAINEE: MUCHOKI MBUITU   GDO/NYI/17

WHEREAS, in pursuance of Regulation 2 of the Emergency
Regulations, 1952, a detention order was made against the
above-named MUCHOKI MBUITU   on the 16th   day
of December   1952 and the said Muchoki Mbuitu
is now detained at   Hola   and is shortly being transferred
to Mathira Division

AND WHEREAS I am satisfied that the operation of the said
detention order may now be suspended subject to certain conditions
which I think fit to impose;

NOW THEREFORE, in exercise of the powers conferred by
regulation 2 of the Emergency Regulations, 1952, I hereby direct
that the operation of the said detention order be suspended from
the time of Muchoki Mbuitu's arrival at   Iriaini Location
subject to the following condition

(a) That he remains in his home location until such time as the said
Detention Order is cancelled

(b) That his conduct is to the satisfaction of his Chief and
Divisional District Officer

(c) That he does not engage in any secret meetings.

(d) That he does not join any political body.

(e)

(f)

(g)

(h)

(i)

(j)

(k)

In this order "District Comissioner" means the District
Commissioner NYERI   or any District Officer appointed
by him to act on his behalf.

GIVEN under my hand at   NYERI   this day of 20th July 19 59

A. J. FOSTER

DISTRICT COMMISSIONER

Appendix 7:

This is a copy of the letter written by Manda Camp detainees to the Minister of Community Development and Rehabilitation on 24 September, 1954.

COPY

Manda Island Detention
Camp
P.O. Lamu
24-9-54.

The Rt. Honourable,
The Minister for Community Development and
Rehabilitation,
The Secretariat,
NAIROBI.
(At MANDA)

Your Rt. Honourable,

We, Manda Detainees, humbly beg to petition your right honourable as follows:—

1. FOOD. That your petitioner's scale of food has been drastically reduced such as to render the same insufficient for the upkeep of normal health. In that the constituents of the scale go up to make only one meal per diem, mainly composed of carbohydrates.

2. WORK, REHABILITATION AND RELEASE. That your petitioners are unsuitably employed on projects not in conformity with their previous experiences and professional qualifications. Your petitioners

④

pray that they be employed on works in conformity with their several trades and callings make fit to take their places once more in their respective communities.

3. SICKNESS. Several of your petitioners are aged, some infirm, and others have contracted diseases of which they have not had the opportunity to acquire adequate environments and treatment. Two have died here in this way. Your petitioners pray that the aged ones, the infirm and

247

the incurables sick, be transferred to suitable environments within reach of adequate treatment and cure. Owing to lack of various important ingredients of foodstuffs, various of your petitioners have contracted loss of sight, impaired resistance to diseases and various other ailments.

4. CORRESPONDENCE COURSES. A certain number of your petitioners were allowed to incur expenses on correspondence courses. Your petitioners pray that they be helped to

(2)

continue their courses smoothly and be allowed to sit for their respective examinations when due.

5. CAMP STUDIES. Most of your petitioners are pursuing studies in the Camp, in an effort to combat illiteracy, and your petitioners pray that they be encouraged in the way of provision of time, books, stationery and equipment.

NEWSPAPERS. Some of your petitioners are pursuing courses in journalism. As you may be away aware, suitable newspapers for the purpose are not allowed in the camps, and your petitioners pray that they be allowed to subscribe to the East African Standard, Nairobi for the same.

6. FAMILY MAINTENANCE AND COMMUNICATIONS. Your petitioners families and dependants were left desolate since two years ago, without provision. Your petitioners therefore pray that their destitute families be provided by Government with means of livelihood, education for their children and relaxation of restrictions on

(3)

communications.

7. CLOTHING AND WEARING APPAREL. Some of your petitioners have not been clothed since their detention, and the few clothed have been provided with inadequate and unsuitable blue drill, i.e. blouse and shorts. Your petitioners pray that they be adequately clothed with better

248

material, e.g. khaki drill, footwear etc.

8. *RELEASE* Your petitioners pray for immediate release and compensation for their losses both morally and materially sustained through detention.

And your petitioners will ever pray.

Signed by:-
  B.H. K Attan
  M.C. Chokwe
  Joel Warui
  R.N. Gikonyo
  Gakara Wanyau
  V. MWokati
  John K Cege

④

Thutha wa mania maya kwandikwo matamgitio manoo Minister for Community Development and Rehabilitation gukir Manda Camp kuri agwikite kwono kambi, andu atandatu ni maruitwo gukir kambi ini matii kuirithwo gitakaini ndakaa kuirukira. Nao ni ayo – B.H. Kanau, M.C. chotwe, Joel Warui Gakara Wanyau V MWokati na Skoite.

24. 2. 64.

249

Appendix 8: The Creed of Gikuyu and Mumbi

Authorship and publication of this Creed was one of the grounds for detaining Gakaara wa Wanjaū. A free translation in English of the Gĩkũyũ Creed is given below:

I BELIEVE IN GOD THE ALMIGHTY FATHER, CREATOR OF HEAVEN AND EARTH. AND I BELIEVE IN GĨKŨYŨ AND MŨMBI OUR DEAR ANCESTRAL PARENTS TO WHOM GOD BEQUEATHED THIS OUR LAND. THEIR CHILDREN WERE PERSECUTED IN THE ERA OF CEGE AND WAIYAKI BY THE CLAN OF WHITE PEOPLE, THEY WERE ROBBED OF THEIR GOVERNMENT AND THEIR LAND AND RELEGATED TO THE STATUS OF HUMILIATED MENIALS. THEIR CHILDREN'S CHILDREN HAD THEIR EYES OPENED, THEY ACHIEVED THE LIGHT OF A GREAT AWARENESS AND THEY FOUGHT TO RESTORE THEIR PARENTS TO THEIR SEATS OF GLORY.

AND I BELIEVE IN THE HOLY RELIGIOUS CEREMONIES OF GĨKŨYŨ AND MŨMBI, AND I BELIEVE IN THE GOOD LEADERSHIP OF KENYATTA AND MBIYŨ AND THE UNBREAKABLE SOLIDARITY BETWEEN THE MWANGI AND IRŨNGŨ GENERATIONS AND THE ONENESS OF THE NINE FULL GĨKŨYŨ CLANS AND THE EVERLASTINGNESS OF THE GĨKŨYŨ NATION.

Thaai Thaithaiya Ngai Thaai—God, let it be so, Amen! God let it be so!

Appendix 9:

A facsimile from the author's detention diary, copied by camera from one of the
exercise books containing the original diary.

Appendix 10 : The Charge Against Gakaara Wanjaŭ

THE LAW COURTS,

NAIROBI.

13th July,   1954.

Mr. J. J. Gakaara Wanjau,
Through:
  The Officer-in-Charge,
Manda Island Detention Camp.

Sir,

Whereas the Governor, being satisfied that for the purpose of maintaining public order it was necessary to do so, has made a detention order against you under the provisions of the Emergency Regulations, 1952, and whereas the Governor has powers under sub-regulation (2) of Regulation 2 of the said Regulation to vary and revoke any such order and has appointed a Committee, known as the Advisory Committee on Detainees, to advise him in the exercise of such powers, notice is hereby given you that you will be accorded an opportunity at an early date to appear before the said Committee in support of the petition for your release which you addressed to the Governor on the 27th March, 1954.

2.   In order to furnish you with such particulars as, in the opinion of the Chairman, are necessary to enable you to present your case, you are hereby notified that the allegations against you are to the effect that, up to the date of your arrest, you were an active supporter of Mau Mau and, in particular:-

  (a) In November *1948* wrote and published a pamphlet entitled (in the English translation) "The Spirit of Manhood and Perseverance for Africans" containing charges of a highly inflammatory nature against the European Community;   and

  (b) in 1952 wrote and published a booklet entitled (in the English translation) "The Belief of the Kikuyu" containing a "Creed" which was a clear incitement to rebellion against Government.

3.   The date upon which you may attend before the Committee will be notified to you in due course.

4.   The Committee will not hear Advocates.

EXECUTIVE OFFICER
To the   ADVISORY COMMITTEE ON DETAINEES.